From Austerity to Affluence

Also by Richard T. Griffiths

DE ECONOMISCHE GESCHIEDENIS VAN NEDERLAND IN DE TWINTIGSTE EEUW 1920–1985 (*co-author*)

THE ECONOMIC DEVELOPMENT OF THE EEC (*editor*)

THE ECONOMY AND POLITICS OF THE NETHERLANDS SINCE 1945 (*editor*)

EXPLORATIONS IN OEEC HISTORY (*editor*)

THE GREEN POOL AND THE ORIGINS OF THE COMMON AGRICULTURAL POLICY (*co-editor*)

JOHN F. KENNEDY AND EUROPE (*co-editor*)

THE NETHERLANDS AND THE INTEGRATION OF EUROPE 1945–1957 (*editor*)

Also by Toshiaki Tachibanaki

INTERNAL LABOUR MARKETS, INCENTIVES AND EMPLOYMENT

LABOUR MARKET AND ECONOMIC PERFORMANCE (*editor*)

PUBLIC POLICIES AND THE JAPANESE ECONOMY: Savings, Investments, Unemployment, Inequality

WAGE DETERMINATION AND DISTRIBUTION IN JAPAN

WAGE DIFFERENTIALS: An International Comparison (*editor*)

From Austerity to Affluence

The Transformation of the Socio-Economic Structure of Western Europe and Japan

Edited by

Richard T. Griffiths
Professor
Department of History
University of Leiden
The Netherlands

and

Toshiaki Tachibanaki
Kyoto Institute of Economic Research
Kyoto University
Japan

First published in Great Britain 2000 by
MACMILLAN PRESS LTD
Houndmills, Basingstoke, Hampshire RG21 6XS and London
Companies and representatives throughout the world

A catalogue record for this book is available from the British Library.

ISBN 0–333–72466–6

First published in the United States of America 2000 by
ST. MARTIN'S PRESS, INC.,
Scholarly and Reference Division,
175 Fifth Avenue, New York, N.Y. 10010

ISBN 0–312–23228–4

Library of Congress Cataloging-in-Publication Data
From austerity to affluence : the transformation of the socio-economic structure of
Western Europe and Japan / edited by Richard T. Griffiths, Toshiaki Tachibanaki.
p.   cm.
Includes bibliographical references and index.
ISBN 0–312–23228–4 (cloth)
1. Europe, Western—Economic conditions. 2. Europe, Western—Social
conditions. 3. Japan—Economic conditions. 4. Japan—Social conditions. I.
Griffiths, Richard T. II. Tachibanaki, Toshiaki, 1943–

HC240 .F77   2000
303.44'094—dc21

99–056424

This book is printed on paper suitable for recycling and made from fully managed and sustained
forest sources.

10   9   8   7   6   5   4   3   2   1
09   08   07   06   05   04   03   02   01   00

Printed and bound in Great Britain by
Antony Rowe Ltd, Chippenham, Wiltshire

Contents

List of Tables   vii

List of Figures   x

Preface   xi

1 From Austerity to Affluence: the Turning-Point
  in Modern Societies   1
  Richard T. Griffiths and Toshiaki Tachibanaki

2 Growing Together? The Internationalisation of the
  West European Economy, 1950–71   25
  Johnny Laursen

3 Internationalisation and Economic Development:
  the Case of Japan   41
  Kazumasa Iwata

4 Economic Growth and Overfull Employment
  in Western Europe   60
  Richard T. Griffiths

5 From Rapid Growth to the End of Full Employment
  in Japan: 1945–70   82
  Takenori Inoki

6 A New Sensibility? Affluence, Disposable Income
  and Politics of Private Consumption, 1955–75   99
  Brian Girvin

7 Postwar Private Consumption Patterns of Japanese
  Households: the Role of Consumer Durables   120
  Atsushi Maki

8 The Affluence of Social Democracy in
  Western Europe (1958–69)   138
  Frederico Romero

9 The Realisation of Affluence and Stability
  through the Shifting Political Climate:
  a Comparison of Postwar Japan and West Germany   153
  Hideo Otake

v

10 The Politics of Collective Consumption in
   Western Europe   173
   Bo Stråth

11 Japan Was Not A Welfare State, But…   188
   Toshiaki Tachibanaki

12 The Transformation of the European Countryside   209
   Wendy Asbeek Brusse

13 Changes in Rural Society in Japan   236
   Kamon Nitagai

Index   252

List of Tables

1.1: GDP per capita in Western Europe and Japan, 1953–73   5

1.2: Consumption per capita in Western Europe and Japan, 1953–73   6

1.3: Percentage of households with a radio in Western Europe and Japan, 1953–73   7

1.4: Percentage of households with a television set in Western Europe and Japan, 1953–73   8

1.5: Percentage of households with a car in Western Europe and Japan, 1953–73   8

1.6: Consumption per household in Western Europe and Japan, 1953–73   9

3.1: Intraindustry Trade Index on Japan, 1959–88   53

3.2: Intraindustry index by industry   57

4.1: Indices of economic growth in Western Europe, 1953–64   63

4.2: Comparative levels of real per capita GDP in Western Europe 1953–65   63

4.3: Comparative levels of real per capita consumption in Western Europe, 1953–65   64

4.4: Composition of population increase in Western Europe, 1950–70   65

4.5: Participation rates by country in Western Europe, 1950–65   66

4.6: Participation rates by sex and age in Western Europe, 1950–65   68

4.7: Unemployment and vacancies in Western Europe, 1955–65   70

4.8: Changes in dependent and independent employment in Western Europe, 1953–64   72

4.9: Wages and wage earnings in Western Europe, 1952–65   73

4.10: Index of real earnings in manufacturing in Western Europe, 1953–65   75

4.11: Sectoral distribution of the active labour force in Western Europe, 1953–65. (a) Changes in the sectoral distribution of the labour force during the two growth cycles. (b) Changes in the sectoral and gender distribution of the labour force 1950–70   76

4.12:   Structure of employment income in Western Europe,
        1953–64   78
5.1:   Total population increase and composition by age,
        in Japan, 1945–70   84
5.2:   Birth rate, death rate and reproduction rate in Japan,
        1947–70   84
5.3:   Participation rates by sex and age in Japan, 1950–70   85
5.4:   Breakdown of employed persons by status in Japan,
        1953–67   86
5.5:   Japanese employment structure by industry, 1950–70   87
5.6:   Latent unemployment in Japan, 1946   89
5.7:   Main labour indicators in Japan, 1955–70   90
5.8:   Unemployment rate (%, seasonally adjusted) and
        employment exchange ratio (annual average) in
        Japan, 1955–70   91
5.9:   Distribution of incomes in Japan, 1951–70   95
6.1:   Ownership of certain consumer durables in the US,
        1952 and 1956   104
6.2:   Ownership of certain consumer in the UK in 1959   106
6.3:   British working-class house ownership and consumption
        patterns, 1957 and 1960   107
6.4:   Public opinion in West Germany   108
6.5:   Ownership of certain consumer goods in France by
        household   111
6.6:   Car ownership in France by socio-economic category   111
6.7:   Ownership of certain items in France by socio-economic
        category, 1955   111
7.1:   Population and the number of households in Japan,
        1950–80   124
7.2:   Necessary goods and services in Japan, 1960 and 1970   127
7.3:   The stimulus for purchasing consumer durable goods in
        Japan, 1953–68   129
7.4:   Normal prices for automobiles and television sets and
        financial assets for households in Japan, 1953–80   131
8.1:   Popular vote in national elections (major parties in
        West Germany, Great Britain and Italy), 1957–72   140
10.1:   The development of social insurance expenditures as a
        share of GNP, 1930–74   180
10.2:   The financing of social insurance in 1950 and 1974.
        Sources of finance in the European OECD countries   184
10.3:   The growth of the GNP and of transfers in the
        European OECD countries, 1951–75   186

11.1: Take-up rates of income support in Japan and the UK,
       1950–70   200
11.2: The rate of tax burden, social security contribution
       and their combination over national income in
       1970 and 1991   204
12.1: Comparison of economically active populations in
       Western Europe at various times of the population
       census   211
12.2: A typology of the European countryside, 1990   212
12.3: Timing of the decline in the agricultural labour
       (male and female) force for various Western European
       countries, 1851–1947   215
12.4: Changes in rural and urban population in European
       regions, 1950, 1960, 1970 and 1975   217
12.5: Rural and urban population developments in
       Western European countries, 1950–70   218
12.6: Female activity rates in Sweden and Switzerland,
       1950–70   220
12.7: Rural and urban population older than 55 years of age,
       in France and Sweden   221
12.8: Active population by economic sector in
       Western Europe, 1950, 1960 and 1970   222
12.9: Land fragmentation and area in need of consolidation
       in Western Europe, 1950   223
12.10: Uneconomically viable units as a percentage of all
       farms in Western Europe, 1971   224
12.11: Change in active agricultural population by category
       of farm worker and change in the number and
       average size of holdings in Western Europe   227
12.12: Male wage earnings in agriculture relative to male
       wage earnings in manufacturing in Western Europe,
       1938–64   228
12.13: Indices of average total consumption expenditure
       per household in France, Denmark and Sweden,
       1955–75   230
13.1: Distribution of farm families by size of area
       cultivated   236
13.2: Percentages of full-time and part-time farm
       households   238
13.3: 1970 levels of consumption   242
13.4: Population of cities of 100 000 or more and percentages
       of total population   247

List of Figures

3.1: Iso-intraindustry trade line energy (Japan)   52
7.1: Diffusion of consumer durables in Japan, 1957–80   133
7.2: Contents of saving in Japan, 1951–80   135

Preface

This book originates in an idea to encourage Japanese and European historians to discover more about each others' histories and, through the comparison, to learn more about their own. It was also concerned that much of traditional historical writing focused on conflicts between the two areas: the conflict of overlapping imperial ambitions and the confrontation in times of war, death and destruction. However, the lives of most people most of the time are not dominated by the political and territorial ambitions of their leaders. Rather they attempt to raise their families and live often in familiar circumstances but ones over which, from time to time, they can exert little control. Long-term structural changes such as industrialisation and urbanisation and short term shocks of recessions and price falls determine the contexts and outcomes of these lives, lives separated by thousands of miles of land mass and oceans. And, just occasionally, the confluence of events join within a short period to transform the economic, social and political contexts of peoples' existence. This is what happens in this book. Within 20 years of an outburst of frenzied destruction and bestial slaughter, of deprivation, misery and hopelessness, the majority of the population in Western Europe and Japan found themselves suddenly, unprecedently rich. How this happened and how it was experienced is the subject of the following chapters.

This work would never have been realised without the unstinting support of the Japan Foundation, which funded the original conference in Kyoto in March 1996 and which also provided the funds to prepare the revised papers for publication. This volume was inspired by the ideals that the Foundation represents and we hope that it repays their trust in us. In addition we would like to extend our thanks to the European Union Delegation in Tokyo for its moral, intellectual and additional monetary support. Our appreciation must also be recorded for the staff and organisation of the University of Kyoto for their work in preparing and hosting the original conference, and to the Schuman Centre of the European University Institute, Florence, for its logistical and administrative backing. Finally we would like to reflect on the memory of two great Europeans, Marcello Buzzonetti and Emile Noël, respectively the secretary-general and the president of the European University Institute when this project was conceived, and who gave it their unswerving support.

Richard Griffiths
Toshiaki Tachibanaki

1
From Austerity to Affluence: the Turning-Point in Modern Societies
Richard T. Griffiths and Toshiaki Tachibanaki

It has become increasingly appreciated that for Western Europe the years 1950–73 marked a unique period in modern history. The spectacular growth of collective and individual prosperity, and the increasing confidence that this condition was normal, stood in stark contrast to the depression that preceded it and the stagflation that followed. In Japan, albeit from a lower base, this growth was even more impressive, averaging over 10 per cent a year. Moreover, in contrast with Europe, after a lull in the mid-1970s, strong growth resumed for over another decade. This unprecedented economic growth revealed in the statistics, however, implies more than simply the provision of an ever greater supply of goods and services. It embodies a shift in their composition and their distribution. This book argues that, during the quarter century or so following the Second World War, one particular transformation occurred that sets the period aside from all others in modern history – a metamorphosis we have characterised as one from austerity to affluence for the mass of the population. Suddenly, within a relatively short space of time, the mass of society discovered that it had become historically very rich. How this occurred, and its impact on social and political organisation, is the subject of this volume.

Without elevating it to the status of a definition, one could describe austerity as a situation in which the majority of the population lived at or near a socially determined level of subsistence, or were at risk of returning to that level. In other words, disposable incomes of the majority of the population allowed for few non-essential items of consumption, employment was vulnerable to seasonal or cyclical changes and social security provisions were minimal. In the 1940s, against a backdrop of postwar hard currency shortages and import restrictions, the term austerity also enjoyed a more specific usage: the restriction of consumption of basic goods below levels otherwise dictated by disposable incomes. By contrast, *affluence* prevailed when the majority of the population, having satisfied a socially determined level of basic need, still disposed of significant (and growing) purchasing power and were confident that this situation would continue. This definition called for a lag between rising real incomes and the attainment of 'affluence' while the population compensated for the backlog in consumption of consumer durables. It also called for a situation of full employment and a confidence, however misplaced in retrospect, that this situation would prevail.

The passage of European society from austerity to affluence was a complex process of economic, social and political change, and this volume does not pretend to define the exact moment for the transformation. However, we would like to place some boundary limits on the period within which the transition took place, even though some parts of the process (with respect to female emancipation and in the countryside) still remained to be completed. In the United States, a situation of affluence already prevailed by the late 1940s, although the skewed income distribution still left large pockets of poverty. Real disposable incomes had been high for some considerable time before that, but true 'affluence' only occurred when the conversion to a peace-time economy and the first postwar recession had passed without any major upswing in unemployment.

In Western Europe the changeover occurred later. It is possible that for a minority of countries this may have started already in the late 1940s: Sweden, Switzerland and possibly Belgium. These were economies which, whether through neutrality or luck, emerged from the war with little damage to the economic infrastructure and which had favourable export structures, with concentrations in sectors previously supplied by West Germany. This combination would have conferred relatively high incomes, low (or non-existent) reconstruction costs and an absence of hard currency restraints to imports. However, given the prevailing uncertainty in the major neighbouring export markets, it is doubtful whether there could have been much confidence in the permanence of the situation. Had there been, it is unlikely to have survived the shocks to the European trading system that occurred in 1950–53 when, successively, West Germany, the United Kingdom and France were forced by balance of payments crises to restrict imports and to reintroduce rationing for domestic consumers.

Although the events of the early 1950s could have tilted Western Europe into a 1930s-style depression, they did not do so. Indeed, by

1953, equilibrium had been restored to the system and the continent was set for a considerable upsurge in economic growth. The year 1953 marked the start of a cycle of growth that lasted until 1958–59. It is also the year that we have chosen as marking the initial boundary for our analysis of the transition from austerity to affluence. The boom witnessed a rapid expansion in incomes throughout Western Europe that, in a few countries, allowed a shift in consumption patterns towards those associated with affluence. For some societies, therefore, the transition to affluence began in 1953, but it was the fact that Europe weathered the 1958 recession almost unscathed that cemented it into place.

Before then, where it had occurred, full employment had been a phenomenon from which to make political capital. It was something aspired to, and enjoyed when it happened, but it had not become an article of faith. After 1958 that began to change and Western Europe entered the age of 'high-Keynesianism'. Permanent full employment seemed to become a reality and voters demanded that governments create conditions to ensure its continuity, and believed that they could do so. The years 1958–59 also witnessed the start of a second cycle of economic expansion that persisted until 1964–65. In these years, the last remnants of persistent unemployment disappeared and everywhere income levels, and consumption patterns, crossed the threshold to affluence for most of the population. Although the final surge of growth, from the mid-1960s to the early 1970s, reinforced the attainment of affluence (and were accompanied by the appearance of the cultural icons associated with 'the sixties' in popular memory) the essential transformation had already occurred.

For Japan, the transformation from austerity to affluence came later than it did for Western Europe. Even without the war and its aftermath, it was less developed economically than the advanced economies of Western Europe, although its industry was already displacing European competition for 'first generation' industrial goods in Asian markets. The Second World War, however, probably entailed heavier losses in social, economic and human capital than in Europe and reconstruction was slower to get underway. The US occupation forces played an important role in reconstructing the economy and society. They made sweeping proposals, accepted by the Japanese people, for democratisation in the political system and throughout society, including land reform and the dissolution of the Zaibatsu. The government also initiated a strong industrialisation policy, focused on exports.

This strong export-led economy is useful when it comes to discussing the postwar Japanese reconstruction and subsequent rapid economic growth: it has two important implications. First, since Japan has few natural resources, it is necessary to export manufacturing goods in order to earn currency to purchase them from abroad. Second, the lack of natural resources dictates the optimalisation of other resources (human capital and technology) for economic strength.

The emphasis on industrialisation entailed several unacceptable policies, and required sacrifices from the Japanese people. For example, immediately after the war the government adopted a heavily protectionist policy and maintained it throughout the period under discussion. Moreover, Japanese citizens had a high savings rate, which contributed to the high growth economy but muted its impact on high living standards and consumption levels. Furthermore, the postwar governments never accorded a high priority to welfare provisions such as health, pensions and housing facilities. Finally, it neglected the agricultural sector in the interests of promoting manufactures, finance and services. This is the shadow side of the Japanese miracle and it will be interesting to investigate them in the course of this book.

Despite these reservations, high levels of savings and investment and a growth rate exceeding 10 per cent per annum enabled Japan steadily to erode the productivity gap with the West and when, in the mid-1960s, existing labour reserves appeared exhausted, there was a rapid surge in disposable incomes and a spreading of welfare. Japan shed the final shackles of austerity and entered fully into the age of affluence.

The turning point

We have now reached a position in our argument where we can construct a comparative framework within which to place the analysis. For these purposes we have selected, in addition to Japan, the three large European economies (France, Germany and the United Kingdom) and two of the smaller ones (the Netherlands and Sweden). This also allows us to capture a spread in the chronology of the European experience ranging from a high income country with an early transformation (Sweden), one which certainly started its transition in the boom of the early 1950s (the UK) and three which were to make their transition in the upswing of the late 1950s–early 1960s.

Table 1.1 shows the relative levels of per capita GDP as they developed over the 20 years under consideration expressed in constant (1985) dollars and prices. The series is derived from the Penn World Tables, itself the outcome of a massive project initiated by the United Nations and designed to provide truly comparable national income statistics by

Table 1.1 GDP per capita in Western Europe and Japan, (1985 US dollars) 1953–73

	1953	1958	1963	1968	1973
Sweden	6260	7300	8926	10415	11890
UK	5791	6340	7220	8265	9520
Netherlands	4694	5389	6650	8508	10301
France	4545	5463	6788	8468	10763
FRG	4278	5787	7248	8556	10681
Japan	1884	2505	4008	6358	9048

Source: http://datacentre.chass.utoronto.ca:5680/pwt.

correcting for structural differences in price levels for different categories of consumption and for variations in real exchange rates over time. The series themselves are available (free) on-line at several sites, and we would recommend the particularly user-friendly site maintained by the University of Toronto. The countries are ranked in Table 1.1 according to their levels of per capita GDP in 1953.

The data reveals the high initial starting position of Sweden and its subsequent high growth, which allowed it to maintain its leading position, albeit by a reduced margin, throughout the subsequent two decades. It also illustrates eloquently the poor growth performance of the British economy, although it was still high by comparison with previous periods. While in the 1950s, British commentators might have been able to console themselves that the differences in performance represented a catching-up by the rest, this illusion was shattered by the mid-1960s, when it was overhauled by its neighbours on the continent. Finally, the data illustrates both the low starting position and the subsequent rapid growth attained by Japan. Nonetheless, it is only by 1964 that Japanese per capita GDP reaches the level prevailing in Germany at the start of our period. The fact that growth continues scarcely undiminished then transforms the situation. By 1969, Japan reaches the levels achieved by France and the Netherlands in 1963 (when we argue that their transformations towards affluence were well established) and by 1972 it has reached the level achieved in Western Europe in 1968 (by which time their transition had certainly been completed). It is worth pausing at this juncture to place these developments in a wider perspective. In 1950 comparable American per capita GDP was $8660, a level reached by Sweden in 1962 but not attained by the rest of our European sample until 1969 and Japan by 1972. The fact that it took 20 'golden' years of 'super-growth' during the European 'miracle' simply to catch-up to American levels merely underlines what a fabulously wealthy country America was immediately after the war.

The growth of the Western European and Japanese economies facilitated the shift towards affluence but it was not synonymous with its achievement. A better indication of the trajectory is provided by looking at consumption levels among European economies, where the performance is conditioned both by levels of income and by levels of savings and investments. This information is provided in Table 1.2.

There are several points of interest in this data. First, the gap between the highest and lowest starting positions is greater for per capita consumption than it was for GDP, although it had closed significantly already by 1958. Second, although the UK's investment ratios were among the lowest in the industrialised world, and were probably a contributory factor in its poor growth record, they did allow the maintenance of relatively high consumption levels throughout the entire period. Whereas, for example, Germany surpassed Britain in GDP in 1963, it only does so in per capita consumption by the early 1970s. Only by looking at consumption data can we reconcile the pessimistic tone of contemporary economic analysts searching for the reasons behind the failure of comparative growth performance and the fact that the 'swinging sixties' is identified with London and Liverpool rather than Bonn and Munich. Finally, the fall in the share of consumption in Japanese GDP from 66 per cent in 1958 to 57 per cent in 1973, retarded the effect of its high growth in reaching European (and American) levels of consumption. While in 1973 Japan had exceeded the 1950 US level of per capita GDP by 4.4 per cent, its per capita level of consumption remained 5.1 per cent below.

The fact that Europe seems to pass through its transformations to affluent societies at lower levels of per capita consumption than did

Table 1.2 Consumption per capita in Western Europe and Japan, (1985 US dollars) 1953–73

	1953	*1958*	*1963*	*1968*	*1973*
Sweden	4113	4650	5418	6228	6932
UK	3585	4077	4635	5075	5912
Netherlands	2809	3349	4073	4988	6232
France	2770	3212	4050	5105	6211
FRG	2383	3189	3936	4654	5939
Japan	1255	1668	2485	3694	5157

Source: http://datacentre.chass.utoronto.ca:5680/pwt.

the US, and that Japan was to do so at levels lower than those of Europe, is not so perplexing as it may seem at first sight. Most new consumer durables enter the market as luxury items, carrying heavy development costs and not yet able to reap benefits of scale economies associated with mass marketing. By the time they had reached Europe or Japan, their costs had often fallen in real terms. However, real disposable incomes and relative prices are but two of many factors that one would expect to influence patterns of expenditure. The stage of development of the ancillary infrastructure, the range of alternative expenditures (for example, larger housing), the age distribution of the population and the composition of households are among others. Nevertheless, to give an impression of the spread of affluence through the possession of consumer items we have chosen to provide evidence on three consumer goods:

- radios,
- television sets,
- passenger vehicles.

These products were chosen because comparative data was readily available and because they each represented a different type of charge on the household budget.

The data in Table 1.3 on radios reveals early universal take-up rates, with a distribution broadly in line with the consumption data. There is also a rapid universal acceleration with the appearance of miniaturisation, in the form of transistor radios, and a concomitant drop in price. Moreover, after an initial lag, Japan rapidly caught up with the rest of Western Europe and by the end of our period, diffusion is almost universal.

Table 1.3 Percentage of households with a radio in Western Europe and Japan, 1953–73

	1953	1958	1963	1968	1973
Sweden	93.2	100+	100+	97.6	93.8
UK	87.0	94.1	90.2	94.2	100+
France	63.0	69.4	94.0	95.3	91.3
Netherlands	98.2	98.8	89.9	82.3	88.2
FRG	70.2	81.0	84.6	87.7	89.0
Japan	64.6	68.9	74.4	92.5	100+

Source: UN Compendium of Social Statistics 1963/ 67/ 77.

Table 1.4 Percentage of households with a television set in Western Europe and Japan, 1953–73

	1953	1958	1963	1968	1973
Sweden	0.02	9.8	66.1	78.3	85.8
UK	22.3	54.4	72.7	82.8	88.3
France	0.5	6.5	28.4	56.7	69.1
Netherlands	0.4	13.4	45.6	68.9	80.9
FRG	0.2	11.4	42.4	69.4	79.9
Japan	0.03	7.6	62.3	78.6	78.9

Source: UNESCO Statistical YBK 1969, 1977.

Table 1.5 Percentage of households with a car in Western Europe and Japan, 1953–73

	1953	1958	1963	1968	1973
Sweden	17.3	37.4	52.2	69.1	77.8
UK	18.8	28.5	43.5	60.7	79.1
France	15.2	29.5	51.4	70.5	81.2
Netherlands	7.9	14.4	25.1	51.8	75.5
FRG	6.7	17.5	35.0	52.5	71.6
Japan	0.6	1.2	5.1	18.7	46.1

Source: UNESCO Statistical YBK 1969, 1977.

The data on television sets in Table 1.4 demonstrates that early take-up rates were determined partly by the development of national broadcasting (or access to that of a neighbouring country). Second, the diffusion of television sets was much slower than was the case with radios (probably reflecting their relative higher cost). Third, the behaviour of Japan in this respect from the late 1950s is very precocious since, despite its relatively low consumption levels it captures second place among the countries we analyse, a performance presumably attributable in part to the small living space and to the age composition of households.

The data on cars in Table 1.5 confirms initial take-up rates in line with initial incomes. The subsequent diffusion is slower than with either radios or televisions, probably because the purchase of a car represented a higher charge on family budgets. The rate of the Netherlands belies the economy's ranking in terms of incomes and is at least partly attributable to the relatively high number of infants per household as a result of high birth rates. Finally, on this measure at least, we could pinpoint Japanese affluence as beginning from the late 1960s, although the poor state of infrastructure (roads and parking) may have played a role in reducing the attraction of car ownership.

The data on consumption generally confirms the shift to affluence among our group of countries over the two decades under consideration (and this is corroborated in Chapters 6 and 7). But in the low- and middle-range price items, it suggests an earlier transformation for Japan than one would expect from the per capita consumption figures. We implied at the start of this section that part of the explanation might lie in the development of prices, but there is another explanation. Most consumer durables data is expressed in terms of households because, initially at least, one fridge, one freezer, one television and so on is considered adequate to satisfy household demand. But if the household, rather than the individual, is the preferable unit of analysis, should we not take household income, rather than per capita income, as the explanatory variable? The relevant data is presented in Table 1.6.

The data for levels of household consumption reveals a far smaller differential in experience among the countries under consideration than does the per capita data, especially between the Japanese and European experience. Moreover, the chronological lags between the two are far shorter. In sum, it provides a data set more consistent with other quantitative and qualitative materials available to historians.

The content of the book

Both Europe and Japan suffered from the destruction of the Second World War, although Japan was a loser in the war, and Europe contained both winners and losers. The economy in two regions was also devastated by the war, particularly those of countries such as Germany,

Table 1.6 Consumption per household in Western Europe and Japan (1985 US dollars), 1953–73

	1953	*1958*	*1963*	*1968*	*1973*
Sweden	11973	12964	14137	15021	16967
Netherlands	12241	12301	14053	16846	19504
UK	11845	13253	14954	16442	17538
France	9044	9779	12585	15262	18197
FRG	7053	9311	11217	12846	15916
Japan	6048	7274	9890	13409	17741

Source: http://datacentre.chass.utoronto.ca:5680/pwt.

Italy and Japan. Europe and Japan, nevertheless, succeeded in reconstructing and reindustrialising their economies with the direct help of the US but largely through their own efforts.

There is a significant difference between Europe and Japan, when we look at the effect of international trade on economic development. While Europe adopted a free trade and capital movement strategy, which resulted in the expansion of trade and international payment, Japan embraced a lopsided trade policy, namely temporary import protection and restricted capital mobility, which resulted in an export-led expansion of the economy. Laursen and Iwata elegantly present this difference between Europe and Japan. It is possible to suggest several reasons for this distinction. First, with some exceptions, Europe had already experienced industrialisation and democratisation before the war, while the degree of industrialisation and democratisation had been underdeveloped in Japan. Europe could enjoy free trade and capital mobility, while Japan's policy options were restricted because it was in the process of preindustrialisation. Second, Europe consists of many countries whose territories are located on a continental landmass (or just off-shore), while Japan is an island country. Third, since many European countries were already developed, they could enjoy intra-trade in manufactures with near-by, rich neighbours. By contrast, in Asia, many neighbouring countries were economically relatively underdeveloped.

In Chapter 2, Laursen discusses a process of internationalisation and separates the period 1950–71 into two distinct phases, namely 1950–58 called the 'silver fifties' and 1959–71 called the 'golden sixties'. The first phase witnessed the re-emergence of economic growth within the framework of austerity, while the second phase saw an unprecedented acceleration in economic growth and major qualitative changes in the international economic system. The second phase, he argues, can also be characterised by a shift from austerity to affluence. Laursen shows several changes in trade patterns in Europe such as the growing interdependence among the countries in Europe, intra-European trade with manufacturing products and the importance of the EEC countries in the 1950s and 1960s. These patterns indicate that the countries in Western Europe are each others' major trading partners and that intra-regional trade within manufactures is its main feature. One important phenomenon in the 1960s is the emergence of Japan as an important exporter of manufactures to Western Europe, although North America remained a more important trading partner in this period.

Laursen, then, describes American direct investment in Europe as another important development in the 1950s and 1960s. American enterprises started to establish factories in mining, smelting, petroleum, transportation (mainly car industries) and computer industries. There were mixed feelings about the American direct investment. One side favoured it because of the inflow of hard currency, capital and technology, while the other was reluctant for the fear of foreign influence. Finally, Laursen examines foreign direct investment by European nations in other regions and shows that the major country in this activity changed from the UK to West Germany and Italy. International money transfers increased among European nations, and between the US and Europe. In these foreign direct investments the US was always the major partner. Therefore, the US dollar played an important role in international money transactions, creating the so-called 'Euro-dollar' market, and thereby furthered Europe's internationalisation.

In Chapter 3, Iwata examines the relationship between internationalisation and economic development in Japan. He breaks down the entire economic history since the Meiji Restoration into three periods. The first is from the early Meiji Restoration to the end of the Second World War, the second is from the postwar period to the end of the 1970s and the third is after the 1980s to the present. Iwata focuses on the second period which encompasses the shift from austerity to affluence. As reasons for the rapid recovery from the war, he suggests the role of the market economy, the importance of government planning, the employee-oriented corporate governance, the predominance of an indirect financial system and the close relationship between business circles and bureaucrats. He presents several interesting illustrations of the importance of the last item – particularly how at the top-level meetings government and business collaborated in promoting strong industrialisation and economic growth.

Iwata, then, argues that foreign trade policy in reality implied a forced import-substitution policy and the expansion of exports which facilitated the importation of basic materials and energy. The process of internationalisation in the rapid economic growth era (1950–73) was not only asymmetric but also lopsided. Trade liberalisation and capital imports were delayed – the latter postponed until the 1960s, or even 1970s – and this despite pressure from abroad, in particular the US, encouraging Japan towards more free trade and capital mobility. Iwata discusses the implication of the temporary protection policy adopted by Japan from the viewpoint of strategic trade policy *à la* Krugman, who in his *Rethinking International Trade* (1990) pointed out that, under some circumstances, import protection leads to export promotion. He suggests caution in applying Krugman's theory to all Japanese industries, by raising the ignorance of acute domestic competition, the entry deterrence effect and the avoidance of the dynamic inconsistency problem. Finally, Iwata investigates the reasons behind the low level of manufactured imports and of intra-industry trade in Japan, by employing a theoretical economic model which takes into account the economies of scale and product differentiation.

Economic growth in both Europe and Japan provided a motor for the transformation from austerity to affluence, by guaranteeing nearly full employment in the two regions. Both Griffiths and Inoki examine the issue of employment in this period. Both authors investigate similar subjects such as labour supply, labour demand, employment, unemployment and wages and/or income. Two differences in interests, however, may be observed. While the role of immigration is evaluated for Europe, the effect of human capital investment is discussed for Japan. Each subject has a unique implication for each region.

Since there are so many countries in Europe, it is difficult to examine all countries. Thus, in Chapter 4, Griffiths selected four countries, namely the UK, Sweden, West Germany and the Netherlands. These countries cover several features of the countries in Europe, which are distinguished by size of country, income level, growth rate, and cooperativeness and/or regulation in the labour market.

Griffiths examines changes in the labour force, by paying attention to total population, population by age, participation rate and employment. He finds that the Netherlands occupies a considerably different position in these variables in comparison with the other countries. One important remark is that the effect of international immigration is significant in the determination of labour force in Europe. In fact, the growth of immigration has a stronger effect on economic growth than that of natural population. Another interesting observation is that female labour participation rates differ considerably from country to country in the 1950s and 1960s. This is a big contrast to the recent high figures in Europe. The most important implication of the high economic growth rates in these periods is the high growth rate of employment and thus the low rate of unemployment in Europe, although some degree of mismatch is observed. It is possible to claim that economic prosperity did not produce any disadvantaged people who are unemployed. This again is a big contrast to the contemporary experience in Europe where many countries suffer from very high unemployment rates. Another important effect of the high growth economy which was induced by rising productivity appeared in the relatively high growth rate in earnings, reflected in the increase in living standards of many individuals.

It is noted that wages, which contribute most importantly to total income, climbed rapidly once full employment was achieved, in particular in Sweden where the labour market is centralised and regulated.

In Chapter 5, Inoki examines the workings of the labour market between the defeat of the war and the end of the rapid economic growth in the early 1970s. This period is characterised by a drastic and rapid change in lifestyles and living standards. He breaks down the period into three phases; a dramatic increase in the number of unemployed in the immediate postwar period, a large increase in labour demand between mid-1950s and mid-1960s, and a tightening of the labour market in the late 1960s.

Inoki, first, examines the overall profile of the labour force in Japan from 1945 to 1970 in the fields of total population, composition by age, labour force participation, characteristics of employment and employment by industry. The most noteworthy observations are: no international immigration in population, the emergence of baby-boomers, almost constant male and female labour force participation rates during the period with the M-shaped (that is, bimodal) age participation rate for females, the increase in the percentage share of employees with a decrease in self-employed and family worker, and the support of the Petty–Colin Clark Law about the shift in employment by industry.

The first period (1945–55) witnessed an increase in both population and labour supply. There was much disguised unemployment and inflation was high – a combination that signified 'miserable' conditions for much of the population. Production, however, in steel, coal mining and textile industries started to increase in the early 1950s, and it absorbed labour from agriculture. Despite some balance of payments problems, the second period (1955–65) was marked by large-scale technological progress and rapid economic growth. This was accompanied by a very low rate of unemployment and a significant increase in wage payments which resulted in an increase in living standards. The third period (1965–early 1970s) shows the annual growth rate over 10 per cent. Due to excess labour demand, the economy soon experienced acute labour shortages.

Inoki, finally, discusses the importance of human capital investment as a source of economic growth. Since Japan lacks natural resources, human resources are crucial for the determination of technical progress and the efficiency of production. He demonstrates the effect of formal secondary and tertiary education on the upward mobility of the society. He also emphasises the importance of on-the-job training in comparison with formal education regarding the effect on skill formation, productivity of employees, career development and wage payments. This leads him to stress the importance of length of service in the firm and in industrial relations.

The effect of high growth and high earnings was to boost the role of private consumption in inducing conditions of affluence in the 1950s and the 1960s in both Western Europe and Japan. It should be noted that living standards in Europe were considerably higher than those in Japan because the economy in Europe, in particular Western Europe, was considerably stronger. Japan was almost in the pre-industrial development age in the 1940s, while Europe had already reached considerable levels of economic development and industrialisation by the 1940s. In other words, the achievement level of economic development had been significantly different between Europe and Japan before the period of 1955–75, although higher growth enabled Japan rapidly to catch up with European living standards. Girvin discusses the relationship between politics and private consumption in Europe, while Maki investigates the pattern of private consumption with emphasis on the role of durable goods in Japan. Girvin is a political scientist, while Maki is an economist. This difference in specialism explains the difference in treatment each author gives the subject, although both are concerned with private consumption. More importantly, in Japan the Liberal Democratic Party (that is conservatives) held power during the entire period, whereas political power in Europe shifted between right and left from time to time. Therefore, it is interesting to inquire into the relationship between politics and private consumption in Europe.

In Chapter 6, Girvin describes how continuing expansion, high levels of employment and rising standards of living led to affluence in Europe from the consumer boom of the late 1950s through to the 1970s. He emphasises that the involvement of the US in European affairs altered the mind of European people significantly, especially in the direction of acceptance of mass production and mass consumption. He also provides various examples of the governments and the countries in Europe which had different policies towards consumption, illustrated by various writers on the subject of the politics of private consumption.

Girvin explains how the American model and the European experience worked in determining the consumption pattern for durable goods. He examines the example of the major European nations, namely the UK, West Germany and France, in respect to various durable goods. It is interesting to see his analysis on the difference in the growth rates among the three countries and the effect of class in the society (working class, middle class, and bourgeois class) on consumption patterns.

He concludes that living standards of people in the country became central to the electoral considerations of most political parties in most European nations: governments were changed frequently by the electoral choice of voters. Finally, he presents a new trend in the politics of consumption in this period – the public representation of youth as a cultural participant and consumer of new products, say clothing, records, rock concerts. This new trend created not only new businesses but also a new sensibility in society.

In Chapter 7, Maki examines the postwar private consumption patterns of Japanese households with emphasis on the role of consumer durables. He starts with his own overview of the Japanese growth economy, investigating, in particular, the relationship between the Kuznets' modern economic growth theory (namely the importance of three factors industrialisation, urbanisation and technological innovation) and the Japanese experience. He then shows the growth in the standard of living during the era of rapid economic growth, the change in household composition and some other statistics. The advance of living standards encouraged the following three changes; the substitution of households' labour by labour-saving consumer durable goods, the shift from household production to purchasing external services and the decrease in Engel's coefficient.

Maki is concerned with the change in consumption patterns, finding significant changes in the demand for goods and services. These centred on a shift from necessary goods and services to luxury ones, which were influenced in turn by the rapid increase in income, the change in relative prices due to industrialisation, the decrease in family size and habit formation in consumer preferences. He also examines the role of consumer durables and emphasises changes in the major consumer durables from time to time, as seen for example in the priorities shifted from refrigerators, televisions and washing machines to colour televisions, video televisions, automobiles and houses. Needless to say, the level of per-capita income determines the major durable goods demanded by consumers, but the price of each consumer durable good was also influential.

One interesting hypothesis proposed by Maki is the contribution of durable goods to the high savings rate in Japan. The mechanism is as follows: high demand for consumer durables requires a considerably large amount of cash not only for down payment but also funds because there has been liquidity constraint in the capital market. If the capital market had been perfect, it would have been possible to borrow funds to buy consumer durables. However, it was imperfect, and thus it was necessary to save a lot in order to accumulate the necessary funds. This high amount of savings deposited at banks was transferred to firms which could finance their investment activity easily. And this channel helped Japan to its high economic growth rate.

Political considerations are important when we evaluate economic policy. The government economic policy reflects the voters' preference because they elect politicians who form the ruling party and thus the government. In other words, voters decide which political party, more precisely political ideology, should govern the country. Both Romero and Otake examine such political processes for Europe and Japan. They evaluate the relationship between politics and affluence, focusing mainly on the role of social democracy in European affairs, while Otake compares the effect of political parties and government on the formation of economic policy for reconstruction and during the period of affluence in Germany and Japan.

In Chapter 8 Romero provides a brief overview of economic prosperity from the late 1950s to the late 1960s. He describes this period as one of prosperity and optimism, certainly when set against the upheavals of the previous decades. After the immediate reconstruction years and the initiation of the cold war, centre-right coalition parties dominated the politics in Europe. In the late 1960s, however, a gradual shift towards the centre-left coalition parties (that is, social democratic parties) was observed. Romero evaluates this shift extensively and carefully. He examines the experience in three countries, namely West Germany, the UK and Italy, and asks why centre-right parties lost power and how centre-left gained it. He concludes that, except for France, the presence of social democracy created a new political climate which supported the idea of the mixed economy. Nonetheless, he warns against assuming a hegemonic role for social democracy because centre-right forces occasionally held sway. Occasionally left-wing parties blocked social democratic policies and if public expenditure and investment on welfare items were to be continuously raised the centre-left needed help from other parties. Romero conceives social democratic policy as deriving from Keynesian doctrine. The economic system should be a mix between private enterprise and government. The government should adopt positive policies aimed at attaining full employment, rationalising rather than reforming the economy, providing various welfare services and so on.

The results of ruling social democracy are manifest in three fields. First, persisting inequalities could be reduced by government policies. Second, total public expenditure, in particular on social programmes, increased significantly as a percentage of GNP in many European countries, indicating the development of their welfare states. It is, however, worth noting that coalitions with conservatives were keener on social expenditure than socialists alone. Third, full-fledged neo-corporatist arrangements among government, industry and labour were developed.

Finally, Romero investigates voters' attitudes towards social democratic parties in this period. He emphasises the importance of an increasing number of employees in most countries as a result of processes of industrialisation and urbanisation. Both working-class and white-collar workers voted for social democracy. Although there is a slight difference in political interests between working-class and white-collar workers, they may be seen as a vast new middle class, fond of the improved and extended provision of public services on health, pension, education and so on. Another interesting phenomenon, which supports social democracy is the decline of religious belief. Rationalism and materialism accompanied this phenomenon.

In Chapter 9, Otake compares the successful experiences of West Germany and Japan regarding postwar economic policy and politics. He suggests that, in many respects, the two countries share common features. They are late comers in comparison with other industrialised countries. They had totalitarian regimes in the 1930s and 1940s. They were occupied by the US after the war and influenced by American idealism and political preferences. He is concerned, in particular, with the distinction between laissez-faire and social democracy (or conservative and mass democracy) in determining the transition from austerity to affluence. The immediate postwar period can be regarded as the predominance of social democracy in both Germany and Japan. Because of their role in resistance before and during the war, leftist groups gained power. It is no wonder that socialists formed the government and that the slogan of a revised capitalism was advocated in both countries.

Economic liberalism, or the free market economy, however, came to power after the temporary socialist regimes for several reasons. First, there was a strong feeling in both countries that it would be necessary to reconstruct the economy quickly. Second, the American government thought it important to strengthen the economy in these countries in view of the emergence of communist power in world politics and the cold war. It is interesting to note that Germany adopted the Currency Reform, and Japan adopted the Dodge Plan, both on American recommendation to restore the economy. He writes in some detail on the role of leading politicians and economic ministers in this period: Konrad Adenauer for Germany and Shigeru Yoshida for Japan as the political leaders, and Ludwig Erhard for Germany and Hayato Ikeda for Japan, as those responsible for the economy.

Otake, then, discusses the increasing democratic pressure from various groups on social and economic policies after they had successfully reconstructed the economy. The ruling Adenauer government made several concessions in response to this pressure, such as the co-determination scheme between firms and unions, monetary compensations for refugees during the wartime and postwar periods, tax cuts for interest groups such as farmers and small business people and massive payments on welfare benefits. It is interesting to recognize that some of these developments lie at the heart of what we consider the German model of postwar growth. Otake also argues that similar pressures invoked government concessions in Japan. The first example is observed at the level of planning and control of the government. The second is the relationship between central government and local government. The third and fourth examples are farmers wanting heavy subsidies and ex-soldiers wanting high pensions. They were able to receive favourable treatment because of the budget surplus generated by postwar economic recovery.

There is a consensus that Europe is the symbol of welfare state development, characterised by a large amount of collective consumption (that is, government expenditure). Japan, by contrast, is not a welfare state at all. It is an interesting subject to inquire why the two regions had different policies towards collective consumption and to examine whether Europeans enjoyed a higher level of welfare provision than their Japanese counterparts. Stråth and Tachibanaki address this issue.

In Chapter 10, Stråth discusses various aspects of the politics of collective consumption in Europe. First, he emphasises the emergence of mass production and mass consumption after the war. He attributes the birth of welfare states to economic prosperity, to neo-corporatist organisation of interests and to Keynesian economics. He argues that there are significant variations in the timing of welfare state emergence, and in the quality and size of their provisions (especially on a north–south/east–west axis). This difference was caused by the difference in the process of industrialisation and whether the country was a battle-field or not. Another important cause is the political and economic conditions during the war and the postwar period.

Stråth examines social insurance as an example of these variations. He investigates in detail how each country adopted the social insurance programme – whether it is compulsory or voluntary, what kind of risks were covered, the coverage of participants, the amount of insurance and so on. He then evaluates the implication of universalism in social insurance. Initially, the social insurance system was intended for the poor or the working-class, but universalism implies that everyone may participate. He examines the effect of political parties in various countries on this universalism and finds that social democracy exerted a crucial influence in Scandinavia and to a lesser extent in Britain. He also examines the increase in taxation which guarantees the working of welfare states in Europe, but shows some resistance from conservatives like Thatcher because of the slower economic growth implied.

In Chapter 11, Tachibanaki examines the case of Japan and explores the question whether or not Japan is a welfare state. The answer is obviously 'no': Japan has never been a welfare state in any period or in any respects. In this Japan is similar to US, which is a symbol of a non-welfare state. Compared with the situation elsewhere, the size of governments in both countries is kept to a minimum. Having defined the welfare state mainly in economic terms and outlined its various purposes (such as efficiency, supporting living conditions, the reduction in inequality and social integration) he evaluates the Japanese achievement in each area.

Tachibanaki's most important proposition is that, although Japan was not a welfare state at all, the welfare level of the Japanese people was not very much lower than that provided by European welfare states. This is because, to a large extent, enterprises and families were responsible for welfare provision. Enterprises prepared several programmes in welfare such as healthcare and housing. At the same time, families paid a considerable amount of money to help each other in welfare. In sum, both enterprises and families were providers of welfare to employees and family members, substituting for the public sector which is the provider of welfare in Europe. There are two important caveats. There is a considerable difference in welfare provision between employees in larger firms and the rest (including employees in smaller firms, self-employed and retired people) which Tachibanaki calls the 'dual structure' in social security. Second, the level of welfare provision is, probably, somewhat lower in Japan than that in Europe, and certainly considerably lower than that in the typical welfare state economies in Scandinavia. Although the rapid economic growth of the 1950s and 1960s contributed considerable tax revenues to the public sector, Japan only started to prepare various welfare systems in 1973. The two oil-crises, and subsequent slower economic growth, torpedoed such plans. Businesses criticised the possible detrimental effects of social welfare on the working of the private economy. It is an irony that such criticism is made despite the fact that Japan has never been a welfare state. Tachibanaki concludes that such criticism has no scientific basis and that it is only part of a political campaign.

When we investigate postwar industrialisation or economic growth in economic and historical studies, little attention is given to the countryside. There are several reasons for this. First, the engine for economic growth is industrialisation and urbanisation. Second, since industrialisation and urbanisation imply that the share of agriculture in GNP, and the share of farmers in the total labour force, has been declining, no major interest is shown for agricultural development. Nonetheless, most historians would agree that the role of countryside is not unimportant in this period. Asbeek Brusse examines the change in the countryside in Europe and Nitagai examines it in Japan. Both authors are concerned with farmers' social and economic life such as income, living standards and so on in comparison with urban residents who work in non-agricultural pursuits.

After warning about the problem of defining the countryside, in Chapter 12 Asbeek Brusse classifies the major European nations into three groups. She emphasises that urbanisation, rural depopulation and declining agricultural production have already been observed since the early 20th century and, of course, this prevailed into the postwar period. Two notes are worthwhile. The phase and degree of such changes differ considerably from country to country in Europe. Second, technological improvements in agriculture encouraged the use of labour-saving production techniques which pushed farmers to change their professions to urban employees.

The development regarding urbanisation, rural depopulation and agricultural modernisation in the 1950s and 1960s is remarkable. The use of tractors and combine harvesters become the symbols of technical progress, and capitalisation and family cars are common in rural areas. Various governments took action aimed at increasing productivity in agriculture, enforcing land consolidation schemes and so on. Some countries adopted income support programmes for farmers, by supporting relatively high prices for agricultural products. These changes, together with efficiency in agricultural production and income support programmes, raised the per-capita income level of farmers substantially. In the past earnings and incomes in rural areas were far lower than those in urban areas. The gap in incomes between rural households and urban households was closing rapidly and so too were their consumption levels. This is true, in particular in Sweden, Norway, Germany and Austria, where strong government policies were successful. For France and Italy, the gap remained constant in the 1950s, but it declined substantially in the 1960s because of a large outflow of rural workers into urban employment.

In Chapter 13, Nitagai compares rural and urban society in Japan. Before the war, Japanese farming units were extremely small and worked by hand. Also, half of all cultivated land was owned by landlords and thus the majority of farmers were tenant farmers. Overall, farmers were a symbol of poverty. Postwar land reform altered agriculture drastically. Productivity increased substantially. Farmers' numbers fell substantially as strong industrialisation and rapid economic growth pulled farmers from rural areas to urban areas, and into work in factories and offices in the manufacturing and service sectors. One important phenomenon of this period is the emergence of part-time farmers who also worked in factories and offices close to home. This raised the income level of rural households substantially and also consumption levels, leading to a substantial reduction in differentials in the living standard between town and country. Even in villages the number of non-farming residents who work in factories and offices exceeds that of farming residents. This affects the traditional village life considerably. For example, there now exists in one village a wide variety of interests among different households, making it difficult to have policies which favour traditional farmers. Occasionally, conflicts between them occur.

Nitagai proposes the integration of the two communities – the traditional community mainly of farmers and the urban community mainly for non-farmers. The role of the public sector, in particular local governments, and planning and development programmes, are crucial in achieving success. Farmers must be incorporated into a co-operative system where both farmers and non-farmers enjoy common community life. This too would benefit the urban sector. Large cities are already overcrowded and all regional urban centres are expanding into the countryside. In sum, Japan is already an urban society with all the serious problems caused by rapid urbanisation, such as oversized and overcrowded cities, industrial pollution and urban pollution, garbage wars, lack of parks and playgrounds, traffic jams, high land prices and rents. He attributes such problems to the lack of planning. Finally, he argues against imbalances in urbanisation. The problems in central urban areas and those in suburban areas are different, and thus need different policy recommendations.

Concluding remarks

The motor for the transformation from austerity to affluence was provided by the uninterrupted *economic development* of Western Europe and Japan at rates of growth unprecedented in modern economic history. The causes of this quarter-century boom are only imperfectly understood, although economists are a little better at accounting for differences between the economies experiencing it. By the end of the 1950s, indigenous labour reserves had been absorbed and further expansion was accompanied by increasing inflationary pressures. Everywhere un- or under-employment had given way to (over-)full employment, whereby posted vacancies exceeded numbers seeking work. Real wages accelerated and, with higher participation rates and the trickle down effect in 'youth wages', family disposable incomes rose faster still. As affluence spread and the backlog of demand for basic household goods was satisfied, so consumption patterns changed and the new consumerism further fuelled economic expansion.

Macroeconomic analysis tends to treat national income as a homogeneous whole and pays little attention to consumption shifts between different levels of income, and thus is rarely related to the social *transformation* that comes in their wake. One area in which the extra income was spent was in means of communication (personal means of transport, televisions, telephones and radios, and tourism) which, in turn, broke up old patterns of social relations (especially the relationship between community and workplace and in work and leisure). It also helped break the isolation of the countryside from the town. The rewards for youth labour also enabled the emergence of a counter-culture (transistor radios and record players) and allowed for greater generational emancipation (the break-up of multi-generational households and the lowering of the voting age). Finally, the increased role of collective consumption diminished the impact of personal risk (especially in the fields of healthcare, unemployment insurance and pension provision) and provided an anchor for the growing affluence experienced throughout the populations of Western Europe.

The emergence of affluence contributed to a shift in *political culture*. Thus far, the experiences of Europe and Japan followed broadly similar paths. However, when we ask the question about the demands made by these newly affluent societies of their political systems, we note sharply contrasting outcomes. In Western Europe, the collectively supplied 'soft-landing' was also a collectively financed one, and the increasing spread of (especially direct) taxation gave a broader section of the population a stake in the political process. The basic welfare provision largely reflected working-class aspirations and formed part of the immediate postwar settlement. Then middle-class pressures were added and there emerged a new coalition that demanded, besides a consolidation of welfare, a continuation of rising incomes and employment

opportunities. As the economic boom appeared unquenchable, political parties were inclined to promise it. Keynesianism became the intellectual legitimisation of the politics of affluence. A mixed managed
economy, shored up by neo-corporatist institutions and backed by big
government, appeared the key to ever growing prosperity. The Japanese
example provides a stark contrast. It was not that collective welfare was
not an aspiration, but the means to provide it were less sought in the
state. Instead, the policy mix was sought in a low level of basic state provision, a reliance on family and kinship networks and the provision of
social security by firms, as part of their labour-market strategies and an
attempt to cement the allegiance of the citizen.

Although we argue that there was a common process of transformation from austerity to affluence, we should emphasise also that there
were significant differences between the experiences of Japan and
Western Europe. For example, we could mention the persistence of protectionism in Japan as opposed to Western Europe. Overfull employment provides another area in which responses differed, with Europe
promoting large-scale immigration and Japan seeking a solution in
direct foreign investment in plant abroad. Finally, there was a major
difference in communal welfare provision with Europe seeking to create
a welfare state, whereas Japan relied on the private sector to underpin a
state of welfare. The key to these differences needs to be sought in one
of three categories of explanation:

- timing
- external environment
- historical particularism.

This volume has emphasised a common thread: economic development
beyond a threshold of high incomes and full employment to higher
consumption and new demands on society. We have constructed the
volume as though the process was largely autonomous and the only
difference was one of timing: Europe is later than America and Japan is
later than Europe. However, we need also to bear in mind that these
differences in timing also mean that each transition takes place against
a different external constellation. We have down-played the external
environment, largely in reaction to the swathe of 'Americanisation'
literature in both Japan and Western Europe which has long dominated
discussion on the subject. Nonetheless, the environment of Europe and
Japan differed in the availability of consumer goods in terms of size,
price and quality, in the development of radio and television broadcasting and the possibilities of travel. Finally, as historians, we have to
recognise that many of the social and political changes analysed in this

volume are 'path dependent', stemming from long differences in religion and social structure and, more recently, a different set of 'lessons' from the preceding years of depression and war.

None of the events described in this book were secret at the time and most aspects of the ideas we develop have been the subject of scientific analysis and scholarly writing. But the literature is highly fragmented, and there have been few attempts to synthesise these into a coherent and cohesive view of the postwar era. Moreover, little of this analysis has been historical in nature, with the result that much of the writing reflects the same perspectives (biases and delusions) as exhibited by contemporary commentators. But we do not live any longer in the 1960s.

Western European governments actually came to believe that they had found the key to continuous, crisis-free growth. Most of the population accepted that too. The recession and slow growth after 1973 in Western Europe only gradually made an impression in that mind-set. The realisation that there were more profound structural changes in the world economy (particularly in the economic upsurge in the Pacific basin) gave an impulse to supply-side analysis and led, in turn, to a rolling-up of government intervention in and responsibility for the economy. The rising levels of unemployment, that quickly surpassed thresholds previously considered untenable for political stability and that remained stuck there, began the erosion of affluence. The return of Japan to a (relatively) high-growth trajectory perpetuated the faith in the efficacy of the Japanese model for a further decade, but that too gradually crumbled amid the bank crises and stagnation of the past decade.

These changes have allowed the 'distance' necessary for a new historical analysis, shorn of the conceits and self-assurance of contemporaneous analysis. We can now view the period in which societies experienced the transformation from austerity to affluence as a special episode in modern history. We should be able to view its rich texture and interrelationships in the same way as we would, for example, analyse the *fin de siècle* of the nineteenth century. And, since a return to the achievements of the years 1950–73 remains an unspoken goal for contemporary politicians, a more satisfactory appraisal of what that involved is long overdue.

Reference

Iwata, K. (1990) *Rethinking International Trade*, Tokyo.

2
Growing Together?
The Internationalisation of the
West European Economy, 1950–71

Johnny Laursen

One of the most remarkable features of the West European economy during the period of high and sustained economic growth in the 1950s and 1960s was the degree to which the economic and social destinies of the Western European nations became intertwined. At the beginning of this era, in 1950, the austerity economies of the Western European countries were still locked into the framework of single nation-states by regulations, trade barriers, currency controls and national economic planning. At the close of the period, in 1971, the affluent, growth-sapped Western European economies appeared highly dependent on international economic factors beyond the control of national governments. The simple explanation is that the era of economic growth in Western Europe, and the move from austerity to affluence, had been accompanied by a process of internationalisation of the national economies and of the West European economy as a whole. As Andrew Shonfield put it in 1976: 'The fact is that the advanced industrial nations are together engaged in the operation of an international society which most directly affects their economic transactions. Any policy which tended to disintegrate this society would involve high costs and penalties' (Shonfield, 1976: 110).

The fact that a process of internationalisation of the West European economy did take place can be demonstrated by a few figures. Since 1948 the volume of exports and imports of Western Europe had risen twice as fast as the gross domestic product (GDP). The volume of West European exports rose between 8 and 9 per cent per year in the 1950s and 1960s. Between 1959 and 1965 alone 5 million workers migrated to industrial Northwest Europe. This internationalisation process took place during the most extraordinary growth period in West European history. Between 1950 and 1970 the European GDP experienced an

average 5.5 per cent growth per year while industrial production rose
7.1 per cent per year. In 1970 the per capita output was two and a half
times that of 1950 (Aldcroft, 1994: 136–7).

This era of economic growth, 1950–71, encompassed two distinct
phases. The first phase, between 1950 and 1958, saw the re-emergence
of economic growth in Western Europe within the framework of a
policy of austerity and a slow liberalisation of intra-European trade
and payments. Thus, in a sense the 1950s began in 1950 and ended
in 1958. The following phase – or 'decade' – saw the return to convertibility between the West European currencies and the American dollar,
the creation of the EEC (European Economic Community) and EFTA
(European Free Trade Association) and the emergence of new forms of
co-operation between US and Western Europe. These changes constituted the background for not only an unprecedented acceleration in
economic growth, but also for major qualitative changes in the international economic system such as the rise of the multinational corporation, new technology, new consumer goods, mass tourism and a
surge in international trade and payments. This period can be said
to have begun in 1958/59 and to have ended in 1971 with the breakdown of the Bretton Woods system. What role did the economic internationalisation play in this transformation and what can a study of
this process tell us about the change experienced by Western Europe in
1950s and 1960s?

The existing syntheses on the economic history of the period or on
international economic relations offer few answers. In contemporary
economics and political studies the period gave rise to some discussion
of the increasing interdependence of the Western liberal democracies
(Cooper, 1968; Keohane and Nye, 1977). The expansion of international
trade, foreign labour, foreign technology and investments also plays an
important role in many studies on the growth and development of the
international economy in the period. The interest has, however, primarily been motivated by the relevance of some of the elements in the
internationalisation process to the discussion about the causes of the
exceptional economic growth (Aldcroft, 1994; Kenwood and Lockheed,
1992; Van der Wee, 1987). On balance, the internationalisation of the
West European economy has not only been neglected as a field of
study in economic history; it has also been disregarded as a phenomenon in the development of the politics and economics of the postwar
European nation states in the era of affluence. One of the few exceptions is the double volume *International Economic Relations of the Western
World 1959–1971* edited by Andrew Shonfield (1976).

The breakthrough of economic interdependence in the West, its role in the coming of affluence and its repercussions for the national economies is still largely an open field. But what might a new interpretation and a better understanding of the internationalisation of the European economy contribute to the research strategy for the history of the era of affluence? Firstly, on the European level it is important to map the phenomenon of internationalisation, to measure its impact and to consider the problem of periodisation. What were the components of this process, when did they start and what was their relative importance? A study of this process can be used to test the traditional periodisation of the move from austerity to affluence in Western Europe in the 'silver fifties' and the 'golden sixties'. A closer look at the phases might provide a more sophisticated picture of the rise of affluent Western Europe and its roots in the 1950s.

Secondly, the internationalisation process allows us to plot some of the structural changes experienced by West European society in this period: it provides important explanations of changes in national economies and of the direction taken by economic development and structural change in Western Europe. Starting a volume on the age of affluence with the international perspective might also provide some of the benefits of comparative history. Put another way: looking at the internationalisation process might tell us as much about what happened at the national level, as it does about what happened at the international level. It might tell us what to look for and where to look for the socio-economic and political changes affecting all Western Europe.

Thirdly, how did economic internationalisation affect the capabilities of the West European nation states to adapt to external change while, at the same time, securing objectives of balanced economic growth and national welfare? What we are talking about here as one phenomenon are in fact several interlocking processes. One involved the changing relationship between the national economies and international markets for goods, money and services. The second is the changing relationship between Western Europe and the major economic power in the world, the USA, through the period (at the end of the period this was becoming still more complex with the emergence of Japan as a major industrial power). Finally, as we shall see, the internationalisation process also embraced a process toward a 'Europeanisation' of the national economies of the West European states. An understanding of these processes is an important requirement for understanding the changing conditions under which the West European states grasped with socio-economic change and with external economic challenges in the period after 1958–59. In this survey, which will focus in operational terms on the European members of the OECD, we will examine three expressions of the internationalisation process: the expansion of trade; international capital movements; and the changes in the international economic system of the OECD countries in the period.

International markets

The literature is agreed on the key role of trade in the growing interdependence between the national economies of Western Europe and the international economy (Pinder, 1980: 367). The expansion of trade in the postwar period was indeed exceptional. In the 1950s and 1960s the volume of West European exports expanded at between 8 and 9 per cent per annum. For no country, other than the UK, was the annual average rate of increase of exports below 5 per cent. West Germany and Italy topped the league (Aldcroft, 1994: 148–9). M.M. Postan observed that, whereas between the wars the foreign trade had hardly grown at all, exports and imports of the West European countries grew at an annual average rate of about 7 per cent between 1948 and 1962. This topped GNP's growth rate of about 4 per cent per year over the same period and even exceeded the growth of foreign trade during the golden age from 1870 to 1913. The trade expansion was particularly strong in inter-European trade, and above all, in trade in manufactures. Between 1950 and 1963 the value of the exports of the European OECD countries grew from a monthly average of $1587 million to $4975 million (more than three-fold), while total world exports increased only by 80 per cent (1967, 90–4):

> ... Western European countries themselves were now absorbing an ever-increasing share of the world's trade in manufactures. In the fifties and sixties the ability of Western countries to take in each other's outputs rose very steeply, with the result that most of them had come to depend more and more on the markets within Europe itself and in the USA.
>
> (Postan, 1967: 94)

This process intensified in the following decade. The rate of growth even accelerated through the 1960s. While Europe became less dependent on imports of primary products from the developing and the developed overseas countries between 1955 and 1969, the intra-European trade with manufactures rose from 18 to 29 per cent of the volume of world trade in all commodities. On the world level total merchandise trade increased from 7.5 per cent of world output to 11 per cent. The bulk of this increase was in intra-European trade which expanded from 5.5 per cent of European GDP to 9.5 per cent. In 1955 intra-trade in Western Europe represented 73.1 per cent of Western European trade. In 1969 this figure had grown to 74.7 per cent. These figures hide an increase in intra-trade with manufactures in Western Europe from 46.8 per cent to 57.2 per cent (United Nations, 1972: 26–7, 30).

The EEC was the main trading group within Western Europe. Intra-EEC trade not only accounted for over one-third of European trade in 1969, but also had the most rapid expansion. Trade among the EEC countries grew by nearly 13 per cent (in constant prices) between 1955 and 1969. Exceptionally, the real value trade with foodstuffs also increased and by 11.5 per cent annually. Trade among EFTA-countries grew slower than total intra-European trade with its share dropping from 9.5 to 8 per cent. This was primarily because of the poor British export performance in the period, including its trade within EFTA. Among the other EFTA states, however, trade expanded by 11.5 per cent per year with intra-Nordic trade accounting for the bulk of the expansion. The share of imports of manufactures expanded from 15 per cent of the consumption in 1955 to 27.5 per cent in 1969 (United Nations, 1972: 31).

The proliferation of trade within manufactures was the more general sign of ongoing structural changes in the international economy in general and in the West European in particular. One change hiding behind the overall figures was the difference in the performance of the branches included under the title 'manufactures'. Through the 1960s by far the most expansive area in industrial Western Europe was the chemical group with output growing at an annual rate of 9 per cent against the general average of 5.5 per cent. The success of the metal-using industries as a whole was less conspicuous, but this group included some of the most fast growing sectors such as automobiles, electronics and electric engineering. While the rate of expansion of output in metal-using industries in industrial Western Europe in the period 1958–60 to 1967–69 was 5.3 per cent, employment only grew at a rate of 1.7 per cent. This was even more pronounced in chemicals and rubber, expanding 9.3 per cent against an employment growing 1.8 per cent. Employment in other branches almost stagnated. Food processing and metal making increased employment by 0.1 per cent and 0.2 per cent respectively, while output grew by 4.4 per cent in both branches. Employment in textiles even fell by 0.7 per cent corresponding to about 700 000 jobs. The explanation must be sought in the extensive

productivity gains in the period. In industrial Western Europe the productivity gain in chemicals, rubber, textiles and light industries were
particularly impressive. In manufacturing output per person employed
grew by 4.8 per cent (United Nations, 1972: 41–3).

Another change hiding behind the increase in intra-trade within
manufactures in Western Europe was a shift in import–export patterns.
The export structures of the four large countries (UK, West Germany,
France and Italy) changed little in the period, as their exports already
were concentrated in the expansive manufacturing branches. Among the
seven small industrial countries (Norway, Sweden, Denmark, Finland,
Belgium–Luxembourg, the Netherlands; data are not available for
Switzerland) the change was more perceptible as the share of manu-
facture exports grew relatively in comparison to the traditional exports
of these countries (food processing, wood, pulp, paper and steel).
The five less industrialised countries (Greece, Ireland, Portugal, Spain
and Yugoslavia) saw even larger changes in the relative share of manufacturing exports. The dependence on exports was, however, growing
among the four large countries. In the area with the highest export
dependence, non-electric machines, the export share grew from 28 per
cent in 1958–60 to 42 per cent in 1967–69. Imports grew in most
branches both in consumer goods and in machinery industries.

The increasing import shares in machinery and engineering industries was a reflection of a particularly fast growth in trade in components, parts and semi-finished product between manufacturers in
Western Europe. In Belgium for example the share of total input in the
machinery industry accounted for by components or parts produced
abroad rose from 12 to 28 per cent between 1959 and 1965. In France
the corresponding figure rose from 3 to 7 per cent, in Italy from 2 to 10
and in West Germany from 5 to 6 per cent. These figures show the trend
of intra-branch and inter-branch specialisation in Western Europe
(United Nations, 1972: 53, 60–1).

The tendency towards economic integration and trade expansion
was furthered by the steep economic growth at the end of the decade
where capacity utilisation in many West European countries increased
the import from neighbouring countries. One feature of this development was a rise in the second half of the 1960s of the import elasticity
which can to some degree be explained with the shift in growth.
Whereas growth among the large countries in 1968 had been higher
than among the small industrial countries, in 1969 the combined GNP
of the seven major economies increased by only 4.8 per cent, while
that of the smaller industrial countries rose by about 5.7 per cent. As the

small countries in 1968 accounted for only 11 per cent of the combined GNP of the industrial areas, but for 28 per cent of their combined imports, the difference in GNP growth rate between the two areas contributed to an intensification of trade (GATT, 1970: 7–11).

Toward the end of the period the commodity pattern and the trade pattern changed. One of the most significant developments was the emergence of Japan as an important exporter of manufactures to Western Europe. The rise of Japanese exports of manufactured goods between 1963 and 1972 was impressive, indeed. Particularly the export of engineering products increased (from $0.24 billion in 1963 to $3.09 billion in 1972). Under this heading not least office and telecommunications equipment, household appliances, motor cars and other transport equipment constituted important commodity categories. The import propensity in Western Europe had by 1972 come to provide one of the major outlets for Japanese exports of industrial goods.

There is a pronounced contrast here to the development of North American trade with Western Europe through the same period. It is true that Western Europe also provided a crucial market for American exports, but while Japanese exports surged, those of North America climbed at a more leisurely rate. The export of engineering products (still the most important category) thus rose from $2.16 billion in 1963 to $6.65 billion in 1972. Nevertheless, in 1972 the economic integration of the West European economy with the North American economy remained closer than that of Western Europe with Japan. In 1972 North American exports of manufactured goods to Western Europe amounted to $10.85 billion against $9.65 billion Japanese exports. The commodity pattern also differed from the Japanese in the sense that commodities, such as chemicals and machine parts, that were common in inter-industry and inter-branch exchanges, were more important in North American exports to Western Europe than they were in the Japanese exports, where consumer goods and household appliances played a relatively central role.

For Western Europe these figures were overshadowed by inter-European trade. In 1972 Western European exports of manufactured goods amounted to $149.95 billion. Of these $99.40 billion were part of exchanges of goods among the West European countries. Goods for $15.55 billion went to North America and only $1.80 billion to Japan. The commodity pattern indicates that both an increase in inter-industrial goods and consumer goods took place between 1963 and 1972. Western European exports of chemicals rose from $3.26 billion to $12.70 billion through this period, consumer goods from $1.77 to

$7.68 and engineering products from $13.82 to $47.30. The lion's share in the latter category is divided between machine parts which grew from $2.13 billion to $7.72, household appliances growing from $1.06 to $3.99 billion and, finally, motor cars performing the impressive growth from $2.71 billion to $10.71 billion in 1972 (GATT, 1978: Tables B1 and B3). Motor cars played a central role in the industrial expansion in Western Europe and in the expansion of West European trade through our period (GATT, 1966: 113–19).

Foreign direct investment

Together with the ever-increasing flow of commodities over European borders additional international transfers of capital began to change Western Europe's economic structures. Foreign capital not only added to the domestic capital available for investments, it also brought new technology, new management forms and influence to large foreign corporations. The most important of these transfers of capital was foreign direct investment. Following in its wake foreign technology, management styles and decisionmaking power began to function as factors changing the production and market structures of Western Europe. The development of foreign direct investment fell in two distinct phases in the postwar period. The first, up till 1957, was characterised by American and West European investment in mining, raw materials and petroleum in the less developed countries and in Commonwealth countries. The second phase from 1958 onwards saw a shift of American investment toward Western Europe in general and to manufacturing in particular. A factor that greatly furthered this development was the restoration of convertibility for non-residents in many countries by the end of the 1950s and European integration. In 1959 the OEEC (Organization for European Economic Cooperation) adopted a code for the liberalisation of capital movements, the customs union of the EEC began to function and EFTA was established. These preferential areas and the general economic expansion in Western Europe induced many American firms to establish a foothold on the European market (United Nations, 1969: 57).

Between 1950 and 1958 direct American investment in Western Europe constituted on average $152 million annually. Of these $68 million were invested in the UK against $63 million in the EEC countries. In the 1960s the destination of American direct investment, having grown to an annual average of $1384 million 1963–66, shifted. Now $837 million went to the EEC countries – mainly West Germany – against

$260 million to the UK. With this shift from the world to Western Europe, and from the UK to the EEC, another shift took place between the branches where investments were placed. In 1950–58 American enterprises placed an annual average of $83 million in mining, smelting and petroleum activities and $54 million in manufacturing in Western Europe. In 1963–66 these figures had changed to $440 million in mining and so on and $649 million in manufacturing. The West European share of US direct investment abroad increased from 17 per cent in 1950 to 30 per cent in 1966.

Even though the proportion of these investments out of overall economic activity in Western Europe was small some sectors particularly felt the impact of American ownership. In 1964 American investment totalled $3102 million (current) in petroleum and $6547 million in manufacturing. Within the latter figure transportation equipment (mainly motor cars) accounted for $1783 million, non-electric machinery $1186 and chemicals accounted for $1073 million. A large part of the production of these American manufacturing affiliates in Western Europe was absorbed by local markets. In 1965 this figure was 77 per cent. While total exports from the US to Western Europe reached $9080 million that year, local sales of manufacturing affiliates in Western Europe climbed to $14 357 million. American firms held a solid grip on the markets for petroleum products, motor cars, chemicals and non-electric machines. In 1966 it was estimated that American affiliates produced 24 per cent of the motor cars in the EEC, 20 per cent of electric engineering and 15 per cent of synthetic rubber. Of more specialised commodities such as computers the market share was even more impressive (United Nations, 1969: 59–61). In 1963 the French Finance Ministry estimated that firms with substantial American influence controlled among other 87 per cent of the production of razor blades and safety razors, 70 per cent in sewing machines and 35.2 per cent in tractors and agricultural equipment (Dickie, 1970: 13–14).

The share of expenditure of American corporations on plant and equipment out of the gross domestic fixed capital formation in the West European countries varied substantially in the period under review. It ranged from 10 per cent for the United Kingdom and 9.3 per cent for Belgium–Luxembourg to a low 4.0 per cent for France. Overall the share was growing for the EEC as a whole from 2.2 per cent in 1957 to 4.5 per cent in 1965. Even though several factors may have influenced this growing involvement in the EEC market, such as lower production costs, lower transport costs and the possibility to circumvent strict US legislation on trusts and market oligopolies the most important factors were doubtless the circumvention of the EEC tariff barriers and the dynamic growth on the EEC market (United Nations, 1969: 67–8).

The West Europeans reacted to the wave of American direct investment in the 1950s and 1960s with mixed feelings. On the one hand the American investment brought hard currency, capital and foreign technology to the host countries. On the other hand it brought foreign economic power, technological dependence and foreign management styles. The French were a classical example of pursuing a policy of strong resistance toward direct American investment, fearing that foreign business would interfere with national economic planning and national policy priorities. Belgium, by contrast, considered that foreign investment supplemented the domestic economy and foreign investment was welcomed. Thus, as foreign firms met difficulties in France in some instances investments were transferred to Belgium, another member of the EEC (Kindleberger, 1969: 74 ff; Servan-Schreiber, 1967).

One of the effects associated with foreign direct investment is transfer of foreign technology to the host country. In the 1960s such technology transfer, however, also began to move independently of direct investment. In 1965 American residents earned more than $1 billion in royalties and licensing fees. More than $300 million of this was not associated with American investment abroad. In 1964 it was estimated that more than a quarter of American results from research and development was transferred to Britain through American firms located in that country. The result of this long-term process was a diffusion of American technology to Western Europe. The American economy relying on new technologies and new products in its export to Western Europe, therefore, began to find it increasingly difficult to rely on its technological lead (Cooper, 1968: 105–6). As firms began to adapt to the potentials of the large Atlantic market both the home and the host countries of the international corporations began to face increasing difficulties with controlling the movement and impact new of technology.

International money

Foreign direct investment, technology transfers and foreign economic influence constituted but some of the changes and challenges confronting West European economies in the wake of changing international economic relations. Another was the awakening of international capital and money markets, and the changes arising from this for intra-European economic relations and US–European relations and for the balance between states and markets in international economic relations.

Through the 1950s the most important West European capital exporter was the UK. British investments in developed overseas countries had primarily been directed to Australia, New Zealand and South Africa. In 1960–62 British investments in the developed sterling countries amounted to an annual average of $198 million and in 1963–65 to $307.6 million. These were also the only developed countries in the world where British capital was more important than American. In addition British investments in the EEC countries were substantial. Unfortunately there are no comparable data for the period prior to 1958, but after 1960 British enterprises invested more in the EEC countries than any of the EEC member countries did. The annual average of British investments in the EEC rose from $72 million in 1960–62 to $105.3 million in 1963–65 (Cooper, 1986: 61–2).

While British capital export was declining in the 1960s, EEC countries with a strong export performance like West Germany and Italy began to emerge as strong capital exporters. In the period 1966–9 the annual rate of West German private long-term capital export was $1.1 billion, against $0.4 billion for Italy and $0.15 for the UK. Contrary to the British case these countries concentrated on portfolio investment and long-term credit facilities. Some of this capital export took the form of European purchases of American shares and bonds. In 1960–65 the flow of European capital to the US amounted to the annual average of $320 million. In 1966–69 the capital movement had reached an annual average of $2.7 billion. Much of this capital had the form of portfolio investment in American corporations investing in Western Europe (United Nations, 1969: 65–6; United Nations, 1972: 37). Thus, there was a changing balance in terms of private long-term capital exchanges between the US and Western Europe in the period. While the American direct investment after 1957 began to exceed West European direct investment in America, a parallel development took place toward increasing private West European portfolio investment:

It may be argued therefore that the United States has in fact acted as a financial intermediary for Europe and that in effect the westward flow of funds into United States securities is in some way related to the eastward flow of direct investment. This appears natural as the Europeans buy equities in the bigger United States companies and it is precisely these companies that invest in Europe. This is to say that European capital merged with American management to invest in Europe.

(United Nations, 1969: 65)

Following the immense expansion of international payments caused by the growing volume of trade, services and international transactions, Western European governments and monetary authorities faced the question of how to control this cosmopolitan money. Already in the 1950s there had been examples of destabilising effects of short-term international capital movements. These problems had primarily concentrated on the UK and had connections to leads and lags in commercial payments related to trade. Before 1958, however, short-term money movements had been strictly controlled by currency controls and non-convertibility of the West European currencies. After the move to convertibility in 1958 and the abolition of the European Payments Union, the gradual freeing of the international capital markets posed a new formidable challenge to national economic policy in Western Europe. Despite a growth of official reserves in West European central banks from $10 billion in 1950, to $20 billion in 1958 and $27 billion in 1962, short-term money movements showed itself as an impetuous and rowdy force. Throughout the 1960s the new strength of West European currencies, economic expansion and the higher interest rates in Western Europe spurred a flow of American private capital to Western Europe (Maddison, 1964: 171–3). This flow posed several challenges to the international economic order.

One of these was the so-called 'Euro-dollars' market. This was the name for the growing trend after 1957 for banks outside the US to lend in and to accept deposits denominated in US dollars. Such international banking operations were involved in financing international trade or were swapped into West European currencies for lending in domestic markets (Cooper, 1986: 116–22; BIS, 1964: 127). Between 1963 and 1970 the amounts handled by this market increased from $7 billion to $57 billion. The rapid expansion of such banking operations not only served to increase and accelerate the interaction between national money markets, but also exposed national economic policies to sudden crises. At times the market helped finance balance-of-payments deficits, thus stabilising economic growth, but at other times it caused severe problems for national economic policies. In 1960 there was a flurry at the London gold market which caused the price of an ounce of gold to rise from $35 to $40 accompanied by a rush of short-term capital 1960–61 from the US to Europe at the size of $3 billion. In 1961 the revaluation of the Deutschmark caused another pressure on the British pound caused by sudden short-term capital movements. (Strange, 1976: 59–62, 176–94; United Nations, 1972: 37; Van der Wee, 1987: 469–72.)

Even though international capital markets developed less rapidly than international money markets, this factor too contributed to the increasing transatlantic links in the 1960s. Between 1950 and 1969 American external liquid liabilities rose from $9 billion to $55 billion, against American assets rising from $12 billion to $41 billion. And while in 1959 more than half of these liabilities were held by public authorities, in 1969 this share had dropped to about one-quarter, the rest held by private corporations (United Nations, 1972: 38). To a certain extent the international capital markets – not least New York – offered advantages for West European governments looking for long-term loans. In 1965 the European Coal and Steel Community raised about two-thirds of its funds at the New York capital market, and after 1960 several West European countries borrowed at the New York market as did many public authorities and private corporations (Cooper, 1986: 131–5; Shonfield, 1976: 113).

The result of these surging flows of money and capital between countries, markets and continents presented a formidable challenge to the international monetary system and to the governments of the countries primarily involved, in both Western Europe and the US. In the 1960s capital assets that had formerly been kept within national frontiers or been able to move only through the sluices of national currency controls, began to move more freely and quickly between different currencies and capital markets. In Susan Strange's words:

> Indeed, the phoenix that rose in those three short years (1958–61 – JL) from long-cold ashes was a bigger and improved version of its predecessor, with distinctive new features that made it even faster acting and more capable of destroying international monetary stability.
>
> (1976: 58)

The reborn international money markets confronted the governments with the dilemma of how to respond to a sudden crisis of confidence in a currency or how to redress sudden balance-of-payments deficits. Deflationary measures of the size seen in the 1930s had become politically unacceptable in the 1960s; and while the speed and volume of international transactions had increased, public reserves had not grown accordingly. In 1971 the US Tariff Commission calculated short-term dollar assets on the international markets to be $268 billion. This was twice as much as central banks and international monetary institutions could muster: 'These are the reserves with which the central banks fight to defend their exchange rates. The resources of the private sector outclass them' (Shonfield, 1976: 110–12). The unification of West Europe and North America into – more or less – one market for money and capital had fundamentally transformed the conditions for national economic policy.

To a certain extent, the surge in international trade and financial transactions was caused by growing international production and by the rise of the multinational corporation as one of the major organising factors behind the international market. In the 1960s multinationals, beyond state control and without definite national allegiance, became crucial actors in the emerging international markets. Transfers of goods or money between the national branches of such corporations accounted for a substantial share of overall international transactions. In the late 1960s 20 per cent of British exports were part of such transactions within single companies. The same held good for movements of money between national currencies or financial markets (Shonfield, 1976: 114–16). In Shonfield's words:

> This case serves to illustrate in an especially acute form the more general problem created for governments by the spreading network of international financial transactions, within and between large corporations, superimposed on the conventional processes of international trade. The means available to governments for acquiring the information needed in order to exercise surveillance over international trade and payments are becoming decreasingly efficient.
>
> (116)

On the other hand it seemed that the multinational corporations tended to bestow some of the advantages of an international division of labour, economics of scale, new technology and modern management techniques on Western Europe (Shonfield, 1976: 117–19). These were exactly some of the trends we have observed in this overview over two of the most significant appearances of the internationalisation of the West European economy.

Conclusion

The economic consequences of the expansion of trade and international payments between Western Europe and the US economy inherent in the re-emerging international economic system in the 1960s not only changed the economic balance between the US and Western Europe, but also allowed the market to strike back. At the close of the era of affluence, in 1971, the main agenda was no longer set by the US, but by a much more vigorous and potentially disruptive force, the international market.

From this preliminary survey it is clear that the 'process of internationalisation' in our period can only be a makeshift epithet for a cluster of interlocking and mutually interrelated processes at the national and international level. Deeply rooted in the 1950s and in the way that Western Europe had made its return to a relatively liberal international economic order, in this decade these processes became tremendous agents of socio-economic and political change in the 'era of affluence'. The growth of international trade opened the way for a torrent of international transactions in the form of payments, portfolio investment, international money and so on. At the national level these forces spurred changes in the industrial economy of the single states towards economies of scale, specialisation, a more refined division of labour and increased productivity. These changes were reinforced by the shifts in the flows of foreign direct investment toward Western Europe and manufactures. Direct investments brought new production techniques, new technology, new management forms and a new organisation of the inter-industrial division of labour. These changes as of yet, have been scarcely colonised by historians. Research both at the national and the international level should aim at establishing the links of causation and interaction between these changes and between national and international history at the socio-economic level.

Future historical research, with national or international perspective, will further have to trace the political decisions, non-decisions and considerations with regard to these changes. How did the West European states meet the challenge of the international market, the power of the multinational corporations and the flood and ebb of international money? International historians will have to trace the shifting relative economic roles of the West European economies and their relationship to the US economy. What were the causes and effects of the shifts between the position of the British economy in Western Europe and that of for example West Germany and Italy towards the end of the 1960s? And furthermore: what was the character of the emerging links between Japan's position in the international economy and that of Western Europe through the era of affluence?

References

Aldcroft, D.H. (1994) *The European Economy 1914–1990*, London.
Bank for International Settlements (BIS) (1964) Thirty-Fourth Annual Report, Basle.
Cooper, R.N. (1968) *The Economics of Interdependence: Economic Policy in the Atlantic Community*, New York.
Dickie, R.B. (1970) *Foreign Investment: France. A Case Study*, Leyden.
GATT (1966) *International Trade, 1965*, Geneva.
GATT (1970) *International Trade, 1969*, Geneva.
GATT (1978) *Networks of World Trade by Areas and Commodity Classes 1955–1976*, Gatt International Studies in Trade No. 7, Geneva.
Kenwood, A.G. and A.L. Lockheed (1992) *The Growth of the International Economy 1820–1990*, London.
Keohane, R.O. and J.S. Nye (1977) *Power and Interdependence. World Politics in Transition*, Boston.
Kindleberger C.P. (1969) *American Business Abroad. Six Lectures on Direct Investment*, New Haven.
Maddison, A. (1964) *Economic Growth in the West. Comparative Experience in Europe and North America*, London.
Pinder, J. (1980) 'Europe in the World Economy 1920–1970' in C.M. Cipolla (ed.) The Fontana Economic History of Europa, Vol. 6, part 1.
Postan, M.M. (1967) *An Economic History of Western Europa 1945–1964*, London.
Servan-Schreiber, J.J. (1967) *Le Défi Américain*, Paris.
Shonfield, A. (1976) 'International Economic Relations of the Western World. An Overall View' in A. Shonfield (ed.) *International Economic Relations of the Western World 1959–1971*, Vol. 1, London.
Strange S. (1976) 'International Monetary Relations', A. Shonfield (ed.) *International Economic Relations of the Western World 1959–1971*, Vol. 2, London.
United Nations (Economic Commission for Europe) (1969) 'International direct investment by private enterprises in Western Europa and North America', *Economic Bulletin for Europe*, Vol 19. no. 1, 1967–68.
United Nations (Economic Commission for Europa) (1972) 'Economic Survey of Europe in 1971', Part 1, *The European Economy from the 1950s to the 1970s*, New York.
Van der Wee, H. (1987) *Prosperity and Upheaval. The World Economy 1945–1980*, Harmondsworth.

3
Internationalisation and Economic Development: the Case of Japan

Kazumasa Iwata

The term 'internationalisation of national economy' is often used synonymously with 'growing interdependence' through movements across national boundaries of goods, services, information, production factors (capital and workers) and culture. Yet it carries different connotations. While growing interdependence encourages the move toward integrating the national economy into the network of international division of labour, and thus facilitates improved resource allocation across the border, the internationalisation causes transformation of values, attitudes and political and economic systems under the circumstance of growing interdependence (see also Ogata (1992)).

The specialisation or assimilation of different economic systems among national economies can bring about the Pareto improvement, as in the case of free trade of goods and services based on difference in technology and natural endowments. Yet international co-ordination is needed to avoid the conflicts arising from the difference in systems and attitudes under the increasing interdependence.

The process of internationalisation can be symmetric or asymmetric. In the first case each nation can engage in exchange of values and attitudes and penetrate the other. In the second case, one hegemonic nation influences the other, while the latter adjusts to an international circumstance or international standards and accepts the attitudinal changes in harmony with the values of the hegemonic country.

Throughout history Japan has been exposed to the imported values and systems from China and then Western countries. Japan's internationalisation process scarcely involved the Japanisation of other nations: the exception was the short period during the Second World War when Japan embarked on the establishment of the 'Great East Asian

Co-prosperity Area'. This passivity forms a sharp contrast to the history of hegemonic countries like China, the UK and the United States.

The process of internationalisation

In the process of modernisation since the Meiji Restoration following the seclusion under the Shogunate after 1639, Japan has attempted constantly to assimilate or reject the Western ideas and systems by trial and error. Although international trade and information exchange did take place under government control during the seclusion period (seclusion therefore implying independence from the hegemonic trade regime of China (Shinbo, 1995)), we can discern three prominent waves of internationalisation of the Japanese economy in the subsequent period.

The first was the period of the early Meiji Restoration (1868–85) when the modernisation process was initiated. The second was the immediate postwar period (1945–50) when Americanisation proceeded in the socio-political and economic spheres, through implementation of various reforms aimed at democratisation and demilitarisation of socio-political structures. The third wave came after the 1980s when the internationalisation has been developed in a more fully fledged way.

The postwar reforms in the second wave of internationalisation were superimposed on the prototype of the Japanese market economy, which was formed during the war. It was the prototype system, combined with postwar reforms, that allowed Japan to achieve the transition from austerity to affluence. Immediately after the war Japan lost about 41 per cent of national wealth, while the production level of consumption goods was only 24.4 per cent when compared with the prewar level. Hunger threatened the people. The per capita national income was only $14 in 1946, yet it grew by 15 per cent on average during the period from 1950 to the early-1970s. Compared with the prewar growth process postwar development was characterised, until 1973, by high and stable growth under the favourable international circumstances of liberalised trade and investment and stable energy prices. By the early 1970s, Japan had caught up with the income level of advanced economies and, by 1987, had overtaken US per capita national income, if the current exchange rate is used for the comparison (though not if purchasing power parities are taken into account).

Between the first and the second waves, due to the war, there was interruption in the movement toward growing economic interdependence. Yet even during the Second World War Japan transplanted the practice and institutions of economic planning from the American New Deal, from the control economy of Nazi Germany, as well as the Soviet plan economy.

Possibly in common with other developed countries, the movement towards economic planning emerged in the early 1930s. It was founded on the need to build a base of heavy industry and petrochemicals in preparation for total war, forming the prototype for the postwar Japanese economic system (Okazaki and Okuno, 1993). Noguchi named the prototype system the 'Year-1940 regime' to distinguish it from the laissez-faire capitalism of the 1920s (1995).

There is some controversy over the extent to which postwar reforms affected and transformed the Year-1940 regime. Several authors argue that the Japanese-style labour–management relations were formed as a result of councils and struggles between labour and management in the late 1940s, reflecting the introduction of concepts of democracy and human rights into postwar Japan. Another point of controversy is the change in corporate governance, where one author has emphasised the crucial role played by the Japanisation of the American impact in the 1950s in the formation of the contemporary Japanese market model (Hashimoto, 1995). Nonetheless, the main features of the Year-1940 regime lie in the employee-oriented corporate governance coupled with the subcontractor system, the predominance of an indirect financing system (notably the main bank system), the centralised fiscal system, the close relationship between business circles and bureaucrats through the intermediation by trade associations (which was founded in an attempt to facilitate technology transfer from abroad in 1885).

Given the institutional and strategic complementarities among the various subsystems, it survived the postwar reforms and persists even to this day with certain degree of transformation and refinement. For instance the origin of Toyota's 'Kanban system' (the 'just-in-time-inventory management system') can be traced back to the system connecting the first subcontractor companies with the assembly factory of trucks for military use in the war economy. The JIT system was elaborated and completed in the early-1970s (Nagao, 1995).

Long before others 'discovered' the origin of the Japanese-type market economy, Nakamura had drawn attention to the continuity of economic institutions and the key industries (Nakamura, 1993). Typical among industries was the establishment of an automobile industry. Before the war, General Motors (GM) and Ford dominated the Japanese passenger car market and held 98 per cent market share of domestic production in 1930. Although in the 1920s there had been no restrictive measures on foreign direct investment, after the Manchurian Incident in 1931 the

government attempted to promote the production of domestic passenger cars (by Toyota and Nissan) and exclude the production by foreign
firms in Japan, to which end it promulgated the 'Law for Controlling
Automobile Manufacturing' in 1936. GM first reacted by embarking
on a joint venture with Nissan, but abandoned ownership in 1936.
Ford initially expanded the plant in Yokohama (1925), but eventually
withdrew from Japan due to the pressure by the Japanese Army (which
had close connection with Nissan). The 'Law of the Import Quotas',
issued in 1939, terminated the production of cars by foreign firms in
Japan. Due to the bitter inter-war experience, the US automobile industry
became hesitant in making foreign direct investment in postwar Japan.
Economic management was no exception. The idea of 'production
doubling' was conceived in 1936 by a military staff officer, Kanji Ishihara,
who considered it necessary to catch up with the production level of
Western countries, notably the US, within 20 years in order to prepare
for total war (Kobayashi, Okazaki and Yonekura, 1995). He concluded,
during his visit to Germany, that victory in the First World War had
depended critically on industrial power centred on heavy industry and
petrochemicals. His proposal was not endorsed by headquarters, since
warfare loomed more rapidly than Ishihara envisaged. However his
idea was partially implemented by the Manchurian government within
the framework of the 'Five-Year-Plan on the Construction and Expansion
of the Military Industry of Japan integrated with Manchuria' (1932–37)
and the subsequent 'Five-Year Plan on Industrial Development in
Manchuria' (1937–41). The exercise of the control economy in
Manchuria after 1932 was carried out by pro-reform bureaucrats – one
of the leaders was Nobusuke Kishi (the Prime Minister at the time of
the amendment of the Japan–US Security Treaty after the war). The
experience of a control economy through a newly-created legal system
and the practice of administrative guidance was transferred from
Manchuria to Japan and the direct control method developed in
Manchuria replaced the indirect method for controlling the economy
based on cartel formation by the private sector (Shinbo, 1995).

Somewhat paradoxically Ishihara's idea was realised within the
framework of the 'National Income Doubling Plan' under the Ikeda
cabinet after the political turmoil at the time of the amendment of
the US–Japan Security Treaty. There is some debate about the origin of
the idea. It has been suggested that Ikeda's interest had been caught by
an article on 'wage doubling' published in Yomiuri Shinban in 1959,
subsequently underpinned by a theoretical vindication published
in 1961 (Kanamori, 1995). Using the Harrod-Domar model in 1961

Osamu Shimomura made surprisingly precise predictions for the 1960s of a 2.69-fold increase in real GNP – the outcome was a 2.76-fold rise (Shimomura, 1961). Yet it was Prime Minister Kishi (not Mr Ikeda) who charged the Economic Council in 1959 with investigating the feasibility of an economic plan aimed at doubling the scale of the economy. And while one may surmise that Ikeda's idea was taken up by Kishi, Kishi had been familiar with the idea of production doubling since 1936. Moreover Teruhiko Iwasaki, who was in charge of the rationalisation policy for the steel and petrochemical industries in the early 1950s, also suggests that it was Kishi who first set the goal of income doubling (Kobayasi, Okazaki and Yonekura, 1995). Such arguments notwithstanding, the plan is regarded as the most successful of the various postwar plans by the government in catching up with advanced affluent economies.

Trade structure and trade policy

The Year-1940 regime was strongly growth- and production-oriented, was biased toward an autarchic production system in the manufacturing sector and was unfriendly towards imported manufactured goods except for the purposes of technology catch-up. Its continuity after the war conferred particular features on the internationalisation process in post war Japan.

Leaving aside the systemic socio-political changes caused by the war, Ohkawa, looking at changes in the international trade structure, distinguished four development phases since the start of modernisation (Ohkawa and Kohama, 1989):

- 1870–1900 traditional product export and primary import substitution of non-durable consumer goods;
- 1900–19 primary export substitution mainly by light manufactured goods;
- 1919–60 secondary import substitution by durable consumer and producer goods;
- 1960–75 secondary export substitution mainly by machinery manufacturing industries.

Before the Second World War, Japan was very successful in import substitution with respect to cotton, textiles and steel. This process gained momentum through the preparation of the war-time economy as exemplified by passenger cars and electric machinery. Propelled by the need to create an autarchic system, there was a tendency to establish a self-sufficient production system within the manufacturing sector except for raw materials and energy, and it was the shortage of energy, notably oil, that drove Japan to military invasion into South-East Asia. What is important is the fact that the tendency toward an autarchic production structure was consolidated not only during the war period but also continued in the period immediately afterwards (1945–49).

The informal study group on 'the Fundamental Problems of Recon-struction of the Japanese Economy' was formed within government on the day after the end of the Second World War. The main participants were prominent scholars, including Marxists, backed-up by bureaucrats (Yonosuke Goto, Saburo Okita, Shokichi Namiki and Yutaka Oda) as the secretariat. The study group envisioned the further development of the international division of labour as well as movements toward planification and socialisation of the Japanese economy (Arisawa and Nakamura, 1990).

Given the energy shortage for reconstruction, a 'priority production scheme' was implemented in 1946 and 1947, based on Arisawa's pro-posal in response to the question posed by Prime Minister Shigeru Yoshida on the most urgently needed items of imports for reconstruc-tion. Yoshida asked the SCAP (Supreme Commander for Allied Powers) to allow the compensation of warfare loss for enterprises. The SCAP rejected it, but it proposed instead allowing the priority import of cer-tain items needed for industrial reconstruction.

Arisawa's supply-side (production-goods-augmenting) oriented scheme aimed at a target of domestic coal production of 30 million tons (from the level of 22.52 million tons in 1946) by concentrated use of imported heavy oil for increasing production in coal mining. The increased coal production was seen as critical for restoring production of steel and fer-tilisers. In reality, it implied a 'forced import substitution policy' under the circumstance of commercial blockade (Kosai, 1984). The imple-mentation of the scheme was so successful for Japan that it recovered more than 60 per cent of the prewar production level by the time of implementing the (deflationary) Dodge Line in 1949, without relying much on imported oil and manufactured goods. It should be stressed that domestic prices tended to decelerate before the Dodge Line due to the supply increase of production goods.

The first plan – the 'Economic Rehabilitation Plan' covering the period from 1949 to 1953 – set the framework for restoring prewar pro-duction levels (1930–34) and establishing the petrochemical industry. During its preparation there arose a debate over development strategy. The controversy involved the issue of whether one should adopt a domestic-development-first strategy ('kaihatsushugi') or a development strategy through expansion of trade ('boekishugi'). The New Deal democrats had supported the somewhat socialist domestic-development-first policy, given the past history of Japan's imperialistic invasion abroad. Hiromi Arisawa, among others, envisaged an urgent need to socialise the economy through the introduction of new technology by government-owned capital and the comprehensive development of land and resources in the domestic economy (Arisawa, 1989). In reality, because of food shortages, overpopulation and scarce natural resources, Japan has taken the development strategy of expansion through exports, which facilitated the import of basic materials and energy. But one should note that the pro-trade strategy is not identical to a free trade strategy, since it was biased toward export promotion combined with temporary import protection. Several economists argue that mild export protection combined with import protection is neutral with respect to resource allocation. Yet this static view dismisses dynamic aspects of export and import protection as discussed below.

The process of internationalisation in the high growth era (1950–73) was not only asymmetric but also lopsided. The growth–production oriented (developmental state) strategy both at a national and at an enterprise level had a pro-trade tendency, or more precisely a pro-export tendency, but at the same time its great success made Japan a low absorber country of manufactured goods.

According to the detailed analysis on the long-term development of Japanese trade structures by Ohkawa, postwar development can be described through successive stages of simultaneous import and export substitution, thereby reducing the dependence on imported basic materials as well as manufactured goods. It should be noted that the remarkable success of simultaneous import and export substitution processes was supported by the government policy of temporary protection from import and foreign direct investment.

The trade liberalisation process in postwar Japan was not only piecemeal but also hesitant and protracted. Trade liberalisation was actively pursued only after the early 1960s coupled with the high growth policy adopted by the Ikeda cabinet. Japan lagged substantially behind the European countries where the trade liberalisation took place in the latter half of the 1950s.

It was no coincidence that both the 'National Income Doubling Plan' and the 'Trade and Capital Liberalisation Plan' were announced in the same year (1960). The latter envisaged a goal of 80 per cent of trade liberalisation by 1963, and 90 per cent after the liberalisation of trade in oil and coal from the level of 40 per cent in 1959. In the face of the opposition by the small and medium-sized firms, Ikeda firmly believed that trade liberalisation was indispensable for sustained economic development. The government saw trade liberalisation as necessary to expand export markets and this position was endorsed by Taizo Ishisaka, the leader of the business circle (the Keidanren).

After joining the IMF (1952) and GATT (1955) discriminative measures against Japanese exports remained in place. Britain strongly resisted Japan's entry into GATT on the ground that it would disrupt the world market because of the competitive edge of the Japanese textile industry, itself the result of an 'Indian level of wage combined with Western technology'. Several Western countries invoked Article 35 against Japanese exports. After Article 35 was rescinded, Japan still faced quantitative restrictions on exports by some Western countries (Akaneya, 1992). In order to dismantle the protective measures by foreign countries against Japanese exports, it was deemed essential and urgent to liberalise the domestic market.

Moreover the implementation of trade liberalisation was closely linked to the security issue; in particular the enactment of the US–Japan Security Treaty in 1960. At the time of the visit of Prime Minister Ikeda in 1961, President Kennedy proposed creating the Japan–US Joint Committee on Trade and Economic Affairs, aimed at achieving economic co-operation and trade promotion as well as dismantling discriminatory measures against US exports by Japan. The Joint Committee served as an engine of trade liberalisation. At its first meeting, the US representative asked Japan to raise the trade liberalisation ratio from 44 per cent in 1960 to 90 per cent in 1962. In fact, Japan achieved 92 per cent trade liberalisation in 1963. In 1962 Japan became a GATT Article 11 country. By 1965 a first round of trade liberalisation was completed and the competitiveness of certain Japanese industries came close to other developed countries. It was in 1965 that Japan started to register a structural trade and current account surplus.

Yet there had been exceptions to import liberalisation such as synthetic fibres, machine tools, passenger cars and computers. The liberalisation of automobile imports was postponed until 1965, while the liberalisation of computers and related equipment was realised in 1975. It may be noted that the liberalisation in banking and agriculture was further postponed until the 1980s. With respect to the automobile industry, MITI in the 1950s attempted to reorganise the industry into three groups specialising in different types of cars. Although it failed to achieve the goal, the Japanese automobile industry gained a competitive edge by temporary import protection.

It is important to note that the implementation of capital liberalisation came after the trade liberalisation. The delay reinforced the protection of the domestic market from foreign producers. Even so, Japan regarded trade and capital liberalisation as the price for joining the circle of developed countries (Nakakita, 1993). Yet the membership of the OECD required capital liberalisation. In 1964 Japan joined the OECD. At the same time it became an IMF Article 8 country and abolished the foreign currency allocation system. Yet it held a reserved position on the 18 items of the OECD liberalisation code. Responding to the mounting criticism by other OECD member countries, Japan announced the first capital liberalisation programme which aimed at liberalising the direct investment of 50 industries. During the period from 1967 to 1973 capital liberalisation was implemented in five major steps. Anticipating the capital liberalisation, and the concomitant direct competition with foreign firms in domestic markets, MITI designed a 'new industrial system' and proposed the introduction of the 'Law for Promotion of Designated Industries' (including automobiles, special steels and the petrochemical industry). It was presented three times to the Diet from 1962 to 1964. The new industrial system had been rooted in the proposed creation of a new industrial order in the 'National Income Doubling Plan' (1960). It was modelled after the French-type 'concerted economy' where the representatives from industry, bureaucracy and banks co-operate to discuss the criteria, goal and desired amount of investment. The government was assumed to back-up the implementation of investment plans by tax and financial measures.

However the Law was not supported by business and financial circles (notably the Keidanren headed by Taizo Ishisaka) for fear of strengthening the control powers exercised by MITI. Business and financial circles were convinced that they could deal with the liberalisation issue by the 'self-adjustment' efforts of industrial reorganisation without MITI's control, provided that the 'excessive competition' among domestic firms could be avoided. This notion of 'excessive' competition is somewhat dubious. Avoidance of 'excessive' price competition usually resulted in the downward rigidity of wholesale prices on products by big companies. Still, they asked the Fair Trade Commission (FTC) to allow cartels and mergers aimed at maintaining competitiveness of industries and they strengthened the practice of crossholding of shares, and embarked on amalgamation of big corporations to prevent the take-over and merger and acquisition by foreign firms. Thus, the by-product of the failed attempt by MITI to introduce a new industrial system, was relaxation of the Antimonopoly Law. The FTC relaxed its attitude towards mergers among firms presumed to be facing an increased competitive threat from foreign producers. This was the second time the FTC relaxed the implementation of competition law – the first was in response to the need to facilitate the rationalisation of major industries (notably steel, coal mining, shipbuilding) in the early 1950s. The relaxation of the Antimonopoly Law culminated in the merger between Prince and Nissan in 1966 and the birth of the New Nippon Steel corporation through the merger between Fuji Steel and Yawata Steel corporation in 1969.

Originally transplanted from the US, the Articles of the Antimonopoly Law were similar to those of the US, but its implementation was deformed by the pressure of business circles placing emphasis on self-adjustment in the process of rationalisation and internationalisation. An alternative strategy (which was adopted by postwar West Germany) was to implement capital liberalisation more quickly and allow the entry of foreign firms into the domestic market, thereby strictly applying the competition law equally to domestic and foreign firms.

The case of the computer industry was different from other industries because the IBM Japan Corporation had advanced in prewar Japan, though its operation was prohibited during the war. In response to the move by MITI to raise import tariffs on computers and related equipments, IBM Japan attempted to start the production of computers. It asked MITI to permit the production of computers in Japan, threatening that it would otherwise prohibit the use of patents by Japanese companies. Yet MITI countered with the argument that the provision of patents held by the IBM 'elephant' to 15 Japanese companies or 'mosquitoes' (the words of Shigeru Sabashi, then Vice-minister of MITI, who was the leading promoter of the new industrial system) was the precondition for domestic production. After long negotiations IBM Japan was permitted to start production of computers in 1963 under the condition that it observed MITI's guidelines on the quantity and types of computers to be produced and accepted decisions on the introduction of new model computers into Japan. The guideline was effective until 1979 (Eto and Yamamoto, 1992).

Postwar protection differed from the permanent protection in the war-time economy: it was temporary with the commitment of future liberalisation. The temporary protection policy had been powerful and instrumental in promoting the import and export substitution process and nurturing infant industries by triggering vigorous expansion of business investment.

Strategic implications of temporary protection, domestic protection and export promotion

The temporary protection policy can be interpreted from the viewpoint of strategic policy. Within the framework of an imperfect competition model with economies of scale, Krugman pointed to the possibility that import protection leads to export promotion, given the technological circumstance of scale economy, learning and doing, and R&D investment. He took up the case of integrated circuits and argued that the domestic protection by the Japanese of non-tariff barriers actually led to promotion of exports, although the welfare of Japanese consumers was reduced due to higher product prices arising from inefficient resource allocation (Krugman, 1984). Yet it seems too early to generalise the case to all industries under temporary protection since the analysis neglects important aspects of temporary protection policy adopted by MITI.

First, one of the secrets in Japan's success of temporary protection was active domestic competition. MITI promoted the development of several firms ('polipoly' in the terminology adopted by Murakami (1994)) and fostered competition among them. Domestic competition among firms with similar technological positions enhanced investment for cost reduction aimed at expansion of market shares (developmentalism at the firm level). It may be noted that the monopoly firm has no incentive or strategic motive for investment. The main aim of Japan's industrial policy was to exploit economies of scale to the maximum extent – in the early-1950s MITI aimed at achieving 'bigness' through a policy of rationalisation, in the 1960s similar results were achieved by avoiding 'excessive competition'.

Second, it is known that free entry may cause a 'market fragmentation effect' of competition, which works to reduce the R&D expense, thus increasing the unit cost of production. Moreover, investment for technological efficiency and cost reduction has the commitment value of producting market competition under an oligopolistic market structure. As a result, the strategic motive for investment may be enhanced by pre-announced import liberalisation ('strategic effect of competition'). A shorter protection period may induce a jump in technological efforts and cost reduction because of the possibility of adopting an entry deterrence strategy to the extent that the strategic effect dominates the market fragmentation effect (see also Sadaoka, 1990). In addition, the entry deterrence effect may be reinforced, if the investment in distribution and customers' reputation is made by domestic firms before trade liberalisation since it may pre-empt the entry from abroad after protection has been lifted.

Third, the temporary protection policy was credible and avoided the dynamic inconsistency problem of economic policy, because of the pre-commitment by the government to a trade liberalisation programme and the existence of a competitive threat among domestic firms. Enterprises were convinced of import liberalisation within a limited time-frame and embarked on fierce competition for domestic market shares through expanding investment. Domestic competition among a limited number of firms in the protected industries (for instance, 11 automobile firms, 11 ethylene producing firms and seven major steel firms under polipoly market structure) enhanced the effort for exploiting the economies of scale and promoting rationalisation. During the high growth era, in sharp contrast to the export-led growth in the prewar period and the early 1980s, the spurt of business investment induced by dynamic and strategic motives brought about investment-led growth (see Figure 3.1).

On the other hand we observe the downward rigidity of product prices in the downswing of the business cycle during the high growth era (the downward rigidity was indicated by stable development of wholesale prices). The cut throat competition of price reduction on the domestic market seemed to be avoided by self-adjustment among the domestic firms concerned, while investment competition was fierce and the resulting excess capacity in the downward cyclical phase triggered export drive or razor beam exports.

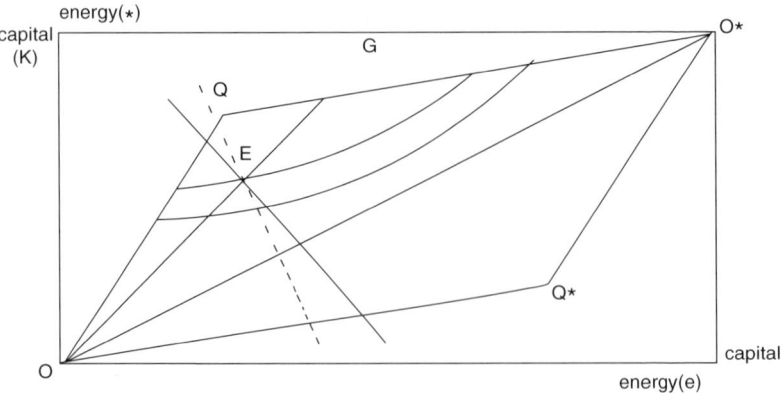

Figure 3.1   Iso-intraindustry trade line energy (Japan)

Tyson and Zysman interpreted temporary protection as the device of a moving band of protection: 'protection lasts only as long as is necessary to develop competitive Japanese suppliers. Once such suppliers appear, imports fall sharply' (1990). The success, maybe too great, of import and export substitution through temporary protection led to economic frictions with trading partners, because of the self-contained product lines which tend to reduce the dependence on imported manufactured goods and lower the level of intraindustry trade.

The development path and the low level of intraindustry trade

Despite the liberalisation undertaken the impression persisted that the Japanese market was closed. The low share of intraindustry trade in total trade and low ratio of manufactured imports to nominal GNP are often cited as evidence of the closed market. Yet these two figures do not necessarily provide direct evidence of import protection. The critical factor is the establishment of a production structure, which is much less dependent on imported capital and intermediate goods, through successive stages of import and export substitution, in line with the change in dynamic comparative advantage.

A typical example was the machinery sector. The import dependence of machine tool industry decreased from 58 per cent in 1958 to less than 10 per cent in the latter half of 1970s (Ohkawa and Kohama, 1989). As shown in Table 3.1, the intraindustry trade index of the machinery sector

Table 3.1 Intraindustry Trade Index on Japan 1959–88: all industry and manufactured sector

year	Japan		US		France		Germany	
	All	*Man*	*All*	*Man*	*All*	*Man*	*All*	*Man*
1959	17		40		46		39	
1964	21		40		60		42	
1970	26	32	53	57	67	78	54	60
1975	19	26	57	62	65	78	52	58
1980	19	28	57	62	67	82	57	66
1985	23	26	54	61	74	82	63	67
1988	(24)							

Note: Figure in parenthesis is derived from Iwata (1991) based on SITC 4 digit, while Lincoln (1991) uses the data of SITC 3 digit.
Source: Lincoln, 1990; Iwata, 1991.

with the US in 1988 is low (except for precision machinery), notably in the transportation machinery (road vehicles and vehicle parts). It may be noted that the intraindustry trade index with Asian NIE's countries is high with respect to cotton spinning, wool spinning, pharmaceuticals, manufactures of metals and domestic appliances. Certainly the import and export substitution process by Asian countries tends to increase Japan's intraindustry index due to the changing comparative advantage, although the increasing possibility of permanent protection of declining industries by the Japanese government also plays a part.

We can argue that Japan has been primarily concerned with exploiting the efficiency in resource allocation based on vertical division of labour, thereby neglecting the benefit of trade based on horizontal division of labour among developed countries.

It seems reasonable to explain the low level of manufactured imports and intraindustry trade and its historical development within the framework of factor endowments and the structural change of Japanese industry in line with the import and export substitution process. It is well known that Japan deviates most significantly in its energy endowment from other advanced economies. Its high import dependence for energy works to lower the share of manufactured imports. The explanation for the low level of intraindustry trade in the manufacturing sector is more complicated and it requires the development of a theoretical model. We assume that there are two sectors, which produce differentiated products, with the production function exhibiting economies of scale at the firm level and that the firms employ two production factors of energy and capital. There is increasing return at the firm level, but at the industry level there are constant returns with the output level of each firm (x) being treated as parameter. Thus, the gross domestic product function and output (X and Y) at the industry level are linear with respect to the production factor, while the output level of each firm plays the role of productivity variable.

$$\text{GDP} = \text{II} (p, K, E; x) \qquad (1)$$

We also assume that demand for differentiated products is determined by the 'love of variety' of consumers; it is characterised by concave and symmetric subutility functions.

$$U = U[u1, u2] \qquad (2)$$
$$ui = ui(Di1, Di2, - - - -), \quad i = 1, 2 \qquad (3)$$

where Din is the quantity of variety, n of product and i what is consumed. The consumer's taste is assumed to be homothetic and identical. Equation (2) can be interpreted as a production function which implies the increasing efficiency arising from diversified intermediate products (the Ethier effect). On the international and domestic market monopolistic competition prevails under the circumstance of full employment.

Helpman and Krugman (1985) took up the case where only capital-intensive goods are differentiated, while labour-intensive goods are assumed to be homogeneous. Here we assume that both capital-intensive goods (X) and energy-intensive goods (Y) are differentiated. Given the symmetric utility function of the 'love of variety' type in the two countries, the export and import of the two differentiated goods are determined simply by economic size. If we denote relative price of X in terms of Y as p and relative economic size of two countries as s and s* (s+s*=1), then we obtain the value of trade in two goods as follows:

import of X^* by country A=export of X^* by country B=spX^*
export of X by country A=import of X by country B=s*pX
import of Y^* by country A=export of Y^* by country B=sY^*
export of Y by country A=import of X by country B=s*Y

The share of intraindustry trade in total trade can be expressed as the proportion of the minimum of two-way trade of capital- or energy-intensive good to total trade. Therefore, the intraindustry trade index (IIT) can be expressed as below:

$$\text{IIT}=2 \ \Sigma\Sigma \ \text{MIN} \ (\text{sp}X^*, \text{s}^*Y, \text{s}^*\text{p}X, \text{s}Y^*) \ / \ 2 \ (\text{s}^*\text{p}X+\text{s}^*Y);$$
$$\text{s}^*\text{p}X+\text{s}^*Y=\text{sp}X^*+\text{s}Y^* \tag{4}$$

Figure 3.1 shows the Edgeworth diagram with the vertical and horizontal axes representing the total size of capital (K) and energy in efficiency unit (E) in world economy; the area of imperfect specialisation is drawn as parallelogram (O–Q–O*–Q*).

If the two countries have an identical factor endowment ratio (K/E), namely they are located on the diagonal of the Edgeworth diagram in Figure 3.1, the IIT index becomes 100, because each country produces and exports X and Y in the same proportion and engages in trade without generating net import or net export of the two differentiated goods; the export of X by country A to B is the same as the export by country B to A (spX^*=s*pX, sY^*=s*Y).

In the extreme case where both countries specialise in different goods, then the IIT index becomes zero at Q and Q*, because trade overlap disappears.

In the case that only the economic size is identical, with factor endowments being different, then the IIT index gets smaller, as factor endowment diverges between the two countries; one country produces disproportionately larger amounts of capital- or energy-intensive goods; it makes the trade overlap of each good smaller, because of the emergence of net import or net export of the two goods. As the factor endowment moves away from the diagonal, the IIT index becomes smaller.

Further if one country specialises in one good, for instance, country A specialises in X, and produces zero Y good, then the IIT index can be expressed as below:

$$IIT = 2spX^*/2s^*pX = sX^*/s^*X \tag{5}$$

The formula is identical with the case of one differentiated good and one homogeneous good which Helpman and Krugman (1985) extensively discussed.

Using the linearity of GDP and output of two goods with respect to factor endowments (E and K) and the definition of the IIT index of Equation (4), it is easy to show that the iso-intraindustry trade line is concave combinations above the diagonal (see also Iwata, 1991). If country A expands along the expansion path OG, the IIT index becomes smaller, because of the larger decline of relative economic size of country B, as compared with the size of increase of relative production of energy-intensive good by country A. Furthermore, if one good is not differentiated, all the iso-intraindustry index curves start from O*.

The endowment point E of Japan is located closer to the line O–Q far away from the diagonal because of the wide difference in capital-energy endowment from the average of trading partner countries. If the world economy grows, then the axis of the box expands due to the technical progress and capital accumulation. Moreover, if Japan follows expansion path OG due to the higher capital accumulation in Japan than trading partner countries, the intraindustry trade index can decline. Only when the energy efficiency increases at the same rate as the capital accumulation rate both in Japan and trading partner countries, will Japan's endowment point remain at E.

The rise of the intraindustry index in the 1960s among developed countries may reflect the outcome of trade liberalisation of manufactured goods (Table 3.2). It is strange that Japan's index showed a decline in the mid-1970s. Yet the model can predict that the oil price shock could bring with it a sharp decline in Japan's IIT. Under the assumption of balanced trade, the IIT index can be written as below:

$$IIT = [(s/s^*)\, pX + Y] / (pX + Y) \tag{6}$$

The oil price hike lowers relative price of capital intensive goods (p). At the same time the relative economic size (s) can be measured by the

Table 3.2 Intraindustry index by industry (Japan SITC digit 4)

Industry	USA	NIEs
Cotton spinning	1	48
Wool spinning	10	52
Synthetic fiber	38	32
Apparel, textile	15	5
Pulp, paper	27	19
Inorganic chemicals	15	38
Organic chemicals	52	29
Oil and detergent	47	29
Tanning and ink	57	30
Pharmaceutical	28	56
Petroleum refinery	4	40
Rubber	36	37
Nonmetallic mineral	30	26
Iron and steel	12	45
Nonferrous metals	27	39
Manufactures of metals	30	57
Industrial machinery	23	16
Metal working machinery	24	14
Machine parts	37	25
Electric machinery	48	30
Domestic appliances	29	58
Telecom. equipment	18	34
Road vehicles	4	9
Vehicle parts	7	13
Railway vehicles	28	1
Shipbuilding	59	1
Precision machinery	56	29

Source: Iwata, 1990.

distance on the diagonal. The oil price hike makes the factor price line steeper and thus reduces the relative economic size of Japan. This is consistent with the actual drop of Japan's IIT after the first oil shock.

In sum, the low level of Japan's IIT and its historical development can be reasonably explained by a model incorporating economies of scale and product differentiation; the model points to the importance of factor endowments and production side explanations instead of a closed market hypothesis.

Conclusion

Japan's internationalisation process during the high growth era can be viewed as a transition from a controlled economy to a market economy.

As the Year-1940 regime, oriented toward the autarchic system, had been deeply imbedded in the mind of policymakers, managers and workers, the transition was protracted and lopsided. The temporary import protection policy combined with protracted capital liberalisation in the postwar era was instrumental in achieving high investment-led growth accompanied by structural change in trade which was guided by simultaneous import and export substitution.

The great success of technology catch-up brings with it a low dependence on imported manufactured goods. The share of manufactured imports remained at a low level during the high growth era, although it showed a rising tendency and reached the level close to the early-1930s by 1970. This resulted in trade frictions with trading partner countries which turned into system frictions in the 1980s (see also Iwata and Fukao, 1995).

The fully-fledged internationalisation of Japan requires a fundamental change in value, attitudes and economic system. Political leadership is essential for the systemic change from the Year-1940 regime. Yet the politics were a side-show notably after the early-1960s. Politicians became concerned more with pork-barrel projects and the protection of agriculture, smaller enterprises and declining industries rather than international political and economic affairs. Politics were internalised, instead of being internationalised in the process of internationalisation. Because of internalised politics the task of systemic change has been postponed to the 1990s.

References

Akaneya,T. (1992) *Nihon no GATT Kanyu Mondai: Rejimu Riron no Bunseki Shikaku ni Yoru Jirei Kenkyu (The Problem of Japanese Accession to the GATT: a Case Study in Regime Theory)*, Tokyo

Arisawa, H. and T. Nakamura (eds) (1990) *Nihon Keizai Saiken no Kihon Mondai (The Fundamental Problem of Reconstruction of the Japanese Economy)*, Tokyo

Arisawa, H. (1989) *Sengo Keizai o Kataru:Showashi eno Shogen(Talk about Postwar Economy: Testify on Showa History)*, Tokyo

Eto, S. and Y. Yamamoto (1992) *Sogo Anzenhosho to Mirai no Sentaku (Comprehensive Security and Choice for the Future)*, Kodansha

Hashimoto, T. (1995) '*1940nen*, Taisei ha Genzai to Chokketu siteinai' ('The Year-1940 Regime Is Not Directly Linked to Present System'), *Ekonomisto*, 2.9, May 1995

Helpman, E. and P. Krugman (1985) *Market Structure and Foreign Trade; Increasing Returns, Imperfect Competition and the international Economy*, The MIT Press

Iwata, K. and M. Fukao (eds) (1995) 'Keizai Seido no Kokusaiteki Chosei'. ('International Coordination of the Economic System'), *Nihon Keizai Shinbunsha*

Iwata, K. (1991) 'Intraindustry Trade and the Japanese Economy', Working Paper No. 21, Department of Social and International Relations, Tokyo

Kanamori, H. (1995) *Watasi no Sengo Keizaishi (Personal View on Postwar Economic History)*, Tokyo

Kobayashi, H., Okazaki, T., Yonekura, S. and the NHK Research Staff (1995), 'Nihon Kabusiki Kaisha' no Showashi: Kanryo Shihai no Kozo, *'Showa History of Japan Inc.:Structure of Bureacrats' Control,'* Sogensha

Kosai, Y. (1984) 'Hukkouki'('Reconstruction Period') in Komiya, R., M. Okuno, and K. Suzumura, (eds) *Nihon no Sangyou Seisaku*, (Japanese Industrial Policy) Tokyo

Krugman, P. (1984) 'Import Protection as Export Protection', in H. Kierzkowski (ed.), *Monopolistic Competition and International Trade*, Oxford

Lincoln, E. (1990) *Japan's Unequal Trade*, Brookings Institute, Washington

Murakami, Y. (1995) *Hankoten no Sejikeizaigaku Yoko:Raiseiki no Tameno Oboegaki (Outline of Anticlassical Political Economics:Memorandum for the Next Century)* Chuo Koronsha

Nagao, K. (1995), *Nihon Kikai Kougyoushi (History of Japanese Machinery Industry)*, Shakai Hyoronsha

Nagaoka, S. (1990) *Dynamic and Strategic Issues of Industrial Policy:Essays from the Perspective of Japanese Experience*, MIT Ph.D., dissertation

Nakakita, T. (1993) 'Trade and Capital Liberalization Policies in Postwar Japan', in J. Teranishi and Y. Kosai, *The Japanese Experience of Economic Reforms*, St. Martin's Press

Nakamura, T. (1995) *Gendai Keizaishi (Contemporary Economic History)* Iwanami Shoten

Nakamura, T. (1993) *Nihon Keizai: Sono Seicho to Kozo (Japanese Economy: Growth and Structure)*, second edition, Tokyo

Noguchi,Y. (1995) *1940nen Taisei (The Year-1940 Regime)*, Toyokeizai Shinposha

Ogata, S. (1992) 'Interdependence and Internationalization', in G.D. Hook and M. A. Weiner (eds) *Internationalisation of Japan*, Routledge

Ohkawa, K. and H. Kohama (1989) *Lectures on Developing Economies: Japan's Experience and Its Relevance*, Tokyo

Ohkazaki, T. and M. Okuno (1993) *'Gendai Nihon Keizai Sisutemu no Genryu'* ('Origin of Contemporary Japanese Economic System'), *Nihon Keizai Shinbunsha*

Shinbo, H. (1995) *Kindai Nihon Keizaishi (Economic History of Modern Japan)* Sogensha

Shimomura, O. (1961) 'Seicho Seisaku no Kihon Mondai' ('Fundamental Problem of Growth Policy') *The Economic Studies Quarterly*, Vol. 11, no. 3

Tyson, L. and J. Zysman (1990), 'Developmental Strategy and Production Innovation in Japan', in C. Johnson, L. Tyson and J. Zysman (eds.), *Politics and Productivity: How Japan's Development Strategy Works*, Harper Business

Ueno, H. (1994) 'Senkanki no Sansigyo to Bosekigyo: Suryo Keizaishiteki Apurochi' ('Wool and Cotton Reeling industry in Interwar Period: Quantitative Economic History Approach') *Nihon Keizai Shinbunsha*

Yakushiji, (1992) 'Japan's Political Change towards Internationalization: Grafted Democracy and Political Recruitment', in G.D. Hook and M.A. Weiner (eds), *Internationalization of Japan*, Routledge

4

Economic Growth and Overfull Employment in Western Europe

Richard T. Griffiths

Economic growth

The motor for the transformation from austerity to affluence was pro-vided by an almost uninterrupted period of economic development that stretched from the end of the Second World War right through to the system shocks of the early 1970s. The causes of this quarter-century boom are only imperfectly understood, although economists are a little better at accounting for differences between the economies experien-cing it. Although it is not essential to our analysis, it is worth reviewing the main genres of interpretation.

On the supply side, the earliest efforts at explanation were afforded by crude applications of 'labour surplus' models to the European expe-rience. These were lent credence by the slow growth of the British and Belgian economies in the 1950s, both of which had slow growing labour markets and low hidden reserves of labour in the agriculture sector, and the correspondingly rapid expansion of Germany, France and Italy which did not face such restraints (Kindleberger, 1967). They would have been at a loss, of course, to explain the acceleration of Belgian growth in the 1960s. At the other end of the scale, there were immensely complex 'growth accounting' exercises comparing European countries with each other, and with the US and Japan over the period from 1950 to the early-1960s. All of these came to the conclusion that the increment of production factors alone cannot account for the observed rates of growth and that most derives from 'unaccountable' increases in productivity. This rather depressing conclusion was modi-fied by trying to 'embody' an element of productivity into factor incre-ments whether it be human capital, which was adjusted for changes in educational background (Denison, 1967) or physical capital, which was adjusted to incorporate a measure of technical improvement (Maddison, 1972). While this all served to reduce the 'residual', the conclusion remained that those countries that grew fastest were those that invested most, and, therefore, were best positioned to harvest the technological gains and organisational economies that accompanied the additional investment. These exercises could not answer the question, however, whether economies grew fast because they invested more, or whether they invested more because they were growing fast.

A second line of approach lay in explaining growth by reference to demand factors. These began by focusing on the fact that everywhere the expansion of foreign demand exceeded that of the domestic market. Not only did this 'export-led' growth pull up the average, but the foreign sector was supposed to impart a cutting edge to the economy that the domestic sector could not. Competition was sharper, stimulating the drive for productivity improvement, while the size of the global market gave room for economies of scale unavailable with domestic markets alone (Lamfalussy, 1963). The *cause célèbre* for this line of reasoning was the case of Italy, where the contrast between an aggressive, modernised export sector and inefficient domestic industries led to its characterisation as 'dual development'. Rapidly expanding production for foreign markets was also supposed to contribute to a 'virtuous circle' development through the mechanism of the balance of payments. High export earning permitted economic growth to expand without hitting balance-of-payments constraints that would force the adoption of deflationary measures restraining growth. Thus, it has been argued, that given its propensity to import, the United Kingdom could scarcely expand beyond its niggardly growth rate of 2.7 per cent per annum over the years 1951–73 without hitting the balance of payments ceilings (Thirwall, 1979). This still left unexplained the observed differences in the key variable, the growth of exports. One effort in this direction lay in relating an economy's export structure to the sectoral growth of demand for world exports. Assuming a 'constant market share', an unfavourable export structure would lead to low export growth. The results were illuminating. The UK in 1953 had one of the most favourable export structures, yet undershot its predicted performance between 1953 and 1962 by 25 per cent. Italy (by 72 per cent), Germany (by 44 per cent), Austria and the Netherlands (both by 23 per cent) all performed substantially better than predicted (Balassa, 1979). Thus a substantial part of export performance was related back to improvements in competitiveness which, in turn, lay at the heart of the unresolved supply analysis.

Economic growth is an important variable in conditioning the changes that accompanied the shift from austerity to affluence. Although everywhere in Western Europe postwar growth rates between 1950 and 1973 exceeded those achieved over any comparable time-span in the continent's modern economic history, there was a considerable variance in achievement among countries and over time. Moreover, there were also considerable differences in the starting levels. In order to capture the diversity of experience, four economies were selected as case studies for more detailed analysis, namely:

• the United Kingdom
• Sweden
• West Germany
• the Netherlands.

This selection was based on information on:

• initial position,
• growth experience,
• size,
• policy orientation.

The UK represents a large economy, with a high initial income/consumption position, with an unregulated labour market, but with relatively slow growth. Sweden illustrates a small(er) economy, with a high initial position (possibly with Switzerland, the highest in Europe), with a co-operative labour market model and with a respectable growth record. West Germany portrays a large economy, with an unfavourable starting position of low income and high unemployment, with an unregulated labour market and with the highest growth rates in Europe. Finally, the Netherlands exemplifies a small economy with a poor initial income position (though less so with unemployment), with the most formalised controls over labour markets in Western Europe and with rates of growth just beneath those of the highflyers.

The data in Table 4.1 illustrates the rapid pace of economic growth through the two growth cycles that spanned the mid-1950s to the mid-1960s. It also demonstrates both the strength of the German expansion and the relatively poor performance of the UK. Although a comparison adjusted for changes in population reflects less unfavourably on the UK, it does not remove the disparity in performance.

However, while British growth appears slow by contemporary standards, it still exceeded that of all previous periods. More to the point, it also built on an initial position that was considerably above those

Table 4.1   Indices of economic growth in Western Europe, 1953–64 (1958 = 100)

	Total			Per capita		
	1953	*1958*	*1964*	*1953*	*1958*	*1964*
West Germany	71	100	141	75	100	132
Netherlands	82	100	137	87	100	127
Sweden	84	100	135	87	100	131
United Kingdom	90	100	124	91	100	120

Note: Real GDP measured at 1970 UD$ and adjusted for changes in purchasing power parities.
Source: Maddison, 1982: Tables A2, A8, B4.

Table 4.2   Comparative levels of real per capita GDP in Western Europe, 1953–65

	1953	*1958*	*1965*
Sweden	2340	2690	3637
United Kingdom	2233	2446	2978
Netherlands	1918	22142	2910
West Germany	1740	2328	3212

Note: Real GDP measured at 1970 UD$ and adjusted for changes in purchasing power parities.
Source: Maddison, 1982: Tables. A2, A8, B4.

of neighbouring economies registering higher rates of growth (see Table 4.2). For much of the 1950s, therefore, contemporaries could console themselves that the difference in performance represented the rest of Europe 'catching-up'. This illusion had been shattered by the end of the second cycle in the mid-1960s when the British economy had been eclipsed, in terms of per capita GDP, by that of West Germany and was rapidly being overhauled by that of the Netherlands. It is worth pausing at this juncture to place our sample of countries in a wider perspective. By 1965, West Germany's per capita GDP has caught up the level achieved by the United States already in 1950, while both the Netherlands and the UK had reached the level attained by the US in 1947. At the other end of the scale, Japan, having grown twice as fast as the European average for a decade and a half, had by 1965 reached a GDP level between those enjoyed by the Netherlands and West Germany at the outset of their transformations into affluent societies (Maddison, 1982).

   The growth of Western European economies facilitated the shift towards affluence but it was not synonymous with its achievement. A better indication of the trajectory is provided by looking at consumption levels among European economies, where the performance

Tabel 4.3 Comparative levels of real per capita consumption in Western Europe, 1953–65

	1953	1958	1965
United Kingdom	1730	1865	2214
Sweden	1646	1853	2310
Netherlands	1347	1429	1871
West Germany	1244	1609	2090

Note: Real GDP adjusted by share of consumption in GDP and expressed per capita.
Source: Maddison, 1982: Tables A2, A8, B4 and UN, *Yearbook of National Accounts*.

is conditioned both by levels of income and by levels of savings and investments. There are several points of interest in the data in Tables 4.2 and 4.3. First, the gap between the highest and lowest starting positions is greater for per capita consumption (40 per cent) than it was for GDP (25 per cent), although it closed significantly already by 1958 (widening somewhat thereafter). Second, although the UK's investment ratios were among the lowest in the industrialised world and were probably a contributory factor in its poor growth record, they did allow the maintenance of relatively high consumption levels throughout the entire period. Only by looking at consumption data can we reconcile the pessimistic tone of contemporary economic analysts searching for the reasons behind the failure of comparative growth performance and the fact that the 'swinging sixties' are identified with London and Liverpool rather than Bonn and Munich.

Labour market tensions

Before we start our analysis of changes in the labour force during the transition from austerity to affluence, it is worth making a few introductory comments. First, we can consider that changes in the labour force depend upon the following dimensions:

- the growth of the population;
- the growth of the population of working age;
- the participation rate of that population in the labour force;
- the availability of employment opportunities.

Second, because much of the information comes from census data, we cannot always isolate the period 1953–64/5. For some elements it is not too important, but elsewhere it does mean, unfortunately, that we have to sacrifice some nuance in the analysis.

Table 4.4 Composition of population increase in Western Europe, 1950–70 (per cent per annum change)

	1950–60					
	(i)	*(ii)*	*(iii)*	*(iv)*	*(v)*	*(vi)*
Netherlands	1.26	1.39	–0.15	0.86	1.19	0.07
West Germany	1.00	0.53	0.50	0.98	1.21	–0.13
Sweden	0.63	0.51	0.13	0.50	3.65	0.17
United Kingdom	0.44	0.45	–0.01	–0.01	0.78	–0.46
	1960–70					
	(i)	*(ii)*	*(iii)*	*(iv)*	*(v)*	*(vi)*
Netherlands	1.28	1.19	0.10	1.51	1.97	3.93
West Germany	0.90	0.57	0.34	0.12	–1.30	–2.35
Sweden	0.75	0.47	0.29	0.50	–0.70	3.60
United Kingdom	0.57	0.61	–0.03	0.06	0.08	2.30

(i) Total population growth
(ii) Natural increase
(iii) Net migration
(iv) Increase population 15–59
(v) Increase population 15–19
(vi) Increase population 20–24
Source: UN ECE, 1979: Tables 1.1, 1.4.

Table 4.4 illustrates, with one exception (the Netherlands), differences in natural rates of population growth were not significant in determining the overall dimensions of population growth. All the other advanced Western European countries (including Italy) had rates of natural increase lying between 0.35 and 0.90 per cent per annum in the two decades covered in Table 4.4. To this extent, the other countries in our sample are clustered toward the lower end of the spectrum. By contrast, the Netherlands experienced rapid rates of increase more commonly found in the less developed Southern European countries (Portugal, Spain, Yugoslavia and Greece).

Generally, the main factor determining variations in population growth lay in differences in the size and direction of international migration. These changes, of course, were not always autonomous. Indeed, with exception of the large in-migration of Germans from other states that determined the West German situation in the 1950s, most of these movements were themselves responses to changes in the labour market. Net emigration was not uncommon in the 1950s. In this respect, the experience of the Netherlands and the UK was repeated in others (for example Denmark, Norway and Austria). In the 1960s, however, heavy emigration was exceptional and most countries gained significantly from net immigration. West Germany is at the top end of the spectrum, with its rate of immigration only surpassed by Switzerland, France and Luxembourg (in that order). The only other advanced Western European country, besides the UK, to experience a net loss in population through migration was Italy, which was wrestling with huge unemployment and underemployment problems in the south.

The degree of international migration had an even greater impact on the growth of the potential labour force (defined crudely as age group 15–59) than it did on the population as a whole. This was because the young and, to a greater extent the old, tended to be underrepresented in migration flows (UN, ECE, 1979 II, Table II.20). Even so, it is noticeable that, measured decade on decade, West German migration barely compensated for shifts in the age composition of the German population and the growth of the potential labour force (here defined as those aged 15–59) was modest. Again, on a decade by decade comparison, the light outflow of population from the UK served to anchor the expansion of its potential labour force at the bottom of the range. Another interesting observation that might help explain why the 'swinging sixties' swung in the UK, is that the 15–24 age group was actually falling in West Germany over that decade, whereas in the UK it grew far more rapidly than the population as a whole.

The Netherlands, again, was the exception to this trend of immigration forming the most important component of population growth. In the 1950s, its population was swelled by the ranks of children and its 'working age' population grew significantly less fast than the population as a whole. The situation was reversed, however, in the 1960s as this generation reached adolescence and hit the 'working age' group and contributed to the fastest expansion experienced anywhere in industrial Western Europe.

Table 4.5 Participation rates by country in Western Europe, 1950–65 (per cent of population)

	1950	1955	1960	1965
West Germany	46.4	47.7	47.4	45.7
Netherlands	39.3	37.5	36.1	36.3
Sweden	44.1	43.4	43.6	44.4
United Kingdon	46.8	46.2	46.2	46.9

Source: ILO, 1977.

If we turn now to the proportion of the population actually engaged in gainful employment, the most noticeable feature is the marked, almost structural difference, between the difference in the Netherlands and the rest, although the uniquely low Dutch participation rate is obviously partially a reflection of the differences in the age distribution of the population. Another feature is that the rates are extraordinarily stable, and this becomes more remarkable still when we observe the trends for demand of labour later on. At the most we can discern a small increase in the participation rate of Germany during the first boom (1950–60) and a fall in the Dutch participation rate over the same period. In both cases, these changes are followed by a levelling during the first half of the 1960s. This stability, however, conceals substantial shifts in the age and sex distribution of the labour force.

Everywhere, the male participation rate declined. Within this picture, the age group 25–65 remained fairly constant near what was presumably the full employment level (everywhere above 90 per cent for the age group 25–54 and above 80 per cent, and in the UK 90 per cent, for 55–64). For those above 65, what is now considered 'retirement age', there was a significant fall in participation rates although even in 1965 those still in employment ranged between 17 and 23 per cent. At the other end of the age spectrum, the share of teenagers in employment fell significantly, reflecting an increase in scholarity. In Sweden and the UK (although from very different starting points and with diverging trends) there are declines in the age group 20–25 throughout the period under review, whereas in the Netherlands and West Germany, these only became apparent from 1960 onwards.

The first striking feature in the female participation rates is the sharp contrast between the Netherlands where it hovers in the range 15.5–18.5 per cent and the other countries in our particular sample which, by 1965 cluster in a range 29–31 per cent. Although low, the Dutch female participation rate was not unique among industrial West European countries, and similar levels prevailed at the time in Belgium, Italy, Luxembourg and Norway. The main factor in the explanation appears to have been the low participation of married women in the labour force. In the Netherlands in 1960 only 7 per cent of married women were economically active, as opposed to levels between 24 and 33 per cent in the other three countries. The rate among unmarried women was clustered in the range of 46 to 52 per cent for all four countries (UN, ECE, 1979 II, Table II.20). The second feature, in marked contrast to the decline in the male participation rates, was that female participation rates either held steady, as in West Germany, or even increased,

Table 4.6 Participation rates by sex and age in Western Europe, 1950–65

	West Germany (male)				West Germany (female)			
	1950	*1955*	*1960*	*1965*	*1950*	*1955*	*1960*	*1965*
Total	63.3	64.5	63.8	61.6	31.7	32.9	32.8	31.2
10–14	5.1	4.7	4.2	2.8	4.0	3.4	2.8	2.1
15–19	84.4	83.0	81.6	74.2	79.5	76.4	73.2	70.0
20–24	93.2	92.2	91.2	89.0	71.4	70.6	70.0	69.0
25–44	96.5	96.7	96.9	97.1	40.8	43.5	46.2	46.9
45–54	95.2	95.1	95.1	95.1	35.4	37.6	39.7	43.0
55–64	81.6	80.9	80.3	79.6	9.4	8.8	8.1	7.0
65+	26.6	24.8	23.0	19.5	9.4	8.8	8.2	7.0

	Netherlands (male)				Netherlands (female)			
	1950	*1955*	*1960*	*1965*	*1950*	*1955*	*1960*	*1965*
Total	60.2	58.2	56.6	55.9	18.6	17.0	15.8	17.7
10–14	6.1	4.4	2.6	2.2	3.2	3.1	2.5	2.2
15–19	70.1	66.5	62.9	53.7	56.4	55.1	53.8	52.6
20–24	92.0	91.5	91.1	87.8	51.2	52.0	52.8	53.8
25–44	98.0	97.8	97.6	97.4	21.9	19.7	17.4	20.1
45–54	97.3	96.7	96.3	95.8	18.4	17.5	16.6	19.1
55–64	85.6	85.3	84.7	84.1	14.8	13.4	11.9	13.3
65+	31.4	25.6	19.8	17.1	5.6	4.0	2.6	2.8

	Sweden (male)				Sweden (female)			
	1950	*1955*	*1960*	*1965*	*1950*	*1955*	*1960*	*1965*
Total	65.3	63.0	61.7	59.6	23.0	24.0	25.6	29.2
10–14	1.2	1.1	1.1	0.9	0.8	0.6	0.4	0.4
15–19	75.4	64.5	53.6	45.9	54.7	50.8	46.9	42.6
20–24	90.3	87.7	85.1	78.8	57.3	57.3	57.3	57.8
25–44	97.7	96.8	95.8	94.6	29.9	33.2	36.9	44.5
45–54	96.4	96.0	95.7	94.5	29.9	33.1	36.2	45.4
55–64	86.6	87.2	87.8	85.0	22.6	24.7	26.8	31.1
65+	36.6	32.0	27.4	22.8	7.9	6.3	4.7	4.4

	United Kingdom (male)				United Kingdom (female)			
	1950	*1955*	*1960*	*1965*	*1950*	*1955*	*1960*	*1965*
Total	67.4	65.9	64.7	63.5	27.3	27.9	28.8	31.1
10–14	0.1	0.1	0.1	–	0.1	0.1	0.1	–
15–19	85.6	80.0	75.5	68.7	79.3	75.3	71.4	64.2
20–24	95.1	94.2	93.4	91.8	65.6	64.2	62.7	61.5
25–44	98.4	98.3	98.2	98.2	35.7	37.8	39.9	44.7
45–54	98.0	98.0	98.0	98.0	33.6	38.0	42.3	50.5
55–64	92.7	92.6	92.4	92.3	21.0	24.7	28.4	33.5
65+	31.8	28.7	25.6	22.7	5.3	5.5	5.6	5.9

Source: ILO, 1977.

as in Sweden and the UK. In the Netherlands, a decline in the participation rate in the 1950s was reversed the following decade.

Behind these patterns, there were some interesting shifts. As with males, the very young were increasingly phased out of the work force and, except in the UK where the trend was upwards, the elderly were allowed their retirement. The proportion of female 15–19 year olds in the labour force declined, but generally not as fast as it did for their brothers. Some of the other age groups substantially increased their participation over the period covered. In Sweden and the UK this involved the entire age range 25–64, and in West Germany those aged 25–54. In the Netherlands, when the upturn came in 1960, it encompassed the entire age range 20–65.

When these trends are translated into absolute terms, we can see that in the decade 1955–65, with the exception of the Netherlands, the growth of the labour force was overwhelmingly female. In the UK 1.3 million women entered the labour force as opposed to 554 000 men. In West Germany the figures for women and men were 516 000 and 143 000 respectively and in Sweden 255 000 and 22 000. Only in the Netherlands was the position reversed with men contributing 311 000 to the growth of the labour force and women 177 000. In terms of the age composition, with the exception of West Germany, young workers formed an important (but not overwhelming) component in the growth of the labour force. They were most important in Sweden and the Netherlands, where they contributed 43 per cent to the extra labour force. In the UK they accounted for 415 000 of the labour market expansion of 1.83 million, but their contribution was eclipsed by the age cohort 55–64 which expanded by 967 000. West Germany, as observed already, was the exception. While its total labour force expanded by 1.94 million, the numbers of young workers fell by 683 000.

The rapid expansion of the economies of Western Europe in the years 1953–65 was the motor behind the growth of employment. This is important not only because it allowed more people to participate in the economic process, but also because it provided a climate of security that underpinned the second part of the definition of affluence. Even at the start of the first growth cycle, the unemployment rate had been low in three of the four countries examined here, ranging from 3.5 per cent in the Netherlands to 2.6 per cent in the UK, and they fell further still, with the greatest drops registered in the Netherlands and Sweden where, by 1957, unemployment had declined to 1.5 and 1.7 per cent respectively. The exception in this relatively favourable start was West Germany, but even there registered unemployment had been reduced from 6.2 per cent to 3.5 per cent by 1958. At the end of the first cycle, unemployment rates tilted upwards but soon resumed their downward trend. Throughout the second growth cycle (1958–65) the unemployment rates were consistently lower than during the first. In 1961, in West Germany and the Netherlands they dipped below 1 per cent, and stayed there until 1966–67. In Sweden unemployment rates remained below 1.5 per cent throughout and in the United Kingdom they fluctuated between 1.5 and 2.5 per cent (OECD, 1973). It is important to emphasise how low these rates of unemployment were in an historical perspective. John Maynard Keynes, for example, when he had written about full employment had envisaged an underlying rate of 5 per cent. Not only were these rates low, they were also of short duration – by 1968 already the trend was deteriorating.

The exceptional nature of the labour market becomes even more apparent when we compare the numbers registered unemployed with the numbers of registered vacancies. Although the OECD made efforts to standardise employment statistics, the data for registered vacancies were susceptible to differences in national practices. However, we can be certain that there were never *fewer* employment openings in the economy than those captured by the official statistics. The extreme tightness in the labour market is illustrated by the appearance of overfull employment – the fact that registered vacancies came to exceed the numbers seeking work and often by a considerable margin (see Table 4.7).

Table 4.7 Unemployment and vacancies (thousands) in Western Europe, 1955–65

	West Germany		Netherlands		Sweden		United Kingdom	
	u	*v*	*u*	*v*	*u*	*v*	*u*	*v*
1955	1080	207	33	90	24.9		239	405
1956	882	227	24	106	19.1		255	357
1957	759	227	33	88	23.5		322	276
1958	769	226	69	44	31.7		442	198
1959	540	291	49	61	26.5		468	224
1960	271	465	29	92	18.9		368	314
1961	181	552	21	119	16.6	339	320	
1962	155	574	21	122	18.8	37.3	454	214
1963	186	555	24	122	20.1	41.5	540	196
1964	169	609	21	131	17.0	47.1	394	317
1965	147	649	25	129	16.6	53.8	339	384

u = unemployed; v = vacancies.
Source: OECD, 1973.

During the first growth cycle overfull employment appeared in the UK until 1956, in the Netherlands until 1957. Although no official data was published for Sweden before 1961, unofficial estimates suggest that vacancies exceeded unemployment until mid-1956 and that this pattern reasserted itself from mid-1959 (Lindbeck, 1975). The UK's experience with overfull employment was confined to the first growth cycle. However, elsewhere the phenomenon intensified and also encompassed West Germany for the first time. Averaged over calendar years, at the tightest points in the labour market, there were 2.7 registered vacancies for each registered unemployed in Sweden (1964), 4.4 for each registered unemployed in Germany (1965) and no less than 6.2 for each registered unemployed in the Netherlands (1964) (see Table 4.7).

This huge mismatch of supply and demand begs the question why there was not a greater change in attitude towards work or why there were not greater flows of migration. Whatever the reason, it played a major role in determining the rewards for labour. And that, in its turn, explains the motor behind the increase in consumption that marked the transition to greater and greater affluence.

Income from employment

As we did in the previous section, we can make some simple assumptions about the mechanisms behind the changes we are analysing. Basically we can assume that the development of the total rewards for employment depend on:

- the numbers in employment;
- the rewards for labour in each sector;
- shifts in the distribution of the labour force between sectors.

Although, put this way, the task seems an easy one, the problems in obtaining comparable information and interpreting it are immense. Even more fraught are the difficulties in explaining any changes observed. The factors behind the increase in the labour force have been analysed in the previous section. As the data in Table 4.8 indicates, most of the labour force comprised of wage and salary earners. Their importance at the start of the first growth cycle ranging from 73 per cent in West Germany to 93 per cent in the UK and, except for the latter where levels were already extremely high, their preponderance in the labour force increased throughout the period 1953–64, largely at the expense of small farmers. Those who hired out their labour constituted the bulk of the labour force, and those dependent upon them, the bulk

Table 4.8 Changes in dependent and independent employment in Western Europe, 1953–64 (per cent)

	(*i*)	(*ii*)	(*iii*)
West Germany			
1953–55	72.7	16.2	11.1
1955–58	75.1	14.2	10.7
1959–61	77.2	12.0	10.8
1962–64	79.2	10.4	10.3
Netherlands			
1953–55	76.3	9.3	14.4
1955–58	78.2	8.3	13.5
1959–61	79.4	7.5	13.0
1962–64	80.4		
Sweden			
1953–55	82.8	9.5	7.7
1955–58	84.3	8.4	7.2
1959–61	85.8	7.4	6.8
1962–64	88.2	6.4	6.5
United Kingdom			
1953–55	92.8	1.8	5.4
1955–58	93.0	1.7	5.3
1959–61	93.1	1.7	5.3
1962–64	93.2	1.6	5.1

(i) wage and salary earners
(ii) agricultural self-employed
(iii) other self-employed
Source: UN ECE, 1967: Table 2.13.

of the population. Moreover, as we shall see later, they made the greatest contribution to total primary earnings by households. Thus, it is upon the fortunes of this group that the transition to affluence turns.

The section of the labour force about which we have the most information is *industrial* waged labour. This is both fortunate, since manufacturing industry tended to be the trendsetter for pay settlements throughout the economy as a whole, and unfortunate, since it was rapidly ceasing to be the main employer. Moreover, although the set-piece bargaining was usually centred on conventional wage rates, employment incomes tended everywhere to grow at a faster rate, as is shown by the data in Table 4.9. Several factors have been advanced to explain these divergent trends. First, one must observe specifically that the high 'drift' observable in Sweden is partly a result of differences in wage bargaining practices. In Sweden (and Norway) increases were

Table 4.9 Wages and wage earnings in Western Europe, 1952–65 (average annual percentage change)

	Wage	Earnings
West Germany		
1952–1958	5.7	6.6
1958–1965	7.2	8.9
Netherlands		
1952–1958	6.5	8.1
1958–1965	5.9	8.0
Sweden		
1952–1958	2.8	5.8
1958–1965	3.3	7.2
United Kingdom		
1952–1958	5.5	6.2
1958–1965	4.6	6.3

Source: UN, ECE, 1967: Table 2.13.

established in terms of actual pay, rather than in terms of contract rates. Thus registered pay increases tended to be lower than elsewhere and the drift component in earnings correspondingly higher. Second, conventional wage rates only refer to part of the activities in any manufacturing sector and 'key' rates need to be translated into piece rates and into comparable pay at other levels. Third, the rates for overtime and unconventional hours tend to be higher and where these increase average earnings will rise disproportionally. This factor, however, is likely to be highly cyclical and while it might be important in year-on-year changes it cannot explain the consistent 'drift' apparent in the data. The final, and probably most important explanation, lies in upscaling within categories (for example, by paying bonuses and extra increments) or between them (for example, through the reclassification of tasks from unskilled to semi-skilled or from manual to supervisory).

One explanation for wage drift suggests that in regulated labour markets (characterised by central wage bargaining and strong, direct or indirect, government pressure) conventional rates establish what is politically acceptable, while 'drift' allows market forces to restore equilibrium. This was certainly a widespread practice in the most centralised labour market, that of the Netherlands. Briefly policy was gradually relaxed:

- to 1954, wage rises only in line with inflation, central norms
- 1954–56, wage rises in line with economic growth, central norms

- 1956–58, wage rises in line with productivity, differential norms within centrally determined limits
- 1959–63, wage rises in line with estimated branch productivity and overall productivity, central supervision
- 1963– , wage rises in line with branch productivity, decentralised supervision.

Yet, from 1957 onwards, 'black wages', 'overgrading' and a shift toward piece rates, which were less easily controlled, were increasingly identified as being responsible for undermining government policy and by the time of the wage surges of 1963 and 1964 it was clear that the government had lost control altogether. The second explanation for wage drift, which is not incompatible with the first, is that insofar as it is caused by shifts within the employment structure in favour of higher skilled classifications, it might simply reflect the increasing sophistication of the production process at a time of rapid increases in productivity. This should come as no surprise given the stress placed upon the development of 'human capital' in the 'growth accounting' literature. Within industry, there was a shift towards supervisory staff among manual workers and, overall, towards salaried clerical and administrative work, both of which (with the exception of mining) were better paid than unskilled or semi-skilled labour. Moreover, the long-term trend towards a narrowing gap between rewards of skilled and unskilled labour, that had been apparent from the end of the 19th century was reversed from the mid-1950s in Sweden and the UK, from the early 1960s in West Germany (Scholliers and Zamagni, 1995) and slightly later in the Netherlands.

Given the lack of information about work definition and rates of pay, it is difficult to give detailed comparisons of earnings with other sectors of the economy. Thus it is difficult to assess the impact of broad shifts in the sectoral distribution of the labour force. Yet, it is clear that other sectors of the economy broadly followed the pay trends set by industry as a whole. Moreover, we can discern the following sectoral differences:

- male earnings in agriculture were a third to a quarter less than in industry, though (except in the UK) the gap was closing,
- female earnings in industry were half to a third less than those of men, though (except in the UK) the gap was closing,
- female clerks and lower administrative grades earned between 20 and 50 per cent more than female unskilled and semi-skilled manual labour, though this might not apply in the Netherlands (where female employment in trade and banking earned slightly less than industry).

With these distinctions in mind, we can begin to trace the shifts in employment structures although, unfortunately, the data on the

Table 4.10 Index of real earnings in manufacturing in Western Europe, 1953–65

	(*i*)	(*ii*)	(*iii*)
West Germany			
1952	68.1	93.5	72.8
1958	100	100	100
1965	181.6	114.4	163.0
Netherlands			
1952	62.7	85.5	78.6
1958	100	100	100
1965	171.4	124.1	138.1
Sweden			
1952	71.3	82.5	86.4
1958	100	100	100
1965	162.7	125.4	129.7
United Kingdom			
1952	69.7	81.2	85.8
1958	100	100	100
1965	153.3	120.9	126.8

(i) Earnings
(ii) Consumer Prices
(iii) i ÷ ii = Real Earnings
Source: UN, ECE, 1967: Table 3.1; Maddison 1982: Table E4.

gender distribution only permits decade-on-decade comparison. Another drawback is that it includes self-employment and this probably has the effect of accentuating the decline in the agricultural sector.

If we start by looking at Table 4.11a, one of the most striking features, with the exception of the UK which already had a relatively small agricultural sector, is the exodus from the land, where earnings were lower than could be obtained elsewhere in the economy. During the first growth cycle, this is most marked in Sweden, which in half a decade lost 14 per cent of its agrarian labour force, followed by Germany and the Netherlands (with declines of 10 and 8 per cent respectively). During the second cycle the pace of shrinkage of the agricultural labour force accelerated in Germany and the Netherlands, registering falls of 27 and 19 per cent respectively, while that of Sweden fell by a further 10 per cent. Turning to the growth sectors, it is the service sector that registers the greatest relative gain over the two growth cycles, though the trend is more apparent in the second growth cycle than in the first. The exception to this pattern is formed by West Germany where industrial employment soared by a staggering

Table 4.11 Sectoral Distribution of the active labour force in Western Europe, 1953–65:

(a) Changes in the sectoral distribution of the labour force during the two growth cycles

	(i)	(ii)	(iii)
West Germany			
1953	4564	9759	7349
1958	4100	12020	8830
1964	3002	12867	10458
Netherlands			
1953	529	1634	1812
1958	482	1739	2020
1965	388	1772	2595
Sweden			
1953	589	1274	1240
1959	504	1330	1332
1964	455	1526	1679
United Kingdom			
1953	1071	11474	10564
1958	994	11731	10948
1964	1014	11399	12109

(b) Changes in the sectoral and gender distribution of the labour force 1950–70

	Male			Female		
	(i)	(ii)	(iii)	(i)	(ii)	(iii)
West Germany						
1950	2328	7648	4493	2807	2113	3184
1961	1625	9731	5532	1961	3330	4639
1970	1025	9410	6570	966	3340	5182
The Netherlands						
1947	579	1127	11349	169	160	597
1960	406	1547	1271	41	211	673
1971	252	1521	1729	39	215	973
Sweden						
1950	579	1058	633	53	209	550
1960	408	1200	661	39	262	662
1970	221	1114	864	56	259	889
United Kingdom						
1951	1091	8525	6372	124	2810	4121
1961	828	8542	6701	97	2767	4868
1971	566	8118	6611	115	2643	6031

(i) agriculture
(ii) industry
(iii) services

Source: OECD (1973); UN, ECE, Economic Survey of Europe 1958, Appendix Table VIII; UN, ECE, 1979 II, Appendix 1.1.

23 per cent during the five years of the first cycle. Finally, one should note the absolute decline in industrial employment in the UK during the second growth cycle and the rapid (10 per cent) rise in service sector employment over the same period.

Table 4.11b allows us to draw some conclusion about the gender balance in these changes. Only in West Germany, and only then in the 1950s, did women enter the industrial workforce in large numbers. The service sector was the largest creator of female employment in every country, although in the Netherlands it created even more male employment opportunities and in West Germany employment growth was evenly distributed between the sexes. On the other hand, in Sweden rather more women entered the service sector than did men. No country, however, matched the UK where over two decades, nearly 2 million women joined the service sector as opposed to 250 000 men.

Throughout the two growth cycles we have seen that increasing numbers of inhabitants were able to earn ever higher real incomes. On the other hand, the largest part of the increase in incomes both reflected the productivity gains achieved in the economies and were absorbed by them. Before looking at the evidence, one comment is in order. The usual way to measure the share of employment in GDP is to include employers' contributions to social security payments. But this 'payment' does not go to employees – insofar as the flow is earmarked for specific purposes, it generally flows to the non-active. Had these payments been levied and collected differently, they would more properly constitute a tax on employers rather than a transfer to employees. Because these contributions increased sharply, especially during the second growth cycle, labour's share in GDP increased less spectacularly than the data would suggest.

The data in Table 4.12 reveals that where the initial share of employment income in GDP was lowest, in the Netherlands, it expanded fastest with most of the increase concentrated during the second growth cycle when wage controls became completely dysfunctional. Even so, by 1962 it does no more than catch up the position in West Germany where growth is surprisingly sluggish. Sweden's rise in employees' share, which is second only to that of the Netherlands, is probably distorted by steeply rising social security payments.

Self-employment and property income

Before we can close the circle and reach the point of consumption, we will have to take several more steps. First we would need to

Table 4.12   Structure of employment income in Western Europe, 1953–64

	(i)	*(ii)*	*(iii)*	*(iv)*
West Germany				
1953–55	47.8	52.9		
1955–58	48.3	54.0		
1959–61	48.9	54.9		
1962–64	51.0	57.0		
Netherlands				
1953–55	42.6	49.2		
1955–58	44.4	51.4		
1959–62	45.1	52.3		
1962	48.9	57.1		
Sweden				
1953–55		64.3	11.9	10.3
1955–58		64.9	10.5	10.4
1959–62		66.2	9.2	10.6
1962–64		70.1	8.5	10.3
United Kingdom				
1953–55	61.9	65.9	9.0	8.3
1955–58	62.9	67.2	8.1	8.1
1959–62	62.6	67.3	7.8	9.5
1962–64	63.4	68.5	7.2	10.0

(i) wages and salaries
(ii) total employment incomes (including employers' contributions to social security payments)
(iii) income from self-employment
(iv) household incomes from property
Source: UN, ECE, 1967: Tables 2.13, 2.15.

complete the elements that comprise primary household incomes (that is before they are affected by taxes and transfers). These comprise the following components, both of which are incorporated into Table 4.12 where data was available:

- income from self-employment (column iii)
- household income from property (column iv).

Unfortunately we only have information for two countries in our sample since the Dutch and German national accounts do not allow a separation of household and corporate income for these categories. What the information suggests for Sweden, is that part of the sharp rise in employees' share in GDP reflects a relative fall in income from self-employment. Add the two together and employment's share of GDP rises by only 2.2 percentage points, and this rise could easily be eliminated were we able to adjust for employers' social security payments. Given that the share of self-employment in the labour force declined equally fast in West Germany, though slightly less in the Netherlands (see Table 4.8) it is probable that a similar development took place there as well. In the UK where the wage and salary share of GDP (for which we have the data) rose only slowly, the effects were more than cancelled out by the slide in self-employment income.

If labour's share of GDP rose only slowly, if at all, we have finally to consider that the 'primary income' of households was augmented by returns from property incomes (rents, interest and dividends). The importance of these varies greatly among the countries for which information is available, but the UK and Sweden, where property incomes made up 11–12 per cent of household incomes, seem to be at the top of the spectrum, together with Belgium (15 per cent dropping to 13) and Switzerland. Moreover, although there is no clear direction in their movement, they do not fluctuate a great deal. In the UK, property income augmented household shares slightly, but the safest assumption for the others is that it remained unchanged.

From income to expenditure: next steps

Households, therefore, broadly kept abreast of the rising real national income over the period 1953–65. On the other hand, the share of consumer expenditure in GDP fell throughout the period and during each growth cycle considered separately. In West Germany (from 71.4 to 65.1 per cent) and the UK (from 77.2 to 74.4 per cent), this decline was spread evenly over both cycles, while in the Netherlands (from 69.4 to 64.3 per cent) it was concentrated in the first cycle and in Sweden (69.9 to 74.4 per cent) it was concentrated in the second.

The resolution of these seemingly contradictory trends lies in two sets of considerations, both of which fall outside the scope of this paper. The first involves the redistributive effects of government policies and hinges on such questions as:

- the level and incidence of taxation
- the nature of income transfers
- decisions on collective consumption
- the impact of these on income distribution.

The second hinges upon decisions made within the household sector on whether to save, to borrow, to buy, to mortgage and to spend.

Conclusion

There can be no doubt that the labour market experienced a profound transformation during the two growth cycles 1953–58 and 1958–65 that contributed to the attainment of affluence in Western Europe. Real earnings accelerated at a hitherto unknown tempo and carried the majority of households well beyond the threshold of (socially defined) subsistence. Moreover, these high and rising incomes were accompanied by 'job security', a phenomenon not associated with previous periods of prosperity. The situation of full employment, however, turned out to be of extremely short duration.

By the late 1960s, the unparalleled expansion of employment was already running out of steam and, by the time the various 'systems shocks' of the early 1970s had reverberated through the European economies, the condition of 'full employment' belonged well and truly to the past. Now, many of the reasons for this change had very little to do with the labour market, but it had been argued that at least two clearly did (Bernabè, 1982). First, although until the mid-1960s the rise in earnings was often seen as a symptom of greater trades unions' bargaining power, the increases had largely been absorbed by rising productivity. After the mid-1960s, this was no longer the case and as labour costs spiralled relative to capital, so the demand for labour adjusted. Second, much trade union bargaining in this period was directed as much at the secondary conditions of employment as at wage levels. The broadened scope of workers' rights secured through industrial agreement and reinforced by national legislation served not only to raise employment costs further, especially in times of downturn, but also to segment the labour market and make it less responsive to changes in both supply and demand.

Thus, the developments in the labour market described in this chapter differed from other trends that accompanied the transition from austerity to affluence in Western Europe. They were not accelerations, beginnings or ends of trends, but were conditioned by a unique constellation of factors that were to prove, ultimately, to be of short duration.

References

Balassa, B. (1979) 'Export Composition and Export Performance in Industrial Countries, 1953–1971', *Review of Economics and Statistics*, Vol. 61, no. 4.

Beckerman, W. (1962) 'Projecting Europe's Growth', *Economic Journal*, Vol. 72, no. 4, 919–25.

Bernabè, F. (1982) 'The Labour Market and Unemployment' in A. Boltho (ed.) *The European Economy, Growth and Crisis*, Oxford.

Denison, E.F. (1967) *Why Growth Rates Differ. Postwar Experience in Nine Western European Countries*, Washington.

Flora, P., F. Kraus and W. Pfenning (1987) *State, Economy, and Society in Western Europe 1815–1975*, Vol. II, Frankfurt, London, Chicago.

International Labour Office (120) (1977), *1500–2000. Labour Force Estimates and Projections*, Vol. IV, Geneva, (2nd edition).

International Labour Office, *Yearbook of Labour Statistics*, Geneva, various years.

Kaelble, H. (ed.) (1992) *Der Boom 1948–1973. Gesellschaftliche und wirtschaftliche Folgen in der Bunderrepublik Deutschland und in Europa*, Opladen.

Kindleberger, C.P. (1967) *Europe's Postwar Growth. The Role of the Labor Supply.* Cambridge Ma.

Lamfalussy, A. (1963) 'Contributions à une théorie de la croissance en économie ouvert', *Recherches économique de Louvin*, Vol. 29, No. 8, 715–34.

Lindbeck, A. (1975) *Swedish Economic Policy*, London

Lutz, V. (1962) *Italy. A Study in Economic Development*, Oxford.

Maddison, A. (1972) 'Explaining Economic Growth', *Banca del Lavoro Quarterly Review*, No. 102, 211–62.

Maddison, A. (1982) *Phases of Capitalist Development*, Oxford.

Organisation for Economic Cooperation and Development (1973), *Main Economic Indicators. Historical Statistics 1955–1971*, Paris.

Scholliers P. and V. Zamagni (1995), *Labour's Reward. Real Wages and Economic Change in 19th and 20th century Europe*, Aldershot.

Thirwall, A.P. (1979) 'The balance of Payments constraint as an explanation of International Economic growth rate Differences' *Banca del Lavoro Quarterly Review*, No. 128, 45–53.

United Nations, *Monthly Bulletin of Statistics*, various years.

United Nations, *Statistical Yearbook*, various years.

United Nations (Economic Commission For Europe) (1967), *Incomes in Postwar Europe: A Study of Policies, Growth and Distribution*, Geneva.

United Nations (Economic Commission For Europe) (1979 I), *Employment, Income Distribution and Consumption. Long-term objectives and structural change*, Geneva.

United Nations (Economic Commission For Europe) (1979 II), *Labour Supply and Migration in Europe: Demographic dimensions 1950–1975 and prospects*, Geneva.

5
From Rapid Growth to the End of Full-Employment in Japan: 1945–70

Takenori Inoki

This chapter delineates the change and development of the labour market in Japan during the years between the defeat in the war and the end of the high-speed economic growth in the early 1970s. This quarter century, characterised by a drastic and rapid change in lifestyles and in living standards, can be sub-divided into three phases. The first phase covers the period in which the economy experienced a dramatic jump in the number of unemployed, mainly due to the demobilisation of the military forces and the cessation of military production. The demand for labour could not absorb all this discharged workforce and consequently the whole labour market remained slack and loose. The second phase covers the ten year period between the mid-1950s and the mid-1960s, when the drastic increase in labour demand derived from expanding private investment tightened the whole labour market in Japan. Finally, the third phase from the late 1960s witnessed the further tightening of the labour market, caused by the serious excess of labour demand.

After delineating such transformation in employment on a macroeconomic level, we will then explore the transition of Japan to an affluent society by looking at the remarkable increase in earnings during this quarter century. Earnings or incomes are not the perfect indicator for measuring the degree of affluence of a society, but definitely the only reliable quantitative indicator we so far possess that allows us to grasp the flow of production and consumption in an economy. For this reason, we are interested in the annual rate of increase in real wage earnings and its distribution in this period.

This chapter also discusses an aspect of the internal mechanism which brought about the high rate of economic growth in postwar

82

Japan, by mainly focusing on two aspects:

- how the shift of labour force from agriculture to manufacturing industry proceeded so smoothly with small adjustment costs of labour, and
- how and what sort of human capital was formed on the production-site.

The overall picture of the labour force: 1945–70

We will first summarise the basic trend and structures of population which not only underwent a drastic change in this period but which also constitute the main forces of supply and demand in the labour market in any period.

Over the entire period between 1945 and 1970, the Japanese population increased by 45 per cent (see Table 5.1), despite the loss of a total of 2.8 million people (2.1 million soldiers) during the war. The large increase in population over the five immediate postwar years was basically caused by 'fukuin' and 'hikiage' (repatriation due to the dissolution of the military force −7.6 million, and loss of business abroad −1.5 million). The annual average growth rate between 1955 and 1970 remained around 1 per cent. Another distinctive feature, although less conspicuous and not shown in Table 5.1, is the relatively high rate of increase, 1.4 per cent, between 1970 and 1975. This was due to the fact that females born in the first baby boom shortly after the war reached the age of fertility in the early 1970s, which, in turn, produced a second baby boom in Japan.

Except for the few years immediately after the war, population increase in Japan has been mainly attributable to natural increase (see Table 5.2). To obtain a total picture of this population change, it is therefore sufficient to observe basic changes in birth rates and death rates. The birth rate, starting from a high level of 34.5 per 1000 population in 1947, has declined steadily, especially since the early 1970s, and reached a level of around 17.1 per 1000 in 1975 and 9.6 in 1993, the lowest rate in the postwar years. The death rate has declined from 14.7 per 1000 in 1947 to 6.9 per 1000 in 1970, which, according to the Demographic Yearbook of the United Nations, was then the lowest rate in the world.

The *age composition* did not change significantly between 1920 and 1950, but as can be seen from Table 5.1, since 1950 there has been a steady decline of young population (age 0–14) from 35.4 per cent to

Table 5.1   Total population increase and composition by age in Japan, 1945–70

Year	Population (000)	Population increase (000)	Annual average growth rate (per cent)	Composition (per cent)		
				Age 0–14	Age 15–64	Age 65 and over
1945	72 147					
1950	84 115	11 052	2.9	35.4	59.6	4.9
1955	90 077	5 595	1.4	33.4	61.2	5.3
1960	94 302	4 225	0.9	30.2	64.1	5.7
1965	99 209	4 908	1.0	25.7	68.0	6.3
1970	104 665	5 455	1.1	24.0	68.9	7.1

Source: Prime Minister's Office, Statistic Bureau, The Census (various issues).

Table 5.2   Birth rate, death rate and reproduction rate in Japan, 1947–70

Year	Birth rate (000)	Death rate (000)	Natural increase (000)	Gross reproduction rate	Net reproduction rate
1947	34.5	14.7	19.9	2.21	1.72
1950	28.3	11.0	17.3	1.77	1.51
1955	19.5	7.8	11.7	1.15	1.06
1960	17.3	7.6	9.7	0.97	0.92
1965	18.7	7.2	11.5	1.04	1.01
1970	18.8	6.9	11.8	1.03	1.00

Source: Ministry of Heath and Welfare, Institute of Population Studies, *Statistics of Population Studies*.

24.0 per cent of total population in 1970, and, conversely, a steady relative increase in the aged population (65 and over) from 4.9 to 7.1 per cent of total population.

It is important to note, however, that the proportion of aged is not high when compared to what is observed in most European countries. What matters is not so much the composition but rather the speed of ageing in the Japanese population. If we measure this in terms of the number of years required for the old aged component to grow from 5 to 10 per cent, Japan's record is remarkable. Japan seems to require only 30 years to make this transformation, whereas France and Sweden require as long as a century, and the UK and the US 40 and 45 years respectively.

According to a projection, made by the Institute of Population Studies of the Ministry of Health and Welfare, of the Japanese population by age for the next 25 years, the proportion of aged people (65 years old and over) will temporarily stabilise at around the level of 25 per cent.

The main findings about *labour force participation* can be summarised as follows. First, the rate of total labour force participation remained remarkably constant between 1950 and 1970 (see Table 5.3). Both for males and females, the advance of secondary education resulted in the decline of the rate for age 15–19, whereas the rate for 50–59 increased over the same period.

Second, the male participation rate for teenagers (15–19) was as low as 38.6 per cent in 1965. The corresponding figures in the same period in the UK, Germany and Netherlands are reported to be well over 50 per cent. On the other hand, the male participation rate of the population aged over 60 in 1965 is 66.2 per cent, which is extremely high compared with Germany (19.5 per cent for 65 and over), the UK (22.7 per cent for 65 and over) and the Netherlands (17.1 per cent for 65 and over). This is mainly due to the structure of the Japanese labour market where the share of self-employed persons in the workforce was relatively large and the job opportunities for the aged were abundant (these and following international comparisons are based on the Japanese Census and ILO Statistics).

Third, the female participation rate by age shows a clear bimodal 'M' shape. This is similar to that of the UK after 1955, though most European countries experienced unimodal distributions. In Japan, the female participation rate before age 30 behaved a little differently

Table 5.3 Participation rates by sex and age in Japan, 1950–70

	Male					Female				
	1950	*1955*	*1960*	*1965*	*1970*	*1950*	*1955*	*1960*	*1965*	*1970*
Total	83.4	85.0	85.0	83.4	84.3	48.6	50.4	50.9	49.8	50.9
15–19	53.0	53.7	51.6	38.6	36.7	46.8	51.8	49.7	37.6	35.5
20–24	90.5	87.4	87.9	87.1	83.9	64.0	67.6	69.4	69.7	70.6
25–29	95.5	95.9	96.9	97.9	98.1	48.3	51.8	50.1	46.4	45.0
30–39	97.1	97.5	97.7	98.5	98.4	50.0	51.6	53.1	52.9	51.8
40–49	97.0	97.1	97.4	98.2	98.2	53.2	54.8	56.7	62.3	64.4
50–59	92.4	93.3	93.4	95.6	95.7	48.2	48.8	49.3	54.1	57.7
60+	65.2	65.9	65.1	66.2	65.3	27.2	26.2	26.9	24.8	27.2

Source: Prime Minister's Office Census various years.

from its counterparts in other counties. It is much lower for age 15–19, a little higher for 20–24 and lower again for 25–29 compared with other countries.

Finally, the male participation rate for the population 20–24 years old decreased between 1950 and 1975 because of the increasingly high college and university enrolments (see Table 5.9). This is in contrast with female participation rates which still show a gradual increase over the same period.

The Japanese government statistics for employment categorise the employed in three groups: self-employed, family workers and employees. Over the period between 1953–67, the percentage share of employees has steadily increased, while the shares of family workers and self-employed have both declined (see Table 5.4). This is not simply because agriculture had been contracting continuously in the postwar years, but also because persons owning and operating unincorporated enterprises have tended to change their legal status to 'corporation' or 'association', thereby turning family workers into regular employees. Even so, the relative share of employees is comparatively low by international standards and that of family workers is high.

One interesting point to be noted here is that the ratio of employees (defined as the number of employees of a certain age group divided by the total employed labour force of that age group) decreases monotonically for both males and females, but the rate of decrease differs between sexes. The ratio for males declines markedly after age 55, whereas that for females decreases are dramatic for age late 20s and early 30s. This implies that, for females aged 25–34, of those who temporarily retire from the labour market maintain their employee status.

The census reports a drastic change in the *distribution of employment by industry* (Table 5.5), which basically supports the Petty-Colin Clark Law about the shifting weight of employment by industry in the

Table 5.4   Breakdown of employed persons by status in Japan, 1953–67

3-year average	total	Self-employed	Employees	Family workers
1953–55	100.0	26.3	40.5	33.2
1956–58	100.0	24.2	47.9	28.0
1959–61	100.0	22.5	53.5	24.0
1962–64	100.0	20.7	58.1	21.2
1965–67	100.0	19.3	61.8	18.5

Source: Prime Minister's Office, *Labor Force Survey*.

Table 5.5 Japanese employment structure by industry, 1950–70

	Composition (*per cent*)			
	Total	Primary	Secondary	Tertiary
1950	100.0	48.5	21.8	29.6
1955	100.0	41.1	23.4	35.5
1960	100.0	32.7	29.1	38.2
1965	100.0	24.7	31.5	43.7
1970	100.0	19.3	34.0	46.6

Note: The industries are classified according to the 1980 Census Code.
Source: Census, 1980.

course of economic development. Employment in the primary sector on the whole has gradually shifted to the aged and to self-employed and family workers. In the secondary sector, manufacturing employment continued to increase until 1970, but it has been decreasing since the first oil crisis. This employment growth was concentrated in the tertiary sector, while employment fell in the primary sector and the rate of increase was lower in manufacturing. The increase in employment in the tertiary sector is most striking in the sector 'Wholesale and Retail Trade and Services'. This is partly due to the increasing efforts by both firms and households to rely on external services in order to reduce their own economic activities in the firm as well as at home.

Three phases of transformation in labour market

The quarter century after the war can be divided into three major phases in terms of labour market conditions:

- the larger increase in labour supply relative to demand before 1955;
- the rapid growth of labour demand that transformed the labour market into a state of nearly full employment between 1955 and 1965;
- the further growth of labour demand with an extreme labour deficit until 1970.

We will review each of these three phases in turn with some micro level observations.

The *first phase* (1945–55) was marked by an increase in population and by excess labour supply. The dissolution of the Japanese military force at home and abroad left approximately 9.4 million people completely jobless when the war was over. Predicting a huge inflow of labour into the market, the Cabinet Council therefore, in November 1945, proposed a provisional employment policy which emphasised two employment policy measures: preferential job replacement for repatriated soldiers and guidance of employed female workers back into household work.

Fortunately, however, the Labour Force Survey which was first conducted after the war in 1947, seldom recorded unemployment higher than 2.5 per cent in the late 1940s and early 1950s. This does not mean that no employment problem existed in Japan. On the contrary, the problem of 'hidden unemployment' was of course very serious. Low wages and short working hours were pervasive among employed persons. The census of 1946, a year before the first Labour Force Survey, showed the latent unemployment of the labour force one year after the end of the war (see Table 5.6). The same survey of 1946 also indicates how much workforce was absorbed into the agriculture sector (3.6 million) and how low the unemployment rate was in agricultural households (1.2 per cent compared to 10.4 in non-agricultural households).

The manufacturing production index had fallen to 30.7 in contrast to 100 averaged in the three year period 1934–36. Such a drastic contraction of the manufacturing sector was accompanied by a large number of discharged workers. To make matters worse, inflation rapidly accelerated. The index of black market prices, compiled by the Bank of Japan, jumped from 100 in September 1945 to 200 in February 1946 and attained a level approximately 40 times higher than official prices.

Thus inflation and unstable employment forced workers' living standards down to virtually poverty levels in the late 1940s. The unions' wage demands during this period were often 3 to 5 times higher than that of previous years and labour disputes, whose slogan was always 'wage for survival', occurred frequently.

Around the year 1950, the entrepreneurial activities, especially private investment, began to recover quickly, stimulated and supported by such governmental policies as rapid depreciation allowances for investment (1951) and the establishment of long-term financial institutions (1950–52). The Industry Rationalisation Policy for steel and coal mining, as well as a special depreciation system ('Tokubetsu Shôkyaku') also gave a strong impetus to the production of steel plate and sheet which is technically linked to electric machine manufacturing, automobiles and the shipbuilding industries.

The textile industry also took the lead in reactivating the Japanese economy in the first ten years after the War. GHQ approved the export of cotton fabrics in 1947 and Japan soon returned to the position of the world-leading exporter of cotton fabrics in 1950.

Table 5.6 Latent unemployment in Japan, 1946

	(000)	*per cent*
Population of age 13–61	47 406	
Labour force	29 720	100.0
Employed	28 130	94.7
for more than 20 days (per month)	21 849	73.6
for 8–19 days	4 320	14.6
for 1–7 days	1 963	6.6
unemployed	1 590	5.3

Source: Umemura, Sengonikon no Rôdôyoku, 1964, p. 75.

During the years between 1950 and 1955 the agricultural sector lost more than 1.1 million of its workforce, while employment in manufacturing and construction grew by 1.7 million people. In addition there was an increase of 2.9 million workers in the tertiary sector (Census, 1950 and 1955). This outflow of labour from agriculture was not primarily due to the direct migration of workers from agriculture to other sectors, but rather to the increased entries of new junior high school graduates who were usually not the 'first children' in agricultural households. In this respect there was virtually no 'friction cost' of migration either between industries or between occupations. The growing demand for labour from manufacturing was basically supplied by new entrants to the labour force directly from school and this tendency remained unchanged during the following ten years from 1955 to 1965.

By the year 1955, personal consumption levels and real wages had returned to prewar levels (1937 standard) and so declared the White Paper on the Japanese Economy in 1956 'the "post-war" period has already passed' (Keizai Hakusho, 1956).

The *second phase* that covers the period between the mid-1950s and mid-1960s was marked by full-scale technological progress and rapid economic growth. This phase was temporarily interrupted by a recession in 1965. Table 5.7 summarises the dramatic economic expansion in this period. Manufacturing production increased four-fold, employment more than doubled and real wages grew by 50 per cent during these ten years.

Economic growth in this period was sometimes slowed down by weaknesses in the balance of payments position. Trade deficits required the imposition of a tight-money policy in order to decrease import demand and thereby to restore the balance-of-payments equilibrium.

Table 5.7 Main labour indicators in Japan, 1955–70

(1970=100)	(1) Production in manufacturing	(2) Employment in manufacturing	(3) Wages in manufacturing (nominal)	(4) Wages in manufacturing (real)	(5) Level of consumption of urban workers	(6) Work hours in manufacturing (regular workers)
1955	12.5	38.5	23.2	44.2	48.1	106.1
1960	27.4	63.8	31.1	54.9	62.8	110.7
1965	48.1	85.9	50.3	65.6	77.7	102.4
1970	100.0	100.0	100.0	100.0	100.0	100.0

Source: (1) Ministry of International Trade and Industry, *Statistical Table of Manufacturing Industry* (Kogyo Tokei Hyo);
(2) Ministry of Labor, *Monthly Labor Statistics* (Maitsuki Kinro Tokei). The figures are for regular workers in establishments employing more than 30 workers;
(3), (4) The same source as (2): wages are monthly average cash payments per regular worker. Consumer price index used for the years 1955 and 1960 are computed for cities with more than 50000 inhabitants;
(5) Prime Minister's Office. *Household Survey* (Kakeichosa);
(6) The same source as (2).

Private equipment investment in general, however, was extremely active, especially in new industries like petrochemicals, synthetic fibres and electronics. In the automobile and machinery industries, the mass-production system was successfully applied to achieve lower prices, which in turn stimulated consumer demand and produced a 'virtuous circle'; a demand–supply expansion spiral. Such a bullish or aggressive behaviour on the business side became the driving force behind economic growth (Nakamura, 1995: 75), but it must also be noted that the unions' demands for higher wages created great effective consumption demand from the workers' side.

By the year 1965, more than 95 per cent of total households owned black-and-white television sets (colour television sets were in more than 90 per cent households by 1975). Washing machines and refrigerators were owned by 90 per cent of households by 1970 (see Chapter 7). Such a rapid change in terms of the possession of consumer goods in households brought about a change in lifestyles, such as in eating habits from a complete rice diet to bread for breakfast and the housing of urban workers in rented homes based on nuclear families (see Table 5.8).

The rapid economic growth, promoted by technological progress and private equipment investment in the 1960s, brought about a tight labour market, in contrast with the more or less over-supply conditions of the 1950s. As shown in Table 5.7, the unemployment rate hovered

Table 5.8 Unemployment rate (%, seasonally adjusted) and employment exchange ratio (annual average) in Japan 1955–70

	UR	EER		UR	EER
1955	2.5	0.22	1963	1.3	0.70
1956	2.3	0.33	1964	1.1	0.80
1957	1.9	0.39	1965	1.2	0.64
1958	2.1	0.32	1966	1.3	0.73
1959	2.2	0.44	1967	1.3	1.00
1960	1.7	0.59	1968	1.2	1.12
1961	1.4	0.74	1969	1.1	1.30
1962	1.3	0.68	1970	1.1	1.41

Note: EER is the ratio of job offers to job seekers at Public Employment Exchange Offices. They are originally collected and computed on a monthly basis, but figures in this table are those of annual averages.
Source: Ministry of Labor, Labor Force Survey, Employment Exchange Statistics.

around 2.2 or 2.3 per cent until 1959. The employment exchange ratio (EER) which is defined as the ratio of job offers to job applicants at the regional Public Employment Exchange Offices, was consistently lower than the 0.5 level before 1960, but we can clearly observe that this ratio began to rise steadily from the mid-1960s onwards. In this period, the labour force increased at an annual rate of 1.5 per cent and labour demand became extremely brisk. For instance, one representative firm (National Electric Company) producing electric home appliances increased its employees from 11 000 in 1955 to 38 000 in 1965 to 60 000 in 1970.

Wage levels also rose rapidly throughout 1955–65 period. The so-called spring-labour offensive ('Shunt'), started in 1955 by an association of eight industrial private sector unions, was a concerted effort aimed at improving general working conditions. Without doubt, however, the most scrutinised issue was wage claims. The number of union members participating in this offensive increased during the era of rapid growth from 0.73 million in 1955 to 5.6 million in 1965.

Wage negotiation in key industries like private railways and the steel industry set the tone for the general amounts and rates of wage increase in other industries. In this sense the spring offensive had not only been attracting special interest from workers, but actually had been determining the macro aggregates of wage incomes in Japan. The size of wage increase has been strongly correlated with such factors as price increases, labour market conditions and business performance.

The general wage increase, including that of medium-small firms, was substantially influenced by the bargaining during the spring offensive by key industries, but when we look into the levels and structure of wages compared to European countries, we find some salient features in Japanese wages which were formed during 1955–65 years.

The White Paper on Wages annually published by Sôhyô, which used to be the most influential National Labour Confederation affiliated with the Japanese Socialist Party, gave an interesting comment on Japanese wages in its final issue in 1963 (Koshiro *et al.*, 1995; Sôhyô, 1994):

> Wages in Japan have increased considerably due to the post-war labour movement.... In spite of such efforts, the post-war wage condition in an international perspective has worsened compared to pre-war period.... While the production index of main industries became almost par with European standards by the years 1955 to 1958, the Japanese wage is still less than half of, therefore far lower than, the European wage.

The Japan Employers Federation (JEF-Nikkeiren) tried to refute this union view by pointing out that the Japanese wage was not as low as generally asserted and that it roughly corresponded to income per capita by international comparison. In other words, JEF did not concede the union view and insisted that the Japanese wage was not unreasonably low. After this dispute, JEF strengthened its interior solidarity and, probably because of its solidarity, the rate of wage increase declined from 13.1 per cent in 1961 to 9.1 per cent in 1963.

Finally, looking at wage structures in this second period, we should observe that major influences on wage structures are usually considered to be sex, experience and age, compared to minor influences of occupation and firm size. Wage differentials in this period are summarised as follows (Tachibanaki, 1996):

- First, the estimated wage differential due to sex seems relatively large and it became slightly wider in this period in terms of coefficients of variation.
- Second, wage differentials are monotonically increasing functions of experience. It means that longer experience provides more skills and it shows relatively stable strength in this period.
- Third, white-collar workers earn higher wages than blue-collar workers, though the effect is not so strong as that of sex, experience and age.
- Fourth, the wage earnings adjusted by bonus and working hours indicate that the size effect is weaker than sex, experience and age, and it tended to shrink during 1955–65.
- Fifth, education had the weakest effect throughout the period and age had a stronger effect than education and size, but it did not show any noteworthy trend in this period.

The *third phase* began with the recovery from the business downturn of 1964–65. The economy soon bounced back, assisted by a long-term public bond policy at the end of 1965 and it began to enjoy the longest economic upsurge in the postwar years that lasted through to the summer of 1970. The average annual growth rate in the latter half of 1960s was as high as 11 per cent. Such a high growth rate finally brought Japan into second position in terms of GNP in the free world.

During these five years, the labour market changed completely from a buyers' to a sellers' market. The market for new school graduates took the lead in this shift. The employment exchange rate (EER) for new junior school graduates had already jumped to a high level of 1.9 in 1960, but it continued to rise as high as 3.7 in 1965 and finally to 5.8

in 1970. New junior high school graduates were in such high demand that they were called 'golden eggs'. The EER for new senior high school graduates also began to rise rapidly after the end of the 1965 recession to the level of 7.1 in 1970. Such a large excess demand for labour then extended to other categories of the labour force in the late 1960s and the Japanese labour market was considered to have reached the full employment state.

Source of economic growth

Already at the turn of the twentieth century, elementary education had been widespread in Japan, but admission to secondary and higher education was still severely restricted even after the Second World War. Yet the sons of poor families, if they had shown superior talent, could aspire to future advancement and were sometimes able to attend university with the financial assistance from a person of means in their village or among their relatives, a so-called 'patron' or 'benefactor'. In this way, those males with ability were often accepted to high school and college without regard to class or status and, upon graduation from college, the way was open to high positions in business or in the bureaucracy.

Open opportunity to education for males thus stimulated the upward mobility of Japanese society. This upward mobility was further stimulated in the 1960s when the economy was expanding rapidly. The main workforce at that time comprised those with only compulsory education (9 years of education) in the 1960s. However, even those who could not afford the upper secondary education had a chance to be promoted to middle management or even higher positions if they showed aptitude and capability in the firm.

In times of high rates of economic growth, the expansion of institutions for higher education synchronised with the tendency toward the acquisition of higher educational qualifications. However, this fact does not necessarily mean that the rise in the general level of education directly led to a rise in labour productivity in the workshops of Japanese industry in this period. On this point, there are two matters that ought to be noted. One is that, considering that the workforce needs 10 to 20 years to acquire skills before they can substantially contribute to productivity improvements, we can say that it was basically the labour force made up of a large number of lower secondary school leavers (and some upper secondary school or technical upper secondary school leavers) that supported high productivity in the workshop during the period of high rates of economic growth in Japan (see Table 5.9).

Table 5.9   Distribution of incomes in Japan, 1951–70

	Wages and salaries	Income from (agriculture)	Self-employment (others)	Corporate income (dividend)	others
1951	38.7	22.3	20.7	12.0 (1.2)	6.3
1955	47.9	20.1	18.7	9.6 (1.2)	3.7
1960	48.4	13.1	14.8	16.4 (1.7)	7.3
1965	53.4	9.4	14.0	13.1 (1.7)	10.1
1970	51.6	6.2	13.6	18.3 (1.4)	10.3

Note: wages and salaries in 1951 does not include allowances and other payments; dividend is included in 'Corporate Income' as shown.
Source: Economic Planning Agency.

This point is related to the question of how much school education itself contributes to actual labour productivity and to what extent it functions as a mere machinery for screening competent human resources (rather than increasing productivity). While it is hard to present a direct answer to this question, we can show some circumstantial evidence. School education (or acquiring knowledge and skill) has two economic aspects: consumption and investment. When we take a look at the investment aspect, it is suggested that the internal rate of return from higher education declined sharply during this period. Since 1965, moreover, it is suggested that the rate was either equal to or below the rate of return from general financial assets. This may be taken as a proof that, supposing (lifelong) wages roughly reflect the level of productivity of the labour force, the rise in the number of years of general education no longer contributes so much to a rise in productivity. This implies that school education now has a strong aspect of consumption rather than investment, and the rise in income level causes an increased purchase of educational services, and, at the same time, higher education has come to play the role of screening machinery for discovering human resources.

Pre-employment competition for acquiring higher educational qualifications represents only a part of the competition process in the Japanese society. Generally speaking, this competition in prestigious universities might be given too much publicity, in an exaggerated form, by the mass media. In fact, more overall (namely, not just a paper test) and protracted competition prevails in the post-employment arena within an enterprise. In other words, overemphasis on the intensity of competition for entrance into universities may possibly make us lose sight of the intensity of post-employment competition within enterprise.

A study which analysed this aspect with respect to white-collar workers employed in large enterprises casts doubt on the popular opinion that finding employment in large enterprises, and promotion to higher posts there, is subject to the reputation and type of university from which the employee graduated. If the brand of university alone can decide on promotion, and there is no competition within the enterprise, then the impetus or the incentive to increase productivity in the workshop will not be maintained. Koike and Watanabe examined this point in positive terms with respect to the rate of employees holding executive posts immediately before reaching the age of retirement, wage differentials by educational qualifications and the scope for promotion to the position of section chief. They showed that the mythology surrounding the relationship between educational qualifications, employment and promotion is exaggerated (1979). This is also confirmed by wage analysis, which showed that school education had the weakest effect on wage differentials (Tachibanaki, 1996: 36–42).

Why is it, then, that educational qualification and performance in the firm tend not to be strongly correlated? The answer seems to be that post-employment education and training really matter, especially on-the-job training (OJT) in Japanese industry. It has already become clear in some literature that OJT as a skill formation system is mutually, closely and organically related to the employment practices of long-term service, internal promotion and the seniority system (Inoki and Koike, 1991). Career progression based on OJT makes internal promotion in the firm basically inevitable. It goes without saying that internal promotion works to elongate workers' length of service for the same firm, compared to other practices. As workers gain experience in their job so they also accumulate seniority and increase their length of service for the enterprise. Moreover, if a supervisory post of intermediate level is filled by internal promotion, the length of service of the worker promoted to that post naturally increases, compared to cases where such posts are filled by persons recruited from outside. Therefore, the 'economy and efficiency of OJT' leads to the phenomenon of 'career formation within the enterprise', and these two are combined to make 'internal promotion' economically rational, with the result that 'elongation of length of service' occurs.

These considerations also help explain why seniority is the most important factor in wage increases. If wages are taken as remuneration for widening and sophistication of the range of skills from easy to difficult jobs through OJT, it is also quite natural that wages are strongly regulated by the length of service (and age in the case of long-term service). No matter how much emphasis is given by personnel or industrial relations managers to 'shifting from seniority to ability' in relation to the question of how wages should be determined, if 'length of service' is an important yardstick for measuring workers' ability, then there is no alternative for the actual wage profile but to take the form of rise of workers' age or length of service increases.

The above arguments do not of course apply to all types of work or all kinds of skills. Some craft based occupations or professional jobs have other characteristics. The central theme of the argument has been the skills learned by workers employed in the heavy and chemical industries or key workers employed in other large manufacturing enterprises, white-collar workers, or workers employed in large enterprises in the tertiary sector. It must thus be said that workers employed in the so-called medium and small enterprises have almost fallen out of the analysis. Many of the statements made above, however, apply basically, but to a varying extent, to cases of medium and small enterprises. It is true that careers are short since jobs are not as fragmented as in large enterprises and that workers move frequently between enterprises due to business fluctuations. It is also true that the possibilities of promotion to important supervisory posts are few because of the strong element of family management. As a result the aspect of long-term service through internal promotion is indeed weaker than in large enterprises. However, various surveys have shown that also in medium and small enterprises OJT is basically the most important method of education and training. And it is this trinity of OJT, internal promotion and long seniority of workers that together basically promoted the unprecedented economic growth of Japan in the quarter century immediately after the Second World War.

References

Inoki, T. (1996) *Gakko to Kôjô*, Yomiurishinbunsha.
Inoki, T. (1997) 'Education, Training and Economic Growth,' *World Bank Report on Social Expenditure and Economic Development* (mimeo).
Inoki, T. and Y. Yasuba (eds) (1989) *Kôdo Seichô*, Iwanamishoten.
Inoki, T. and K. Koike (eds) (1991) *Skill Formation in Japan and Southeast Asia*, Tokyo.
Koike, K. and U. Watanabe (1979) *Gakurekishakai no Kyozô*, Tôyôkeizai Shinpôsha.
Koshiro, K. *et al.* (1995) *Sengo 50 Nen Sangyô, Koyô, Rôdôshi*, Nihon Rôdô Kenkyôikô: 339–41.

Kôzai, U. (1981) *Kôdoseichô no Jidai*, Nihonhyôronsha.

Nakamura, T. (1995) *The Postwar Japanese Economy Its Development and Structure 1937–1994*, (2nd Edition) Tokyo.

Research Institute of Ministry of Health and Welfare (1992) *Nihon no Shôraisuikei Jinkô*, Kôsei Tôkei Kyôkai.

Sôhyô (ed.)(1994) *Sôhyô 40 Nenshi*, Daiichi Shorin.

Tachibanaki, T. (1996) *Wage Determination and Distribution in Japan*, Oxford.

Umemura, M. (1964) *Sengonihon no Rôdôryoku*, Iwanamishoten.

6
A New Sensibility? Affluence, Disposable Income and the Politics of Private Consumption, 1955–75

Brian Girvin

For a brief period between 1955 and 1975 Western industrial societies seemed to discover a formula for meeting all the demands its citizens made of it. Governments were able to manage the economy to assure continuing expansion, high levels of employment and rising standards of living for most of their citizens. Successful economic management led to affluence which in turn led to the consumer boom of the late 1950s, a process which continued despite the economic downturn of the 1970s. Furthermore, technical and scientific advances contributed to this mood of optimism: the availability of antibiotics, contraceptives and computers promised a cornucopia to some, for others it entailed the worst excesses of Huxley's 'brave new world'. The contrast between this subperiod and the ones which preceded and followed it is quite striking in retrospect. Perhaps the most vivid expression of the change which occurred in the 1970s was the acceleration of the 'discomfort index', which added the rate of unemployment to that of inflation. The index which had been low and stable during the 1950s and 1960s increased three fold by the mid 1970s and rose again at the end of that decade.

During this time most liberal democratic governments seemed poised to eradicate the contradictions of industrial society. In 1989 Fukuyama declared the 'end of history' on the grounds that with the end of the cold war capitalist liberal democracy had eliminated its internal contradiction. In the future conflict, where it occurred, would be about the administration of things in the Hegelian–Marxist sense (Fukuyama, 1992). This argument has some strength, but it echoes similar claims made during the 1960s, in particular, that the mixed economies have achieved a means of regulating the boom–slump cycle which had seemed central to capitalism. By technical adjustment it was claimed that a new stability had been secured for industrial society. One cautious exposition of this approach led to the conclusion in 1968 that 'a major set back of Western economic growth seemed on balance unlikely' (Shonfield, 1965, xiv–xv).

The unique character of the 1950s

The unique circumstances, which prevailed up to 1975, were primarily a product of decisions taken during the 1950s. By 1951 postwar recovery had largely been achieved, but the contours of the postwar world were still not settled. The involvement of the United States in Europe after the War marked a profound change in the character of European politics as provider, protector and cultural influence. American dominance in global terms provided a successful example for European states of a wealthy mass democracy enhancing its citizens' incomes and its security. The United States provided confirmation that industrial development in a mass democracy need not be a zero sum game (Ellwood, 1992; Kuisel, 1993). What was not clear by 1951 was the form that economic development would take in Europe. It was conceivable that a uniquely European economic model would emerge under the influence of social democracy; one involving extensive public provision, a high degree of planning, considerable restrictions on private investment and consumption. This had in large part been the model adopted for postwar reconstruction. Yet this did not prove to have the staying power expected by the left. In place of state ownership, rationing controls and public provision the 1950s is characterised by the growing influence of the American free market model emphasising mass production techniques and scientific management, by the expansion of free trade and export led growth, and by the increasing dominance of the consumer over the producer (middle-class consumers in the 1950s, mass consumption in the 1960s).

What now becomes apparent is a new political economy and a new political consensus for Europe. The political economy involved the acceptance by Europe of the American growth model and the completion of Europe's industrialisation. This implied that societies could aspire to and sustain growth and consumption at levels close to those associated with the United States. One of the main criticisms of capitalism from the left historically had been that whatever the ability of the system to generate wealth, this did not ensure that the mass of the population benefited from it. Central to the new political economy was the acceptance that the mass of citizens in society would indeed benefit from their contribution to the economy. There was little disagreement among liberal democratic states about this, what was at issue was how the promise would be delivered. The 1950s stand out in relief from previous periods of capitalist development as a period when not only does national income increase appreciably but the real income of the vast majority of the citizens does also. There was a wide ranging consensus in the 1950s on a limited number of issues: these included a commitment to democracy, the cold war and the need to sustain economic growth. However, the consensus on domestic issues in individual states reflected the balance of power between the political parties. The nature of this balance of power had a significant impact on both policy formation and outcome. The former Labour Party cabinet minister John Strachey claimed in 1956 that the postwar consensus was a reflection of the enhanced political power of the working class. He believed that the advance of democracy and the organisation of the working class had created a situation where no democratic government could continue to govern with high levels of unemployment or declining living standards (Strachey, 1956). While this observation had particular reference to the UK it also had more general application. However, at the time it was written the main political characteristic of Western Europe was the growing dominance of the centre-right both at the political and policy level. Indeed, Nau has argued that successful economic growth between 1947 and 1967 was predicated on Conservative incumbency. On this reading it was centre-right governments which got the policy mix right and this became the dominant mix until the end of the 1960s (Nau, 1990: 9, 41–9).

Three political factors are of importance for the move to affluence during the 1950s. The first is the electoral requirements of the centre-right parties throughout Europe (and in the US). Consumption provided a powerful appeal for most of these parties in competition with their social democratic rivals. This was, secondly, reinforced by the nature of the electorate. Most voters had experienced the depression, the rise of Nazism, the Second World War and the postwar settlement which divided Europe by 1947. In political terms this environment produced a desire for stability, security and higher living standards. The centre-right argued that these could be best provided by the politics of consumption rather than by the left-wing alternatives. A third feature was the way in which Keynesian economics was adapted by the centre-right to justify this move to consumption politics. Whereas Keynesianism was originally conceived as a justification for government intervention in the economy, it could also be utilised to justify enhanced private consumption. Throughout the 1950s the left continued to emphasise a production-led economic policy; while the centre-right did not ignore this, it supplemented it with the view that the expansion of private consumption, especially for the middle classes, could provide better economic benefits than state ownership or planning. There had always been an under-consumptionist element to Keynes and implicitly the centre-right used this feature to justify the rapid expansion of private spending which began to dominate during the 1950s. This was not set in motion by the centre-right, but it was more successful than the left in adopting it as a policy for government. If hedonism was not actually justified by the centre-right, they were quicker to concede to it than the left (Hibbs, 1977; Skidelsky, 1977). There is therefore a certain ambiguity about the rise of affluence in the 1950s. As one of the characteristic features of that decade it was promoted by the centre-right in an effort to outflank the appeal of the left in a political environment where full employment, the welfare state and economic growth were not serious grounds for political disagreement. The centre-right successfully identified the demand for consumer goods and used this to their own electoral advantage. It is no coincidence that not only are the centre-right electorally successful in the 1950s, but that increasingly the social democratic left had to respond to the challenge of affluence in the 1960s by promising more of the same.

From collective provision to affluence

Daniel Bell highlighted the critical significance of the 1950s as a decade in which the lethal politics of the interwar years had been replaced by a new (and more benign) consensus that included, 'the acceptance of a welfare state; the desirability of decentralized power; a system of mixed economy and of political pluralism.' The working class, once the hope of revolutionaries, now accepted the benefits of the new economic and social order (Bell, 1988: 393–407). This optimism was widespread by the early 1960s, but little more than a decade earlier such an outcome might not have been predicted. A UNESCO survey in 1948 reported that while respondents were optimistic about some matters, in other respects there was strong insecurity evident. One in five believed that employment was less secure after the war, while more than 40 per cent in each country reported that they were not in a position to plan for the future (in France 74 per cent) (Buchanan and Cantril, 1953). By 1955 the contours of the postwar order in Europe had become clearer. The division of Europe, the partition of Germany and the cold war remained the fixed certainties of geo-politics, certainties confirmed by Germany's entry to NATO in 1955.

The domestic landscape however was still not as clear-cut, and the future was still not always viewed with optimism. The change in government in the UK in 1951 and the US in 1953 prompted fears that conservative governments would introduce policies which would slow economic growth and even precipitate a recession; fears compounded when just such a recession followed in the US (Girvin, 1994: 169–75).

This pessimism was to change fairly quickly over the next few years. In the Federal Republic of Germany, 1953 was a year of rising prices and this gave cause for concern. However, in the same year the percentage believing that they were worse off than the previous year dropped to a postwar low. In 1951, 56 per cent had considered that they were worse off than the previous year, whereas by 1953 this figure had dropped to 19 per cent. Those saying they were better off had increased appreciably from 12 per cent in 1951 to 24 per cent in 1954 (Noelle and Neumann, 1967: 374–5). Similar figures begin to appear in other liberal democratic states at the same time, especially in Britain and the US. The uncertainties quickly disappeared and the economies of Europe and the United States entered a golden age of accelerated growth and expansion.

It is possible to use the term affluence in a number of ways. At one level it is simply a description of those who have reached a level of luxury not possessed by the majority of the citizens of a society. This is not the use followed here. Affluence here is closely related to the rapid expansion of mass consumption to the majority of the citizens in a state. It is a situation where a majority of the population satisfy, out of their income, a socially determined level of basic needs: food, housing, clothing and leisure (Berry, 1994). After these needs have been satisfied the individual can be considered to be affluent if he/she has purchasing power left over to acquire commodities once considered to be luxuries and traditionally limited to a minority of the population. An affluent society is one where scarcity or want of the basic necessities no longer threatens the majority of the population, and especially a majority of the working-class, the poor and the marginal. This is a society where mass consumption is realised and where most people believe that the conditions which allowed for this process would continue (Mason, 1981: 67–100).

The American model

Affluence does not simply involve an increase in Gross National Income or indeed in per capita income, unless that increase is relatively evenly spread across various social strata. Let me illustrate what affluence is not. Average purchasing power rose by some 40 per cent in the US between 1910 and 1929. Most estimates agree that the surplus was spent on consumer durables, especially on motor cars and radios. However, despite some trickle down, it is questionable how far this new wealth penetrated to the lower classes. Estimates for 1930 suggest that even before the recession, 60 per cent of American families (or 70 million individuals) received less than the $2000 per annum considered necessary for socially determined basic necessities. Of this 70 million some 40 million or approximately one-third of the US population had incomes of $1200 or less per annum (National Bureau of Economic Research, 1929: 625–26; Leven, Moulton and Warburton, 1934; Cross, 1993). The contrast with the 1950s is quite stark. Median income (in constant 1967 $ terms) increased from $4147 in 1950 to $7167 in 1970. In 1950, 50 per cent of the labour force earned $5000 or less, whereas by 1970 this had fallen to 24 per cent. Furthermore, in 1950 some 8.4 per cent had an income in excess of $10 000 per annum, by 1970 this had increased to 44 per cent (Levy, 1988). This change in disposable income is clearly reflected in the nature of consumption. Table 6.1 illustrates the expansion of expenditure on some consumer items between 1952 and 1956. These figures do not reveal other patterns of consumption behaviour. In 1947, 71 per cent of those who purchased cars paid by cash, whereas 29 per cent paid by credit. By 1960 those paying by cash had dropped to 33 per cent, while those paying by credit had increased to 67 per cent. This change in consumer behaviour is accompanied by a significant increase in economic confidence over the same period. By 1955, 75 per cent of Americans believed that the country was prosperous, while 55 per cent now believed that a depression was not

Table 6.1   Ownership of certain consumer durables in the US, 1952 and 1956

	1952 %	1956 %
automobiles	65	71
television	38.5	76
fridge	86.7	94.1
vacuum cleaner	55.7	64.3
washing machines	73.5	84.1
freezer	9.3	16.8

Source: Eisenhower Library, Abiline Kansas; Presidential Papers, Administrative Series, Box 9, Burns to Eisenhower, 17 August 1956.

inevitable after a period of high prosperity. Furthermore, fully 72 per cent considered that it was the government's responsibility to ensure that prosperity would be maintained (Wattenberg, 1976; Gallup, 1972).

The role of credit is significant because it provides the basis for those without savings or ready cash to purchase the commodities. The economic and employment security of the 1950s provided the basis for purchasing decisions to be taken over the long term without the fear that economic instability would undermine the ability to repay; a fear which the experience of the 1920s reinforced. Thus, the US was the first country to achieve these levels of affluence and to sustain them over time (Girvin, 1994: 175–88).

The European experience

The American model in Europe was especially influential in the first postwar decade, but its cultural and economic example continued to be followed during subsequent decades. Was the European experience different from that of the US?

The return of the Conservative Party to government in 1951 accelerated the movement to affluence. Increasingly, government policy was to promise to secure rising living standards for all, but especially the working class. Real national income increased by about 20 per cent and working class income reflected this change. Furthermore, full employment, the welfare state and economic security enhanced the possibility for increased consumption through the use of the credit system. As a consequence the patterns of consumption expenditure changed during the 1950s. There is a decrease in the proportion of income spent on the traditional 'basics'; such as food, drink and clothing. In contrast, expenditure increases for furniture, radios, televisions and motor vehicles; in this area the volume of sales doubled in a decade, whereas growth in the traditional consumption areas was considerably slower (Hall, 1962: 429–60).

Patterns of consumption continued to differ between classes. The expansion of television ownership is a case in point. Middle-class families appear to have purchased cars before televisions, whereas the opposite is the case with the working classes, a feature which reflects both priority, cost and availability of credit. However, due to credit restriction in the UK during the 1950s the level of indebtedness was low in comparison with other affluent societies. It is not until the 1960s that credit driven affluence becomes a central part of the British (and European) experience (Hall, 1962: 433–9). This class aspect to television purchase is also evident in other European states. In 1950 some 382 000 television licenses were issued, by 1960 this had grown to 10 554 200 and by 1964 90 per cent of all homes in Britain had a television. The patterns of car ownership are slightly different and not as dense in penetration. In 1949 some 7 per cent of people owned a motor car, but ownership is heavily concentrated in the higher income brackets with 26 per cent of those in social category AB owning a car. By 1966 53 per cent of people owned cars, with 50 per cent of skilled workers doing so (Halsey, 1978; Goldthorpe *et al.*, 1969). While a critical mass of car ownership had been achieved, it was not at the American level nor was this the case with other products (see Table 6.2).

Paid holidays are an increasing feature of consumption in the UK. By the end of the 1950s virtually all workers had two weeks paid holidays, which was not the case during the interwar period. There is a class bias to holiday destination, with the middle classes increasingly travelling abroad and the working classes remaining in Britain. By the 1960s a growing proportion of working-class Britons were however travelling abroad on package tours. There is a significant increase in passport possession; from 20 600 in 1931 to 467 778 in 1951 and 563 000 in 1961. While foreign travel may have been a class phenomenon in the 1950s, it laid the basis for the growth of mass foreign tourism in the next decade. However two aspects of the trends are worth noting at this stage. The first is that even within the working class there are clear distinctions to be drawn between those who own their own homes and those in public rented accommodation: Table 6.3 can be roughly compared with Table 6.2, which it relates ownership of consumer good with house ownership for working-class families.

Homeowners seem to be more similar to the middle classes in their consumption patterns, though this may be a reflection of similar

Table 6.2   Ownership of certain consumer durables in the UK in 1959

	Total %	Middle class %	Working class %
house	38	59	27
car	27	47	17
television	78	77	79
fridge	24	46	11
washing machine	40	49	35

Source: Abrams and Rose, 1960: Table 27, p. 43.

Table 6.3 British working-class house ownership and consumption patterns, 1957 and
1960

Percentage of households	1957	1960
living in own house	24	29
in possession of:		
television set	53	78
lawn mower	33	34
washing machine	21	37
car	17	22
fridge	5	13

Source: Tiratsoo, 1991: 44–61 Table p. 48.

residential status rather than class (Goldthorpe *et al.*, 1969). A more important aspect of affluence in the 1950s in the UK is the changing pattern of young people's consumption outlay. The young working class had more disposable income and, though contributing to the home were also in a position to generate their own demand. This focused on leisure to a large degree: clothes, music and transport. It may be no accident that it is in the UK that rock and roll and the new music sensibility gets its strongest grip in Europe; in the form of the 'teddy boys', it also creates its own specific fashion statement.

The West German experience is distinctive, but shares with other European states the general move towards affluence and enhanced consumption. In Germany geo-political, economic and domestic factors interacted during the second half of the 1940s and these affected the nature of policymaking during the 1950s. The most important of these were partition, continued occupation by the Western allies, the establishment of the Federal Republic in 1949, and the need to secure economic reconstruction, political stability and national sovereignty. As a consequence the needs of production took priority over those of affluence at first, but relatively quickly and certainly after 1955, consumption politics played an increasingly significant role in domestic politics. German recovery was based on its successful reintegration into world markets and its increasing share of those markets, particularly in the case of industrial exports (Abelshauser, 1983; Buchheim, 1990). GDP per capita grew in real terms by about 8 per cent per annum between 1949 and 1956, while the unemployment rate declined throughout the decade. Estimates based on Kuznets suggest that the share of national income going to the bottom 60 per cent may have actually increased between 1950 and 1959 after a decline during the Nazi period (Hallett, 1990). There was certainly a substantial rise in real income during the 1950s, though wage earners may not have benefited as much as the self-employed or other sectors of the labour force (Leaman, 1988: 127–9). A further contributory factor to affluence in Germany was its success in reducing the percentage of its citizens living in poverty. By the early 1970s the German figure was significantly below other OECD states such as the US or the UK (Hallett, 1990: 92). By the time of the economic downturn after 1973, German income and consumption levels were among the highest in the world and well above their partners in the European Community.

There had been considerable anxiety during the 1950s about the political stability of German democracy and some scepticism about its ability to internalise the main features of a parliamentary system. However, German democratic institutions quickly took root and were consolidated during this time. The improvement in the economy probably reinforced these trends and this is reflected in public opinion (Otake, 1985: 10–18). Whereas in 1951 public opinion remained, at the very least, suspicious of democratic government, by the end of the 1950s the majority believed that Germany's economic position was good, that income was high and that the working class was better off in the federal republic than in the Third Reich. This change of view can by appreciated in a September 1957 poll which found that 36 per cent of those interviewed believed that Germany had the highest standard of living in Europe and the best economic circumstances. Opinion on these matters show an upward trend: in 1957, 55 per cent believed that workers now earned good money in Germany, a figure which had increased to 66 per cent by 1963 (Noelle and Neuman, 1967: 344–50, 370–9). Further analysis of opinion found that there was a consistently positive

Table 6.4 Public opinion in West Germany

Answers to the question 'Would you say that our economic situation is, generally speaking, good, middling or bad?' (%)

	December 1956	November 1958	April 1959
good	42	37	43
middling	44	49	46
bad	9	8	7
do not know	5	6	4

Source: Noelle and Neumann, 1967: 379.

view of the economic situation as Table 6.4 shows. This also helped to underwrite a more sympathetic view of parliamentary democracy and the federal republic, support for which grew appreciably during the late 1950s (Noelle and Neumann, 1967: 379–80; Conradt, 1980).

Despite the significant changes in the German economy during the 1950s, individual consumption patterns lagged somewhat behind those of Britain until the 1960s. It is not until then that Germany becomes an affluent society in the sense defined above. The spread of consumer goods during the late 1950s was predominantly a middle-class phenomenon, but even here somewhat restricted. In comparative terms patterns of consumption between classes are similar to those of Britain, the middle-class purchase cars and houses while the working-class purchase motorcycles and televisions. The housebuilding pro-gramme, as in Britain, privileged middle-class buyers; in both cases reflecting centre-right incumbency and the commitment to providing the middle class with a stake in property (Hamilton, 1965: 144–52; Girvin, 1994: 110–22). In political terms, a significant proportion of the German electorate were undecided about the policies pursued by Adenauer and his CDU-dominated government between 1949 and 1952, but from the middle of 1952 until 1960 agreement with govern-ment policy rarely fell below 40 per cent (Noelle and Neumann, 1967: 256–63). Despite this, working-class and SPD supporters tended to take a less positive view of their own economic position and that of Germany until the end of the decade.

Notwithstanding these caveats, the overall evidence for Germany in the 1950s is that affluence was a growing feature of society; consump-tion patterns change from the traditional concentration focus to a greater concentration on consumer durables. As in other states produc-tion and sales in this area increase rapidly by the end of the decade and expand exponentially in the 1960s (Wildt, 1993). This can be measured in less direct ways than ownership of cars or other commodity items. The number of individuals who visit the cinema reflects the amount of disposable income available for leisure; in Germany the number of cin-ema visits almost doubles between 1947 and 1957. The decline which follows is due to mass ownership of television rather than a decline in income. A similar point can be made in respect of those playing or attending sporting events and, between 1956 and 1959 these figures increase appreciably. Other features of behaviour during the 1950s become more pronounced towards the end of the decade. Germans take more holidays, increasingly in their own cars and occupy pension or hotel accommodation by the early 1960s. Here, as in Britain, it is already possible to identify the emergence of a youth culture sharing traits with their counterparts elsewhere (Schildt, 1993).

Although similar patterns are detectable in France, the outcome is somewhat different from that of Germany and Britain. French growth rates for the 1950s were high in a comparative context; only Germany grew at a faster rate. The governments of the Fourth and Fifth Republics were strongly committed to modernising France and this led to rapid industrialisation, urbanisation and social change (Kuisel, 1981: 219–71). However, it is probably the case that a majority of French people did not share in prosperity until after the establishment of the Fifth Republic in 1958. According to surveys, in 1954 some 45 per cent of households found it difficult to make ends meet. In 1955, 71 per cent of unskilled workers and 54 per cent of skilled workers were below the median income. In contrast 49 per cent of white collar and 72 per cent of staff were above this level. Throughout the 1950s unemployment remained a fear for significant sections of the working class, even among skilled workers. This can be appreciated by the distribution of consumer goods. However, it should also be noted that between 1949 and 1958 household consumption appears to have grown by around 6 per cent per annum (Hamilton, 1967: 71–5; Rioux, 1987: 360–9).

Tables 6.5, 6.6 and 6.7 highlight the relatively restricted nature of ownership of consumer durables during the 1950s. They also draw attention to the class bias in ownership. The ownership of motor cars is a good example of the class basis of consumption during the 1950s. While there is some growth among the working class in the ownership of motor cars, it is the middle classes who benefit most in the short term. In a 1955 survey of consumption patterns among workers quite clear distinctions can be appreciated. These, and other data, show that ownership of the main consumer goods remained a luxury for the majority of the French working-class until the end of the 1950s and it is not until the 1960s that significant changes take place in such ownership. What it demonstrates in contrast to Britain and the US is that affluence was largely restricted to the middle classes and traditional bourgeois sectors (Hamilton, 1967: 82–6). However, changes were already taking place in consumption, which followed those of other European countries. Even before the dramatic political changes, which ushered in the Fifth Republic, lifestyle changes were already underway. Between 1950 and 1959 there is a noticeable shift in the share of family income committed to food, clothing and furniture, whereas there are significant increases in car ownership, medical products and televisions as a proportion of expenditure. This is what one would expect at the

Table 6.5 Ownership of certain consumer goods in France by household

Households owning (%):	1954	1959
motor cars	21.0	28.4
television set	1.0	9.5
fridge	7.5	20.5
washing machines	8.4	21.4

Source: Rioux, 1987: 371.

Table 6.6 Car ownership in France by socio-economic category

%	1954	1959
farmers	29	35
agricultural workers	3	12
liberal professions/executives	56	74.5
middle managers	32	57.8
workers	8	21.5

Source: Rioux, 1987: 371.

Table 6.7 Ownership of certain items in France by socio-economic category, 1955

	unskilled	skilled	white collar	staff
Percentage having:				
house (owned)	21	17	19	33
washing machine	8	15	24	38
fridge	4	7	23	37
radio	81	91	93	98
television	1	2	5	8
car	8	12	30	50
fur coat for wife	5	8	21	40

Source: Hamilton, 1967: 83.

beginning of affluence and these patterns of expenditure increase rapidly between 1959 and 1968 (Coffey, 1973: 38, 67; Furlough, 1993: 65–81).

In his study of the French worker in the 1950s, Hamilton concedes that some changes had taken place but concludes that these were not as radical in political terms as sometimes asserted. However, he does recognise that an increase in the standard of living might change even the militant worker when he suggests that; 'Where he once sold *l'Humanité* on Sunday, he may now go for a drive in the country with his family' (Hamilton, 1967: 185). (What has not been explored here is the extent to which the movement from collectivist provision and collective political involvement was replaced by increased privatisation of social activities and political action. In a number of European states the growth of television ownership and the possession of a car changed the social context of party membership though not necessarily of party loyalty.) The end of the Fourth Republic provided a basis for stability in French politics and this in turn contributed to the growth of affluence in the 1960s. Notwithstanding differences between French trends and those of Britain and Germany during the 1950s, by the end of the 1960s France had also become an affluent society. The May 1968 events may have captured the attention of the world, but a more prosaic reality existed below the surface. By this time over two-thirds of French families owned their own car, had a television and a widening range of other consumer durables. Private housing became widespread, most people took holidays and mass consumption became prevalent. The shift to affluence may have been a little later than some other European states, but it nevertheless followed very similar patterns of evolution (Bernstein, 1989: 125–52).

The politics of consumption

By the end of the 1950s the politics of consumption had become central to the electoral considerations of most political parties in most European states. While growth was a concern for governments and economists, the affluence that was spreading by this time allowed the political parties to emphasise what they could provide for the electors if they voted for them. This is a subtle shift, but an important one. During the 1959 British general election, Harold Macmillan famously encouraged voters to support the Conservative Party on the grounds that 'You've never had it so good' and Conservative publicity emphasised rising living standards as a key aspect of the campaign. Furthermore, though British economic growth was not comparable to that of Germany, France or Italy, government policy ensured that full employment would be maintained and consumption increased. In 1958 at the mid-term election President Eisenhower and the Republican party suffered defeat, in part because the electorate believed that the administration was not protecting its economic security and living standards (Girvin, 1994: 150–4, 177–9).

This pressure is also evident in France and Germany. Under de Gaulle the Fifth Republic was quickly consolidated, economic policy was broadly expansionist and modernisation reinforced. De Gaulle's electoral base was heterogeneous comprising traditional bourgeois voters, a section of the working class and Catholics. His nationalist philosophy required sacrifices on the part of the population, but also insisted that benefits should be shared. This allowed his Presidency to enhance consumption and to keep together his diverse constituency, but also provided the means for national integration and effective competition with the left. Likewise in Germany, at the 1957 and 1961 Bundestag elections the CDU were able to mobilise support around the issues of prosperity and security. The economic expansion of the 1950s provided the basis during the 1960s for the increasing spread of consumption. Moreover, by the 1960s there is a shift in the economy from manufacturing to services. Not only do the discernible patterns of affluence intensify, but they spread geographically across Europe and penetrate into the social classes which had not shared in the first wave of affluence. This can be appreciated in Italy, which had grown rapidly during the 1950s, but where real wages had been stagnant. During the 1960s income increased quickly and by the end of the decade it is possible to identify the trends of higher consumption and affluence (Ginsborg, 1990: 210–33, 239–47).

A number of factors contributed to the acceptance of the affluent society. American influence continued to be of importance, particularly in terms of fashion, music and television. Full employment and rising living standards also contributed to this sense that a new era had been achieved. Considerable confidence in the economy is detectable from the mid-1950s, a confidence which is maintained until the mid-1970s. This allowed the mass of the population to consider credit commitments without fear of economic insecurity. A further factor was the narrowing of the ideological poles between left and right. In a period of low electoral volatility, relatively strong party identification and few major policy differences, the parties sought to persuade the electorate that they could manage the economy efficiently and provide more growth, higher income and increased consumption. Elections were close and the party which could persuade the crucial floating voter that it fulfilled these criteria was well placed to win (Girvin, 1988; Rose and Urwin, 1970: 287–319).

In a European context the Conservative Party in Britain, the Christian Democratic parties and Gaullism were well placed to take advantage of this opportunity. Affluence and consumption (though not without their own difficulties for the centre-right) allowed these parties to effectively compete with the left in elections. The emphasis on private ownership of housing, for example, reflected the centre-right's belief that a property-owning electorate would not be attracted by the collectivist policies of the left. Furthermore, as consumption goods were provided by private industry, this enhanced the role of that sector in economies where the state sector was strong (as in the UK). In these circumstances individual choice could be given priority, not only on the grounds that the demand for such choice was evident, but because choice in a market situation created the basis for an alliance between liberals and conservatives to exclude the left. Both conservatives and liberals accepted the discipline of the market, though based on different ideological assumptions. This could also be supplemented by a degree of public provision, which would have been unthinkable for the centre-right in the 1930s. It was often the case that spending by centre-right governments until the 1960s was higher than many social democratic regimes (Girvin, 1988: 110–22, 190–5; Van Kersbergen, 1995; Nau, 1990: 5–43). In political terms the emergence of affluence proved fortuitous for the centre-right and allowed them to generate electoral advantage at a time of change for the right in the postwar years.

A new sensibility?

Comment on the new affluence was widespread. Considerable anxiety was expressed concerning the effect of affluence on the working class, the poor and the young. This reflected a degree of superiority on the part of journalists, churchmen and intellectuals, as well as a fear that the new society would not give them the respect they deserved. But the anxiety was deeper than this. It maintained a tradition on the left and the right that the extension of luxury to the mass of the population would lead to decadence and hedonism. Left-wing writers often argued as if an affluent working-class would lose its political and radical identity, and indeed this was a major criticism of organised labour by the new left in the 1960s (Stratchey, 1956; Marcuse, 1964). On the right the fear was that without the discipline of starvation, the poor would not work, social status would be impaired and that the moral order would break down. All of these fears became focused on the emergence of the 'teenager' in the 1950s. Whether in the United States or Europe the young became the social problem in the era of affluence (Bernstein, Sondheim and Laurents, 1957; Goodman, 1960; Pielke, 1988; Rock and Cohen, 1970; for Germany see Schildt, 1993). The young are a new social force in industrial societies. The extension of the school age, restrictions on age of employment, earlier maturity and disposable income generated a new social dimension between childhood and adulthood. The young had historically been hidden and subordinate; either children or being trained to be adults. To be young was a state of transition, whereas by the mid 1950s in the US, and to a lesser extent elsewhere, it became an entity in itself. The main expression of this new dimension was cultural.

Youth culture transformed the culture of the industrial states in a remarkably short period of time. It is in this realm that the changes during the 1950s are most apparent: the beat poets, cool jazz and new wave cinema gave some expression to this. However, it was in the realm of youth culture that it is possible to talk about a revolution. If it were possible to pinpoint a moment when a new force enters the realm of social reality then this might be August 1954 when Elvis Presley entered the Sun Studios in Memphis Tennessee to make a record. The owner, Sam Phillips, had believed for some time that he could make a fortune if he could find a white singer who could 'sing like a black person'. In Presley, he believed he found that person. In technical terms what Presley did was to blend blues and country music and transform the way in which both musical forms were presented. This can be heard on the re-released Sun recordings, with all their technical inadequacies. Indeed it is this very fumbling, which can now be appreciated as the search for a new expression. As has been pointed out by a number of commentators, what was unique about Presley was not that he was the first to record rock and roll, but that he developed a form of the music which transcended its predecessors and located a unique audience for that form. This audience was a predominantly youth audience; one which was rarely seen or heard in the public arena prior to this. In the US alone record sales increased dramatically; from $189 million in 1950 to $227 million in 1955. When Presley moved to the RCA label in 1956, his style had developed and become more sophisticated, but he now dominated the popular recording business. Between 1956 and 1962, 31 of his record releases became million sellers, while nine of his long-playing records sold a million or more. It is estimated that his sales alone accounted for 25 per cent of total RCA sales during that time. Not until the Beatles appeared in the early 1960s was there such a radical transformation of popular culture (Marcus, 1975; Pielke, 1988: 139–56).

The years between 1954 and 1964 can be characterised by the extent to which a new sensibility emerged in the US and Europe. In retrospect, its most enduring feature was the public representation of youth

as a cultural participant and consumer of new products. In very important respects new markets, until then not identified, grew rapidly:
these include clothing, records, rock and roll radio stations and concert
going. In other ways this was a restricted market; for most of the 1950s
it was an American mass phenomenon which gradually permeated
European sensibility. However, by the beginning of the 1960s there was
a clear distinction between the sensibility which had been generated
by rock and roll and that of an older generation, whose cultural and
political environment had been established in quite different circumstances (Lipsitz, 1982: 195–225; Inglehart, 1977).

Once established as a social and cultural force, rock and roll (and
subsequently beat and rock music) took on a developmental logic of its
own. As an autonomous form it developed its own coherence, nuance
and drive. However, this was not an inevitable outcome. As a radical
intrusion into public life, it was resisted and despised. The music was
seen as degenerate, because of its origins in black music, and as vulgar,
because of its debt to country music and its other working-class forms.
Furthermore, because it emphasised hedonism and youth, it clearly
challenged the existing lines of authority whether they were bourgeois
or working class. As a generalisation, it might be claimed that rock and
roll marked a dividing line between the authoritarian family and the
possibility of personal autonomy outside of this social form, not only
for youth but for women and for some minorities such as blacks in
America and gays everywhere.

This dividing line can be better appreciated by the demise of jazz as
the dominant form of popular music for the masses. The dance bands
in the 1930s and 1940s were similar in appeal to rock and roll later; the
origins in black music, the international appeal and dancing. However,
there were considerable differences between the two. Dance bands and
jazz were an essentially adult phenomenon; the young, and especially
teenagers, were not central to its appeal. Indeed, when a mass youth
following did appear, the bandleaders were hostile to the screaming
and the public expression of approval. Both Artie Shaw and Benny
Goodman condemned this behaviour for interfering with the quality
of the music, but it can also be seen as uneasiness about the social consequences of this behaviour (Palmer, 1976: 246–7). Neither in its big
band format or in the abstract nature of postwar bop or cool jazz
was this form able to offer a musical outlet to the majority of young
people. Youth culture not only emerges as a distinctive force in the
1950s, but it generates the cultural context out of which a new sound
emerges. Even before Presley is discovered, the young in many cities

were listening to black and country music stations because they offered a music form not widely heard by white urban audiences: the demand existed before rock and roll emerged in final form. The demand was recognised by a number of entrepreneurs, who quickly marketed a new sound to give effect to this. However, they were not only creating a new market, which they were, but they also gave expression to a new sensibility which was that of a section of society which was young, relatively free, reasonably well educated and affluent. The mix was a potent one and it was to survive the end of affluence at the end of the 1970s when a new recession changed the postwar society beyond recognition (Gillett, 1971: 15–19).

Conclusion

The 1950s and 1960s were the high point of affluence. The end of affluence comes sometime between the election of Margaret Thatcher in 1979 and Ronald Reagan in 1981; for these two politicians represent a new type of politics and successfully impose a new consensus on the politics of industrial society. Growing insecurity, high levels of unemployment and significant exclusion of the poor and the marginal, are characteristics of the new politics. Yet the legacy of the age of affluence remains. Despite the recession a majority in most societies continue to gain significant benefits from the economy, consumption remains the characteristic trait of industrial and many developing societies, while the politics of class and welfare have been overshadowed by other concerns. While we may not live in a postmaterialist society, the claim made by advocates of this view that the affluence, peace and security of the postwar era produced a generation which broke decisively with previous modes of behaviour is surely accurate. The momentum for this change was created under rather unique circumstances, but the impact of the changes which were then effected continue to influence the politics and culture of the late 1990s.

References

Abelshauser, W. (1983) *Wirtschaftgeschichte der Bundesrepublik, 1945–1980*, Frankfurt.
Abrams, M. and R. Rose (1960) *Must Labour Lose?* Harmondsworth.
Bell, D. (1988) *The End of Ideology: On the Exhaustion of Political Ideas in the Fifties*, Cambridge MA.
Bernstein, S. (1989) *The Republic of de Gaulle, 1958–1969*, Cambridge.
Bernstein, L., S. Sondheim and A. Laurents (1957) 'West Side Story' film.

Berry, C.J. (1994) *The Idea of Luxury*, Cambridge.

Buchanan, W. and Cantrill, H. (1953) *How Nations See Each Other: A Study in Public Opinion*, Westport, Connecticut.

Buchheim, C. (1990) *Die Wiedereingliederung Westdeutschlands in die Weltwirtschaft, 1945–1958*, München.

Coffey, P. (1973) *The Social Economy of France*, New York.

Conradt, D.P. (1980) 'Changing German Political Culture' in G. A. Almond and S. Verba (eds), *The Civic Culture Revisited*, Boston.

Cross, G. (1993) *Time and Money: The Making of Consumer Culture*, London.

Ellwood, D.E. (1992) *Rebuilding Europe: Western Europe, America and Postwar Reconstruction*, London.

Fukuyama, F. (1992) *The End of History and the Last Man*, London.

Furlough, E. (1993) 'Packaging Pleasures: Club Mediterranee and French Consumer Culture, 1950–1968' *French Historical Studies* 18: 1, pp. 65–81.

Gallup, G.H. (1972) *The Gallup Poll: Public Opinion 1935–1971*, Vol. 2, New York.

Gillett, C. (1971) *The Sound of the City*, London.

Ginsborg, (1990) *A History of Contemporary Italy: Society and Politics 1943–1988*, London.

Girvin, B. (1994) T*he Right in the Twentieth Century: Conservatism and Democracy*, London.

Girvin, B. (ed,) (1988) *The Transformation of Contemporary Conservatism*, London.

Goodman, P. (1960) *Growing Up Absurd*, London.

Goldthorpe, J.H., Lockwood, D., Bechhofer, F., Platt, J. (1969) *The Affluent Worker in the Class Structure*, Cambridge.

Hall, M. (1962) 'The Consumer Sector' in G.D.N. Worswick and P.H. Ady (eds), *The British Economy in the 1950s*, Oxford.

Hallett, G. (1990) 'West Germany' in A. Graham and A. Seldon (eds), *Government and Economies in the Postwar World*, London.

Hamilton, R.F. (1967) *Affluence and the French Worker in the Fourth Republic*, Princeton, New Jersey.

Hamilton, R.F. (1965) 'Affluence and the Worker: the West German Case' *American Journal of Sociology* 71, 144–52.

Halsey, A.H. (1978) *Change in British Society*, Oxford.

Hibbs D.A. (1977) 'Political Parties and Macroeconomic Policy' *The American Political Science Review* 71, 1467–87.

Kersbergen, K. van (1995) *Social Capitalism: A Study of Christian democracy and the Welfare State*, London.

Kuisel, R.F. (1981) *Capitalism and the State in Modern France*, Cambridge.

Kuisel, R.F. (1993) *Seducing the French: The Dilemma of Americanization*, Berkeley.

Leaman, J. (1988) T*he Political Economy of West Germany, 1945–85*, Basingstoke.

Leven, M., H.G. Moulton, C. Warburton (1934) *America's Capacity to Consume*, Washington DC.

Levy, F. (1988) *Dollars and Dreams: The Changing American Income Distribution*, New York.

Lipsitz, G.(1982) *Class and Culture in Cold War America*, South Hadley, Mass.

Inglehart (1977) *The Silent Revolution*.

Marcus, G. (1975) *Mystery Train*, New York.

Marcuse, H. (1964) *One Dimensional Man*, London.

Mason, R.S. (1981) *Conspicuous Consumption*, Westmead.

National Bureau of Economic Research (1929) *Recent Economic Changes in the United States*, Vol. 2, New York.

Nau, H.R. (1990) *The Myth of American Decline*, New York, 9, 41–49.

Noelle, E., and E. P. Neuman (eds) (1967) *The Germans: Public Opinion Polls 1947–1966*, Westport, Connecticut.

Otake, H. (1985) *Konrad Adenauer und Shigeru Yoshida: Die Wiedergeburt des Liberalismus als Konservative Ideologie*, Tokyo.

Palmer, T. (1976) *All You Need is Love*, London, 246–7.

Pielke, R. G. (1988) *You Say You Want a Revolution: Rock Music in American Culture*, Chicago.

Rioux, J.P. (1987) *The Fourth Republic 1944–1958*, Cambridge, 360–69.

Rock, P., and S. Cohen (1970) 'The Teddy Boy' in V. Bogdanor and R. Skidelsky (eds), *The Age of Affluence 1951–1964*, London.

Rose, R. and Urwin, G.W. (1970) 'Persistence and Change in Western Party Systems since 1945', *Political Studies*, 18, 287–319.

Schildt, A. (1993) '"Mach mal Pause!" Freie Zeit, Freizeitverhalten und Freizeit-Diskurse in der westdeutschen Wiederaufbau-Gesellschaft der 1950er Jahre' *Archiv für Sozialgeschichte* 33, 357–406.

Schildt, A. (1993) 'Von der Not der Jugend zur Teenager-Kultur: Aufwachen in den 50er Jahren', in A. Schildt and A. Sywottek (eds) *Modernisierung im Wiederaufbau: die westdeutsche Gesellschaft der 50er Jahre*, Bonn, 335–48.

Shonfield, A. (1965) *Modern Capitalism: The Changing Balance of Public and Private Power*, London.

Skidelski, R. (1977) 'The Political Meaning of the Keynesian Revolution' in R. Skidelski (ed.), *The End of the Keynesian Era*, London.

Strachey, J. (1956) *Contemporary Capitalism*, London.

Tiratsoo, N. (1991) 'Popular politics, affluence and the Labour party in the 1950s' in A. Gorst, L. Johnman and W. Scott Lucas (eds), *Contemporary British History 1931–1961*, London.

Urwin, D.W., 'Persistence and change in Western party systems since 1945' *Political Studies* 18:3 (1970), 287–319.

Wattenberg, B.J. (1976) *The Statistical History of the United States: From Colonial Times to the Present*, New York.

Wildt, M. (1993) 'Privater Konsum in Westdeutschland in den 50er Jahren' in A. Schildt and A. Sywottek (eds), *Modernisierung im Wiederaufbau: Die Westdeutsche Gesellschaft der 50er Jahre*, Bonn, 275–89.

7
Postwar Private Consumption Patterns of Japanese Households: the Role of Consumer Durables

Atsushi Maki

Recently, Japanese economic power has grown apace in world com-modity and financial markets. Japan's balance-of-payments has been in surplus since 1985 and the country is currently the largest asset-holding country in the world. This rapid emergence of the Japanese economy is one of the more striking developments in the international economy since the Second World War.

The phenomenal economic growth achieved by Japan after the Second World War is referred to as the 'Japanese Miracle'. In the period just after the Second World War, the Japanese economy lay in ruins. About 25 per cent of the capital stock had been destroyed and Japan had to absorb huge numbers of repatriates. At that time, the most impor-tant economic policies of the Japanese government were restoring the capital stock and maintaining security of employment for the swollen labour force.

To promote industrial production in the 1950s, the Japanese govern-ment implemented the Preferential Production Plan and devised an industrial policy based on negotiations between the government (mainly the Ministry of International Trade and Industry), corporate management and labour union leaders. Japanese monetary policy con-ducted by the Ministry of Finance and the Bank of Japan created favourable conditions for the recovery of the Japanese economy. The characteristics of the Japanese financial system after war through to the 1980s include:

(i) A low interest rate policy;
(ii) The establishment of short-term and long-term lending institutions;
(iii) Drawing distinctions between the activities of commercial and trust banks, and security companies;

(iv) The introduction of foreign exchange controls by the government;
(v) A system of collateral security in borrowing money from financial institutions.

Through a combination of industrial and monetary policies, the government created a quasi-closed economy. Despite the government's low interest rate policy, due to its foreign exchange controls, financial funds held by households did not move abroad. Imports of final products were restricted, especially before 1965, by the government's protectionist policies and regulations. On the other hand, the government promoted exports of quality goods such as steel, automobiles and electric appliances.

In the initial period of recovery, households supplied funds to industry through financial institutions. Industries, as the deficit sector, borrowed investment funds from financial institutions. This indirect finance system, relying on bank loans rather than bond or equity markets, characterised the postwar economy. The financial institutions attracted deposits from the household sector at government mandated low interest rates and lent funds to corporations. In this way they had the advantage of access to a large amount of low cost investment funds in the domestic market. At this time, in order to control imports and investment flows, the government imposed strict foreign exchange control. Through such economic policies, the government sought to promote exports, facilitate the import of natural resources, restrict other imports and limit foreign investment.

The process of Japanese economic growth followed the pattern of 'modern economic growth' proposed by Kuznets. Industrialisation, urbanisation and technological innovation were three factors crucial to modern economic growth. Kuznets, writing about the changes in the patterns of consumer expenditures due to modern economic growth, suggested that:

Urban life, with the anonymity of its dense population masses, with the detachment from earlier roots of the large immigrant component, and with the ease of observation and imitation of consumption patterns, may facilitate higher consumption levels by permitting greater play of the demonstration effect and by increasing sensitivity to new consumer goods. Here again the effects may be reflected in the trends in consumer expenditures relative to those of savings and capital formation, and in some components of total consumer expenditures more than others.

(1966: 274)

Further, he argued that:

> Technological changes, the main source of modern economic growth, affect consumer goods by the creation of new types and by major changes in the old. Even in the case of food, modern canning, freezing, etc. are new processes that affect the total demand for food and its distribution among various categories and must be reflected in the processing part of the PTD component (processing, transportation, and distribution). Such technological changes are even more conspicuous when they lead to entirely new consumer goods – synthetic fiber textiles, household electric appliances, radio and television sets, passenger cars, airplane transportation, and the like. The relative technological impact on consumer goods and on capital goods is difficult to measure, but this is not important in the present connection. However, it is important to recognize the continuous and far-reaching effect of technological changes on consumer goods – as would be revealed by a brief glance at the variety of consumer goods used in presently developed countries and resulting from relatively recent technological progress.
>
> (1966: 276–7)

Economic progress since the Second World War led to more rapid changes in Japanese households' socio-economic structure than in either the US or Europe. The phenomena of industrialisation and urbanisation, together with technological innovation, contributed to the advance of living standards of Japanese households within a relatively short period. The postwar economy was marked by three distinct phases: the recovery period of the 1950s, the rapid economic growth era in the 1960s and early half of the 1970s, and the stable economic growth era in the 1980s after the oil shocks in 1973–74 and 1979–80. This chapter mainly focuses on the first two phases.

In a series of works, Kuznets stressed the impact of structural changes in industrial sectors. Applying his hypothesis of modern economic growth, this chapter discusses population growth and per capita GNP growth in the Japanese economy after the war. The focus is on the movements in consumption patterns and consumer durables, and how these led to structural change in the industrial sector. In the 1950s and 1960s the economic objectives for consumers, corporations and the government coincided. Consumers sought an improvement in their standard of living, corporations sought modernisation and industrialisation to increase their productivity, and the government sought to nurture a new economic system through industrial and monetary policies aimed at rebuilding the war-devastated economy and maintaining employment security.

The main economic criteria proposed by Kuznets for modern economic growth are a steady growth of population and a still faster growth in GNP. We then discuss living conditions in Japanese households after the Second World War focusing on changes in GNP, per capita GNP, population and the family composition of the household. This discussion is followed by an analysis of household behaviour, looking at the overall movement of consumption patterns, which leads to an analysis of the reasons why the Japanese household sector maintained a high rate of saving and how this was influenced by the decision to purchase consumer durables. Here, we elucidate the reasons, which stimulated high household savings and how these induced an increase in domestic investment. In considering Japan's economic growth, it is important to consider increases in both national supply capacity and domestic demand. We then discuss the investment and savings balance and their growth from the household standpoint and introduce data on the household savings rate before presenting some conclusions.

The rise in the standard of living

Japanese economic development since the 1950s is frequently referred to as the 'Miracle'. The Long Term Estimates of the National Accounts from 1955 to 1969, compiled by the Economic Planning Agency, reported an annual growth rate of nominal GNP and real GNP from 1955 to 1970 of 15.7 per cent and 10.0 per cent respectively. A growth rate of 10 per cent means that after five years the economy increases 1.6 times compared to the base year, 2.6 times after ten years, and 4.2 times after 15 years. By comparison, a growth rate of 1 per cent would lead to a quadrupling of the size of the economy in 140 years and even with a growth rate of 3 per cent, it would take about 50 years. Although the era of high economic growth in the 1960s and 1970s lasted only 15 years, the economy quadrupled in size. Following the two oil shocks, the growth rate of real GNP levelled out at 4 per cent per annum. In 1955 per capita GNP stood at 94 000 yen rising to 1.329 million yen in 1975, a 14-fold increase during that period. After correcting for price increases, the real level of expansion in the same period was 410 per cent. The average growth rate of real per capita GNP over the two decades between 1955 to 1975 was 7 per cent.

Table 7.1   Population and the number of households in Japan, 1950–80

	Population (000)	No. of households (000)	Household members
1950	84 115	16 425	5.12
1960	94 302	22 476	4.20
1970	104 665	29 887	3.50
1975	111 940	32 877	3.40
1980	117 060	35 338	3.31

Source: Population Census, Statistic Bureau.

Data for population size, the movements in the number of households and that of household members from 1950 to 1980 are presented in Table 7.1. The average growth rate of population from 1950 to 1975 was about 1.5 per cent. The 1975 Population Census reports the population at 112 million with 33 million households. Therefore, the average number of household members was 3.40. Looking back to 1950, the average number of household members was over five, while in 1960 there were slightly over four, indicating a trend towards fewer children in Japanese families. In the US, the decrease of average household size from five to four members took about 50 years whereas in Japan this same change was realised in only ten years. The number of households in 1975 was nearly 33 million, about double that in 1950. The average growth rate in the number of households for 26 years was about 3 per cent, which is twice as fast as the growth rate of population. This trend reflects the rise in urbanisation during the era of high economic growth and consequent shift in the family composition of households.

Per capita GNP in Japan was $477 in 1960, a level one-third of that in Germany and one-sixth of that in the US. At that time Prime Minister Ikeda unveiled his famous income-doubling plan. By 1975, per capita GNP had risen to $4471, a level two-thirds that of Germany and three-fifths that of the US. This was the era of the Japanese miracle. In addition to increases in per capita GNP made possible by rapid economic growth, the national welfare level also increased. For example, as a result of the development of medical care and health systems, life expectancy has reached 75 years for Japanese males and 80 years for Japanese females, a substantial improvement on the average life expectancy of 60 years recorded in the 1950s. By comparison, the life expectancy in the US is currently 72.0 years for men and 78.9 years for women, while in Germany it is 71.5 years and 78.1 years, respectively.

The rapid rise in per capita GNP translated into an enormous increase in Japanese households' consumption levels. Households can now afford to consume many kinds of goods and services, which were either unavailable or unaffordable in the early postwar era.

Overall trends in consumption patterns

In Japan the advance in living standards was reflected in two tendencies:

(i) The substitution of housewives' labour by labour-saving consumer durable goods, and
(ii) The shift from household production to the purchase of external services, namely laundry or food away from home.

With the proliferation of labour-saving consumer durable goods, hours worked by housewives decreased and leisure hours increased. At the same time, advertisements by corporations have increased consumers' knowledge about a variety of commodities and services, stimulating them to purchase goods of ever improving quality at ever lower prices.

Engel's coefficient, indicating the ratio between food expenditure and total consumption expenditure, decreased during the 1950s and 1960s. In the same period, expenditure on food away from home increased rapidly due to income growth and a desire for receiving services instead of home production. Usually, Engel's law is verified in the cross-sectional data. However, since there was an enormous increase in income during the era of high economic growth, the decrease in the budget share for food in the time series data is observed among Japanese households.

In addition to the decrease of Engel's coefficient, the change of consumption patterns, focusing on the changes in necessary goods and services defined by the theory, is also observed in the consumer behaviour of Japanese households. I analysed consumer behaviour for Japanese households from the 1950s to the middle of the 1970s, using a complete demand system called the linear expenditure system (LES) including family size and the habit formation effects in addition to total expenditure and prices. The LES has the following theoretical characteristics: If the price elasticity of the item is inelastic, then the item is classified as necessary goods and indispensable; and, if the price elasticity of the item is elastic, then the item is classified as luxury goods and dispensable (Maki, 1983).

The analysis used the consumption expenditure series data published in the Family Income and Expenditure Survey (FIES) compiled by the

Statistics Bureau. The data covers all households in all cities with a population of 50 000 or more, but it excludes households engaged in agriculture, forestry and fishery, and one-person households. This means that the data covers mainly workers and individual proprietor households. Table 7.2, drawn from Maki (1983), indicates necessary goods and services in 1960 and 1970, respectively. The observation period is from 1958 through 1974. Consumption is measured on a household basis, and data for the family size are obtained by the FIES. Total expenditure is obtained as the sum of fifty-nine expenditures – the classification of fifty-nine expenditures is given in the Appendix. Items which existed in 1960, but not in 1970, are marked by a single asterisk, in the left-hand column in Table 7.2. These include the following six items:

- Barley and other cereals (item 2),
- Bread (item 3),
- Other fuel and light (item 35),
- Cloth and thread (item 40),
- Shoes and footwear (item 42),
- Stationary and writing supplies (item 53).

On the other hand, there were eight items, which became indispensable in 1970, marked by a double asterisk, in the right hand column of Table 7.2. These were:

- Meat (item 8),
- Non-alcoholic beverages (item 21),
- Repairs and maintenance (item 24),
- Electricity (item 33),
- Japanese clothing (item 36),
- Shirts and underwear (item 38),
- User-operated transportation (item 51),
- Other reading and recreation (item 57).

The change in Japanese consumption patterns was dependent on the supply structure in this period. The rapid increase in income, the change of relative prices due to industrialisation, the decrease in family size due to urbanisation and habit formation in consumer preferences contributed to the observed changes in consumption patterns.

Noting the six items which disappeared and the eight items which appeared in the list of necessary goods, it is clear that a rapid change in Japanese consumption patterns occurred during a relatively short span of 11 years. In the food categories, the fact that 'barley and other cereals'

Table 7.2 Necessary goods and services in Japan in 1960 and 1970

	1960	1970
Food	• Rice (item 1) • Barley and other cereals (item 2)* • Bread (item 3)* • Noodles and others (item 4) • Leafy vegetables (item 10) • Root vegetables (item 11) • Other vegetables (item 12) • Processed food (item 15) • Cakes and candies (item 16) • Fruits (item 17)	• Rice (item 1) • Noodles and others (item 4) • Meat (item 8)** • Leafy vegetables (item 10) • Root vegetables (item 12) • Other vegetables (item 12) • Processed food (item 15) • Cakes and candies (item 16) • Fruits (item 17) • Non-alcoholic beverages (item 21)**
Housing	 • Water (item 25) • Tableware (item 26)	• Repairs and maintenance (item 24)** • Water (item 25) • Tableware (item 26)
Fuel and Light	• Gas (item34) • Other fuel and light (item 35)*	• Electricity (item 33)** • Gas (item 34)
Clothing	 • Cloth and tread (item 40)* • Shoes and footwear (item 42)* • Other clothing (item 45)	• Japanese clothing (item 36)** • Shirts and underwear (item 38)** • Other clothing (item 45)
Miscellaneous goods and services	• Medical care (item 46) • Toilet tissue (item 47) • Detergent laundry (item 48) • Stationery and writing supplies (item 53)* • Other miscellaneous (item 59)	• Medical care (item 46) • Toilet tissue (item 47) • Detergent laundry (item 48) • User-operated transportation (item 51)** • Other reading and recreation (item 57)** • Other miscellaneous (item 59)

* Items which exist in 1960 not in 1970; ** Items which had been indispensable in 1970.
Note: Classification of 59 items given in Appendix.
Source: Maki (1983).

(which became inferior goods to rice and side dishes) and 'bread' vanished from the menu of necessary goods, and 'meat' (which had been a luxury good in 1960) and 'non-alcoholic beverages' appeared, reflects the shift in eating habits due to economic growth and higher disposable income while the appearance of 'repairs and maintenance' in housing in 1970 indicates the accumulation of consumer durables during these 11 years. In the fuel and light category, 'other fuel and light' namely coal and charcoal, vanished while 'electricity' appeared in 1970. The emergence of electricity is linked with the diffusion of electronic goods. And the change from 'cloth and thread' to 'shirts and underwear' indicates the shift of consumer behaviour to the purchase of finished products. This change resulted from mass production, reduced commodity prices and the change of marketing channels.

Finally, some interesting variations appeared in the miscellaneous goods and service categories. The fact that 'user-operated transportation' and 'other reading and recreation' became indispensable indicates the improvement in the household standard of living between 1960 and 1970. The 23 indispensable goods and services in 1960 are subsistence oriented while the data for 1970 show marked changes in eating habits and more recreation, reflecting a generally more luxurious household life due to economic growth and consequent increases in disposable income.

The role of consumer durables in the high economic growth era

This section clarifies the characteristics of household consumption and saving behaviour related to the purchase behaviour for consumer durables after the Second World War. Japanese households aspired to the lifestyle prevailing in the US. Since the 1950s, through radio, television, movies, newspapers and magazines popularising the American way of life, Japanese households gained knowledge about various consumer durable goods such as refrigerators, washing machines, vacuum cleaners and automobiles. The movement in consumption patterns is revealing. In 1952, the diffusion rate of radios was 67.6 per cent, that of electric fans 2.8 per cent and that of refrigerators only 1 per cent. The year 1953 is generally thought of as the first year of home electrification. At that time, Japanese households aspired to the purchase of washing machines, vacuum cleaners and refrigerators, calling them the 'three kinds of Jingi'. The concept, 'the three Jingi', is borrowed from the Japanese imperial family. The imperial 3 Jingi are the sword, mirror, and jewel. Another version of three kinds of Jingi in the late 1950s was washing machines, refrigerators and televisions. Before explaining the diffusion of consumer durable goods, the stimulus for purchasing consumer durable goods by households is denoted in Table 7.3 in connection with catchphrases coined by the mass media or advertisements by corporations in the 1950s and 1960s aimed at promoting these goods.

Due to the catchphrases coined by journalists and advertising by corporations, Japanese households identified the menu of desired consumer durable goods and sought to realise their dreams by increasing their saving rates. This is mainly because of the immature financial market and the existence of liquidity constraints due to a system of collateral security in borrowing money from financial institutions. Hayashi (1987) suggests there are three kinds of liquidity constraints:

- cash-in-advance constraints;
- quantity constraints on the amount of borrowing (credit rationing);
- the case in which the loan rate available to consumers is higher than the rate at which they can lend (differential interest rates) (see Maki, 1993).

It is useful to describe one aspect of the liquidity constraint connected with capital market imperfections. For the household, there are two kinds of assets, namely human and non-human assets. Human assets are obtained from present and future labour income streams, and non-human assets consist of present financial and real assets.

With perfect capital markets, human and non-human assets are perfectly substitutable. When households want to buy expensive consumer

Table 7.3 The stimulus for purchasing consumer durable goods in Japan, 1953–68

1953	The first year of home electrification Three Kinds of Jingi (television sets, refrigerators and washing machines) or (refrigerators, vacuum cleaners and washing machines)
1959	Private transportation
1966	Second electric appliances boom 3Cs (colour television sets, coolers (air conditioners) and cars)
1968	New 3Cs (cottages, central heating and cookers (electric ovens))

Source: Weekly Asahi (1988, 1990).

durable goods, there is no difference in borrowing against future labour income streams and against present non-human assets. In this case, the characteristics of human and non-human assets are identical. In the real world, especially in the transition period during the 1950s and 1960s, commercial banks usually discriminated between human and non-human assets for mortgage loans. From the viewpoint of uncertainty, human assets have a high risk compared with non-human assets, through defaults arising from unemployment or death in the household. This means that uncertainty is larger in the case of future labour income streams than present non-human assets.

This capital market imperfection generates liquidity constraints for households. Because of these liquidity constraints, there is a lag between the desire to purchase consumer durable goods and the realisation of such purchases. The accumulation of financial assets, namely the accumulation of savings, occurs between the desire to purchase consumer durables and the realisation of the purchase. However, during our period, this lag in Japan was short because of the price decrease due to technological innovations through new investment, the economies of scale on the supply side and increasing household income.

In April 1959 the Emperor Akihito and Empress Michiko were married. Producers of black-and-white television sets found that consumers were eager to buy them. One week before the marriage, the number of television owners exceeded two million. Live television coverage of the parade accelerated the diffusion of black-and-white television sets. In 1960 domestic-made (Toshiba) colour television sets were sold for 420 000 yen, which was about 90 per cent of the average annual disposable household income. Subsequently, especially after the Tokyo Olympics held in 1964, during which large screen colour televisions were installed at the corners of busy shopping districts like Ginza (Tokyo) and Umeda (Osaka), there was a boom in the sale of colour sets.

The 1960s featured a proliferation of electric appliances in Japanese households. At that time, black-and-white television sets, refrigerators, washing machines and vacuum cleaners became popular and the rate of diffusion was very high. Other consumer durable goods such as shavers, electric pots, electric rice ball steamers and so on, also sold well. This occurred just at the time that the income of Japanese households reached a level sufficient to purchase these kinds of consumer durable goods. However, it took some time for the use of more expensive consumer durable goods such as automobiles to spread due to insufficient household income and financial assets.

The normal prices (i.e. sales price divided by disposable income) of automobiles and colour television sets and the level of financial assets for households are indicated in Table 7.4. The financial assets distribution forms the shape of lognormal distribution, with a different mode, median and mean (average). Because of the characteristics of asset distribution, most households have less than the average amount of financial assets. In the case of automobiles, though they were not a new product, the price in 1955 was about two-and-a-half times the average annual income of households. After eight years, the price and

Table 7.4   Normal prices for automobiles and television sets and financial assets for households in Japan, 1953–80

	Automobiles	b/w-TV	Colour TV	Financial assets
1953		175 000 (0.63)		
54		125 000 (0.41)		
55	800 000 (2.57)	89 500 (0.28)		
56		79 800 (0.24)		
57	675 000 (1.88)	76 500 (0.21)		
58	767 000 (1.99)	66 500 (0.17)		
59	695 000 (1.96)	60 000 (0.14)		275 900
1960		51 000 (0.11)	420 000 (0.93)	297 300
61		46 500 (0.09)		396 500
62		52 000 (0.09)	198 000 (0.35)	365 400
63	583 000 (0.98)		230 000 (0.39)	507 200
64			178 000 (0.27)	560 600
65		489 000 (0.06)		658 900
66				711 900
67	560 000 (0.80)		159 000 (0.18)	777 500
68		428 000 (0.04)	148 000 (0.15)	873 600
69			131 000 (0.12)	1 094 900
1970			108 000 (0.08)	1 262 300
71	694 000 (0.50)		95 000 (0.06)	1 419 100
72			93 000 (0.06)	1 730 400
73	743 000 (0.41)		89 800 (0.04)	1 935 300
74	817 000 (0.36)	39 800 (0.01)	105 000 (0.04)	2 252 000
75	83 300 (0.32)			2 636 000
76				3 151 000
77				3 486 000
78			92 800 (0.03)	3 722 000
79	989 000 (0.28)		87 800 (0.02)	4 023 000
1980				4 734 000

Notes: automobiles; until 1958; Datsun from 1959 to 1970; Nissan Blue bird 4-door sedan; from 1971: Blue bird 4-door sedan deluxe.
Source: Weekly Asahi, 1990. Parenthesis in the table is the price and annual income ratio.

annual income ratio was below unity (0.98), and in 1971 it became half of annual income. In those days, imported cars from the US were a kind of status symbol since they were not suited to Japanese traffic conditions and, therefore, were not intended for a large cross-section of Japanese households.

On the other hand, colour televisions were new products and had no competition. Black-and-white televisions and movies became inferior goods and services due to the improvement of technology for colour televisions. In addition to tariff and non-tariff barriers, the speed of innovation was fast and decreases in prices were rapid, and thus there was no room for US and European corporations to penetrate the Japanese colour television market.

The second electric appliance boom began in the late 1960s. In those days, households wanted to purchase durable goods popularly referred to as the '3Cs', that is, colour television sets, 'coolers' (air conditioners) and cars. The year 1959 was the opening year for private transportation (called family motorisation). The catch phrase of '3Cs' appeared in 1966. The catch phrase of 'new 3Cs' – that is, cottages, central heating and cookers (electric ovens) – appeared in 1968. The realisation of the 'new 3Cs' is still a target for most Japanese households even in the 1990s. The proliferation of these expensive consumer durable goods was due to the rapid increase in household income and the rise of mass production and technological innovations, which made these items more affordable. The diffusion of consumer durable goods is indicated in Figure 7.1. In the figure, there is a gap between 1963 and 1964 because of the enlargement of the sample size in the Consumer Movement Survey by the Economic Planning Agency.

By 1970, the diffusion rate of refrigerators and washing machines was over 90 per cent. By 1975, over 95 per cent of households had refrigerators, vacuum cleaners, washing machines and colour televisions. On the other hand, the diffusion of air conditioners and automobiles was not so rapid as that of other consumer durables due to the high price/income ratio and, in the case of cars, the deficiency of the Japanese road network. Considering the relatively high prices of consumer durables and the number of households, expenditures on consumer durables contributed significantly to an increase in domestic demand.

What is the relationship between the household saving rate and the diffusion of consumer durable goods? As indicated in Table 7.4, the amount of financial assets for households was low in the 1950s and 1960s, totalling 275 900 yen (about $766) in 1959. If households wanted to purchase durable goods, they had to save and accumulate

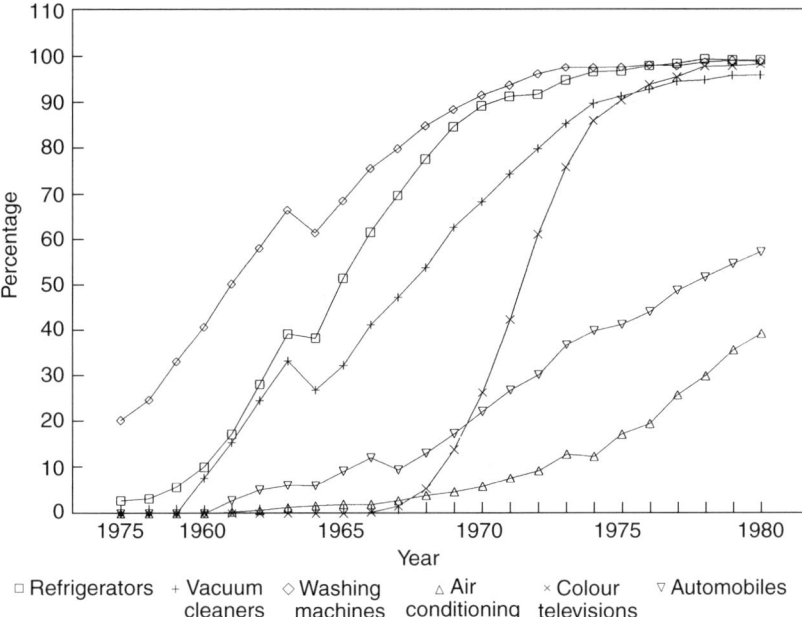

Figure 7.1 Diffusion of consumer durables in Japan, 1957–80
Source: Consumer Movement Survey, EPA.

funds to purchase them. Consumer finance for commodities and services, excluding mortgage loans for housing, began in 1960. However, due to the low level of financial assets, the credit capacity of households was limited. Therefore, when households wanted to purchase consumer durables, they faced liquidity constraints which stimulated saving. In those days, consumer durable goods were new products for Japanese households and households were eager to purchase them. Therefore, due to liquidity constraints, the amount of excess saving was large. Even so, a substitution effect existed. For example, the fund for emergencies would decrease to make room for the purchase of consumer durable goods.

Investment–saving balance and data on the household saving rate

The literature on the Japanese economic miracle suggests that the high rate of saving played a critical role in facilitating rapid economic growth. It was emphasised that one of the main factors contributing to rapid economic growth after the Second World War was the high level of investment facilitated by the high level of saving (Ito, 1992).

However, the investment and saving units are different from each other. The investment unit is corporations. Based on profit maximisation behaviour, they sought increases in productivity. To increase such productivity, corporations introduced R&D investment, technological innovation and expansion of capacity. On the other hand, the main saving unit in the quasi-closed economy was a household. One of the objectives of households is to improve their standard of living through utility maximisation behaviour. To improve their standard of living after the 1950s, they wanted to purchase consumer durables like refrigerators, televisions, vacuum cleaners, air conditioners and automobiles.

Consumer durable goods exert two effects on the investment and saving balance. There is an effect on the investment for production of consumer durable goods by corporations and there is also, due to the existence of liquidity constraints, a stimulus to accumulate financial assets in order to purchase expensive consumer durable goods in the future.

The household saving rate since 1951 has been published in the Family Income and Expenditure Survey (FIES) since 1951, compiled by the Statistics Bureau. The household saving rate of workers' households living in urban areas was only 2.0 per cent in 1951, 4.3 per cent in 1952, 5.8 per cent in 1953, 7.4 per cent in 1954 and 9.2 per cent in 1955, rapidly increasing to 11.8 per cent by 1956.

During the period of economic take-off in Japan, households saved at a high rate compared to the increase in disposable income, and therefore the household saving rate increased sharply. During the high growth era, the Japanese government decreased the income tax rate for households almost every year, an additional explanation for the rise in disposable household income. The increase in the savings rate was attributable to households' desire to purchase consumer durable goods to improve their standard of living. Due to the existence of liquidity constraints, households had to save before purchasing expensive consumer durable goods. In the mid-1950s consumer durable goods were almost all new products for households and many kinds of consumer durable goods appeared in the market annually. Because of this excess-saving due to the existence of liquidity constraints during the time gap between accumulating financial assets and purchasing consumer durable goods, corporations easily obtained funds through financial institutions at a lower rate than that available on world capital markets.

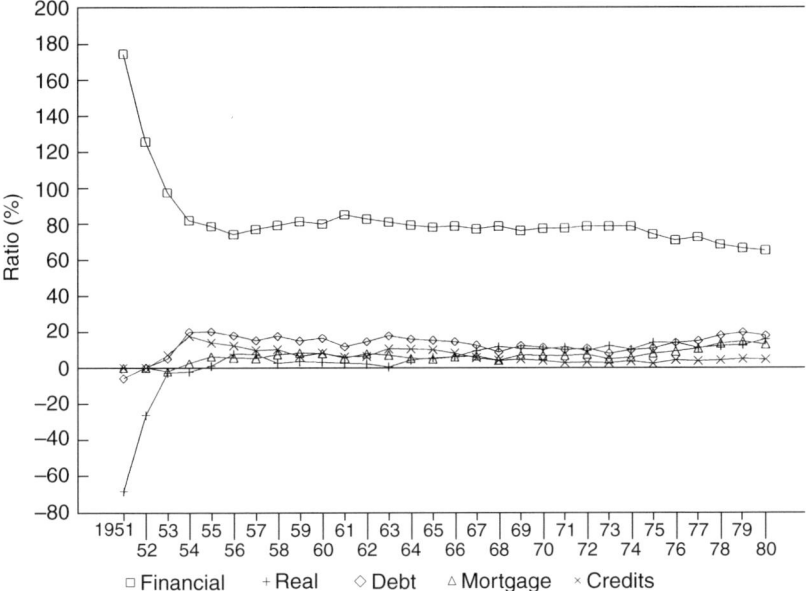

Figure 7.2 Contents of saving in Japan, 1951–80
Source: FIES, Statistics Bureau.

Because of the liquidity constraints faced by households, the rate of debt repayment in the mid-1950s was low. In Figure 7.2, savings are broken down into increases in financial and real assets, and decreases in debt. Decreases in debt are divided into two categories; decreases in mortgage loans for housing, credits and instalments. Repayment of debt for credit and instalments represented a small percentage in this category. It is clear that household saving behaviour was strongly influenced by liquidity constraints.

Concluding remarks

This chapter considered the importance of the consumer demand side in the development process. While most development theories focus on the supply side, especially innovations in technology and the quality of human capital, equally important is the innovation of society as a whole through a desire to improve standards of living.

In the 1950s and 1960s the objectives of the industrial sector and consumers coincided in Japan; the former sought modernisation and industrialisation and the latter sought an improvement in standards of living through the purchase of expensive consumer durable goods. Due to the existence of liquidity constraints, consumers had to save before purchasing consumer durable goods. Focusing on the period of economic take-off in Japan, the correlation between the purchase of consumer durable goods and the household saving rate is clear. The household saving rate was low in Japan before the 1950s but increased sharply during the period of economic take-off. This is, inter alia, because households wanted to buy consumer durables (see also Horioka, 1990), but they had to save first. Thus, the demand for consumer durable goods for households was an important stimulus to the development process, especially in Japan after the Second World War, both in stimulating investment and the supply of financial capital through household saving. In the development process, the government had to funnel these savings to corporations in order to increase the domestic supply of capital at a low price and to enable corporations to satisfy consumer demand. A rising level of disposable income and rising demand for labour-saving consumer durables facilitated a virtuous cycle of rising savings, investment and demand which generated and sustained rapid economic growth.

Appendix: Classification of total expenditure into 59 items

Food category:

Cereals: rice (item 1), barley and other cereals (item 2), bread (item 3), noodles and others (item 4)

Side dishes: 'fresh fish (item 5), shellfish (item 6), dried and salted fish (item 7), meat (item 8), milk and eggs (item 9), leafy vegetables (cabbage, spinach, lettuce, etc.) (item 10), root vegetables (potatoes, carrots, onions, etc.) (item 11), other vegetables (string beans, pumpkin, cucumbers, etc.) (item 12), dried vegetables and seaweed (item 13), processed food (item 14), condiments (item 15)

Table luxuries: cakes and candies (item 16), fruits (item 17), sake and shochu (item 18), beer (item 19), other alcoholic beverages (whiskey, wine, etc) (item 20), non-alcoholic beverages (item 21)

food away from home (item 22)

Housing category:

Rent (item 23), repairs and maintenance (item 24), water (item 25), tableware (item 26), kitchen utensils (item 27), electric appliances (bulbs, cooking appliances and heating appliances) (item 28), radio and television receivers (item 29), electromotive appliances (washing machines, refrigerators, vacuum cleaners, electric fans, and air conditioners) (item 30), furniture (item 31), other furniture and utensils (sewing machines, etc) (item 32)

Fuel and Light category:

Electricity (item 33), gas (item 34), other fuel and light (fuel oil, coal, and liquid propane) (item 35)

Clothing category:

Japanese clothing (kimono, obi, etc) (item 36), Western clothing (suits, dress, etc) (item 37), shirts and underwear (item 38), gloves and socks (item 39), cloth and thread (item 40), bedding (item 41), shoes and other footwear (item 42), umbrellas (item 43), hats, bags, and accessories (item 44), other clothing (sport outfit, cleaning, costume and rental formal wear) (item 45)

Miscellaneous goods and services:

Medical care (item 46), toilet tissue (item 47), laundry detergent (item 48), other toilet care (toilet articles, preparations, barbershops, beauty parlors, and baths) (item 49), purchased transportation, and telephone and telegram (item 50), user-operated transportation (item 51), education (item 52), stationery and writing supplies (item 53), reading (books, newspapers and magazines) (item 54), admission and broadcast licences (item 55), recreational goods (film, flowers, toys, records, and musical instruments) (item 56), other reading and recreation (travelling costs, religious and welfare activities) (item 57), tobacco (item 58), other miscellaneous goods and services (item 59).

References

Hayashi, F. (1987) 'Tests for liquidity constraints: A critical survey and some new observations', *Advances in Econometrics, Fifth World Congress.*

Horioka, C. (1990), 'Why is Japan's household saving rate so high?: A literary survey,' *Journal of the Japanese and International Economies*, 4, 49–92.

Ito, T. (1992), *The Japanese Economy*, Cambridge, Mass.

Kuznets, S. (1966), *Modern Economic Growth: Rate, Structure, and Spread*, New Haven and London.

Maki, A. (1983), *Consumer Preferences and the Measurement of Demand* (in Japanese), Tokyo.

Maki, A. (1993), 'Liquidity constraints: A cross-section analysis of the housing purchase behaviour of Japanese households,' *Review of Economics and Statistics*, 75, 429–37.

Weekly Asahi (1988), Chronological Table of Prices, I, (in Japanese) Tokyo.

Weekly Asahi (1990), Chronological Table of Prices, II, (in Japanese) Tokyo.

8
The Affluence of Social Democracy in Western Europe 1958–69

Federico Romero

In Western Europe, no less than in the United States, the decade from the late 1950s to the late 1960s has by now become almost paradigmatically associated with images of prosperous optimism, of a vast and pacified consensus on economic fundamentals, and of the prevalence of policy management over political conflict. The shared premise of the 'mixed economy' appeared as hospitably wide and functionally efficient as to comfortably accommodate within their bosom a large range of previously conflicting political actors and currents. To be sure, new forms of social and cultural conflict were emerging in Western societies, but until the late 1960s they seemed to remain rather innocuously on the fringe of the predominant liberal, welfarist and productivity-oriented consensus.

It is certainly not surprising that public memory currently contrasts our own uncertain times and choppy circumstances with a rosy, celebratory recollection of those years of rising real wages, full employment and seemingly unlimited prospects of further growth. Between 1960 and 1969 average rates of unemployment in West European countries ranged between 1.0 per cent and 2.2 per cent; the only exception being Italy, which at any rate was at an all-time historical low for that country (Van der Wee, 1983: 77). Even more revealing is the fact that that era is now conceptualised and somewhat canonised, especially by Marxist historians, as the economic and political 'golden age' of capitalism (Armstrong *et al.*, 1984; Hobsbawm, 1994).

The political history of the period has been investigated primarily within the boundaries of separate national histories, so that we do not as yet have a proper comparative picture similar to that provided by the historiography of macro-economic transformations. However, political scientists and scholars of historical political economy have outlined an interpretative synthesis that we can use as an initial frame of reference.

When the major political conflicts of the immediate postwar reconstruction period had been settled – within the rigid mould of the emerging cold war alignments – national politics in Western Europe remained largely dominated, until the early 1960s, by centre-right coalitions. Their conservative ethos stressed the priorities of anticommunism, economic growth and private investment. Leftist parties were in opposition and the influence of labour movements was rather limited. Such a picture does not fully portray the more mixed cases of Holland and Belgium, and does not even pretend to include the diverse situation of the Scandinavian countries (or of Austria), but it is an accurate representation of the cases of Germany, Britain, Italy and, partly, of France.

The 1960s, on the other hand, saw a gradual shifting towards the centre-left, with an enlarged influence and electoral success of social-democratic parties. With the notable exception of France, these eventually came to join new government coalitions intent on developing more extended public services, higher levels of income and employment security, and new systems of social concertation among major interest groups (Maier, 1993).

The social democratic progress towards government

The electoral progress of leftist, and particularly socialist parties, became noticeable at the beginning of the 1960s and continued throughout the decade. As Table 8.1 shows, the German social democrats experienced the clearest, largest and most consistent advance. In Italy a minor but generalised shift towards the left within the electorate as a whole transferred votes from the right to the centre parties, thereby offsetting the losses incurred by the Christian Democrat (CD), while the progress of the left resulted primarily in a constant increase of the communist vote. However, the centre of gravity of the entire party system moved leftward: this precluded any further reliance of the CD on a centre-right alliance, emphasised the urge to contrast the Communist Party with reformist policies, and therefore engendered the new era of centre-left coalitions, which from 1963 onwards saw the Socialist Party associated in government with the CD. The British Labour Party enjoyed only a slight increase in 1964, but the simultaneous drop of the Conservative vote gave Labour a slender parliamentary majority, and the party came back into power after 13 years of Conservative rule. Prime Minister Harold Wilson then led Labour to a substantial advance, and a much more robust majority, in the elections of 1966.

Table 8.1   Popular vote in national elections (major parties in West Germany, Great Britain and Italy) in 1957–72

| | West Germany % | | |
	SPD	CD	FD
1957	31.8	50.2	7.7
1961	36.2	45.3	12.8
1965	39.3	47.6	9.5
1969	42.7	46.1	5.8
1972	45.8	44.9	8.4

| | Great Britain % | | |
	Labour	Conservative	Liberal
1959	43.8	49.4	5.9
1964	44.1	43.4	11.2
1966	48.0	41.9	8.5
1970	43.1	46.4	7.5

| | Italy % | | | | | | | |
	Soc	PCI	Extr Left	Total Left	DC	Centre Parties	Total Centre	Right
1958	18.8	22.7		41.5	42.4	4.9	45.3	9.7
1963	19.9	25.2		45.2	38.6	8.4	46.7	6.8
1968	14.5	26.9	4.4	45.8	39.1	7.8	46.9	5.7
1972	14.7	27.1	1.9	43.7	38.7	6.8	45.5	8.7

Source: Childs, 1992; Ginsborg, 1989; Wegs, 1994.

Coupled with the uninterrupted primacy of the social democrats in Sweden (who kept increasing their electoral majority until 1968), these changes in the polities of the major Western European countries created a new political landscape characterised by the direct association of social democracy in the governmental management of the mixed economy. The major exception was France, where the establishment of the Fifth Republic in 1958 ushered in an era of growing hegemony by the centre-right coalition engineered by President Charles de Gaulle. Its electoral predominance remained uncontested until 1968, when it reached its peak. Throughout the 1960s the Communist Party's electoral results barely managed to recover from the drop of 1958, and hovered around the 20 per cent mark, while the Socialists slipped further from 20.3 per cent in 1962 to 16.5 per cent in 1968. Early signs of recovery surfaced in parliamentary elections in the second half of the 1960s, but the slow march towards power for the reorganised French Socialist Party actually materialised, a significant counter-tendency with most of Western Europe, only in the following decade (Wegs, 1994).

Even if we discount the big anomaly of the French case, it would still be unwarranted to conclude that Western Europe had entered an era of social-democratic hegemony. First, the electoral and political strength of social democracies was far from overwhelming. The Italian socialists were a junior (and as it turned out largely ineffective) partner in coalition governments dominated by the Christian Democracy. In Germany, the SPD entered government only in 1966 and until 1969 it shared power with a more powerful CDU in the grand-coalition formula. Even in Britain, where Labour ran an undivided government, its leadership was seriously constrained by the perceived necessity to broaden its electoral appeal towards the centre. Rather than by an all-out reformist effort, social-democratic strategies in the 1960s were marked by consensus politics and consensual policies.

Second, the now sharply increased risk of antagonising their supporters from the left, and particularly some sectors of the trade union movement, often limited or damaged the social democratic parties' performance once in government. In Italy, for example, a left-wing split cut down their electoral size, and in Britain the effectiveness of the Labour government economic policies was rocked, among other things, by a growing militancy of its own working-class supporters.

These difficulties, that were to grow noticeably sharper and less manageable in the 1970s, bring us to the third, major restraining factor on the influence of the social democrats. They came to power at the height of a prolonged economic boom that created the resources that the social democrats promised to utilise to extend and improve public consumption in a few key areas, most noticeably health, education, transport and housing. And on these issues the social democracies managed, by and large successfully, to push forward new investment and expenditure programmes, in Britain and Germany as well as in Italy.

But in conditions of full employment the boom also ran the risk of slowing down or grinding to a halt if its social and political consequences were not kept under control. This was the primary task that the social democrats were called upon to perform by their partners in coalition governments: to control and restrain the increase in labour cost, by means of concertation with labour which linked the dynamic of wages to the growth of productivity. Whether it was the German '*Konzertierte Aktion*', the British planned growth of income or the Italian '*politica dei redditi*', the socialists were also in government to guarantee that their own voters would accept a political trade-off between wage restraint and (deferred) public consumption for the sake of further growth (Padgett and Paterson, 1991: chap 4).

The experiment initially seemed to work (even though the British Labour government was constantly beset by the 'stop and go' policies imposed by the balance-of-payments deficit, and thus forced to cut down its investment plans), but at the end of the decade there was overfull employment in most economies, overheating set in and the explosion of wage claims brought the consensual co-management of the boom to a halt (Crouch and Pizzorno, 1978).

The political management of the mixed economy

The shift in most party systems, from conservative or Christian democratic dominance to a centre-left configuration, is probably best understood if we focus on the convergence of social and economic theories on a shared paradigm of functional, technocratic Keynesianism. By the early 1960s the era of sharp ideological conflicts was said to be over. The affluence provided by seemingly unstoppable growth had overcome the previous antagonisms and social dilemmas rooted in scarcity. Throughout Western Europe, and even more explicitly in the US, the main political tasks at hand appeared to be the further acceleration of growth rates and the integration of the residual areas of poverty within the economy of affluent consumption (Bell, 1960; Galbraith, 1958).

The means to reach this end were indicated with different emphases in the conservative and in the social-democratic agenda, but they increasingly converged on a set of shared premises. The dispute on private versus public ownership no longer tore polities apart now that conservatives were reconciled to the presence of a few state enterprises within the mixed economy and the social democrats no longer wanted to expand the scope of public ownership. Socialists focused on an enlarged provision of collective goods and income supplements (health services, pensions and so on) while conservatives kept emphasising the primacy of private investments. Their differences were on the type and degree of the welfare that the state was to provide, not on the concept itself.

Above all, the general responsibility of government for managing the economy and assuring constant rates of high growth had become almost axiomatic for a wide range of political and economic opinion. Within a prevailing functionalist culture that posited a positive-sum interplay of social and economic groups, by means of collective bargaining and political pluralism, the rational pursuit of long-range planning by national governments as well as corporations and other private actors appeared as 'the most characteristic expression of the new capitalism' that had so formidably grown into maturity in the postwar period (Lieberman, 1977; Shonfield, 1969: 121).

The changing international context was another crucial factor that smoothed the way towards political convergence, because it dissolved the siege mentality that had hardened the internal divisions of the early postwar years. By the late 1950s cold war tensions had abated in Europe, where the resolution of the Berlin crisis of 1961 highlighted the mutual recognition of an implicit but durable status quo. Destalinisation was well under way in Moscow and in both East and West the previous language of 'total symbolic annihilation' of the antagonist was increasingly replaced by a public rhetoric of peaceful coexistence, which underpinned the newly acquired affluence and stability (Stephanson, 1994: 51). Over the Atlantic, the Kennedy administration extolled the virtues of innovation, enlarged prosperity and social inclusiveness, while its style and economic philosophy magnified the promise of Keynesian managerialism. Besides, with Pope John XXIII even the Catholic Church switched its main public emphasis from anti-communist exclusion to ecumenical progress. In short, a variety of mutually reinforcing factors were suggesting that it was desirable, if not necessary, to 'enlarge the sphere of political legitimization' (Maier, 1993: 335).

In most cases, European social democracies were well prepared to step in and fulfil such a role. In the late 1950s they had come to a major overhaul of their theoretical approaches, policy programmes and political outlooks. The German SPD spearheaded the change with the most thorough revision. At its Bad Godesberg Congress of 1959 it discarded its Marxist heritage, redefined itself as a people's rather than a workers' party, replaced the critique of class-divided capitalism with the endorsement of liberal pluralism and the market economy, and focused its policies on the extension of democracy, via concertation, in the social and economic sphere. In the British Labour Party, left-wing anti-revisionist resistance was more effective and prevented such a clear-cut doctrinal renewal. But the party abandoned its emphasis on nationalisations, acknowledged the vital role of the private sector, eagerly embraced the basic parameters of the mixed economy and adopted – especially under Wilson – a modernising image that stressed the opportunities offered by productivity growth and technological advance. Italian Socialists were even less prone overtly to break with their Marxist tradition, and kept saying that the type of planning they had in mind was meant not to rationalise but to restructure the capitalist system. However, they bridged the gap with the Christian Democracy by accepting NATO and the EEC, and the 'structural reforms' that they suggested did not really amount to anything very different from the management of a high employment economy with a substantial amount of public investment in welfare, housing and transport (Sassoon, 1996; see also Klotzbach, 1982: 402–45; Howell, 1979: 206 ff.; Tamburrano, 1990).

In retrospect, we can now see that the common thread was social democracy's own candidacy to govern the mixed economy, further reflate it along Keynesian premises and, most crucially, steer it towards social and economic inclusiveness. This meant expanding wage earners' bargaining rights and capacities, maintaining high or full employment, achieving regular pay rises, improving the provision of welfare state services. Social democrats' refashioned thinking – perhaps best epitomised by Anthony Crosland's upbeat and influential reassessment the *Future of Socialism* (Crosland, 1956) – emphasised the degree of political control embedded in the new post-depression system of managed capitalism and thus the opportunity for a democratisation of the political economy.

A high-performance economy under Keynesian rules provided the tools and resources to accommodate the conflictual claims of capital and labour, and to engineer a full fledged welfare system. Besides, it legitimised the search for equality as a means to expand economic demand. Capitalism thus appeared to metamorphose into a full-employment regime that actuated social citizenship. Within this framework, what survived of the egalitarian tradition of socialism was something more akin to the American liberals' concept of equality of opportunity. Revisionist social democrats believed that a more balanced social order was in sight; the persisting inequalities could be reduced by government policies aimed at harmonising the workings of the market with a high degree of economic security and welfare. Thus, the keystone of social-democratic policies in the 1960s was an indicative planning aimed at rationalising more than reforming the economy, and particularly at modernising the infrastructure of society. And it is precisely on this ground that the convergence with Christian Democratic, liberal and even conservative parties could take place, within an increasingly similar technocratic culture of pragmatic fine tuning (Padgett and Paterson, 1991: 11–40, 142–54).

The convergence thesis was not simply based on the self-evident establishment of centre-left coalition governments. Its most meaningful verification can be found in the data on welfare state growth. Between 1958 and 1971, total public expenditure as percentage of GNP experienced a significant growth throughout Western Europe, under every type of government, and was particularly strong in Belgium, Denmark, Holland and Norway. In the largest countries it followed a strikingly similar pattern: in France it grew from 33.3 per cent to 38 per cent, in Germany from 33.1 per cent to 37 per cent, in Italy from 29.5 per cent to 38.4 per cent, in Britain from 30.1 per cent to 37.7 per cent. These large increases were totally due to the growth of civil expenditure and particularly of social programmes (most noticeably for health and old age), since defence expenditure decreased everywhere.

When related to the political composition of governments the figures reveal that, as expected, the slowest growth of public expenditures took place under purely conservative governments, but the fastest rates of growth were achieved by coalition governments independently of their centre-right or centre-left character. This suggests that the major factor for increased social spending was not so much the ideological and political pressure from the left as the 'necessity to build coalitions' and 'reconcile competing political priorities'. This becomes evident if one looks at direct social transfer outlays, that grew more markedly under centre and centre-right coalition governments built around Christian democratic parties. Socialist governments were less keen on cash transfers for social security; on the other hand, they were the prime spenders on the direct public provision of social services along the Scandinavian pattern. Naturally, the strongest growth of total social expenditures can be observed in conservative–socialist coalitions, where all these priorities combined (Flora and Heidenheimer, 1981: 327, 338–41; on defence outlays see Armstrong *et al.*, 1984: 262).

The most crucial and specific contribution of the social democracies to the political management of the mixed economy can be easily identified in the development of full-fledged neo-corporatist arrangements for macro-economic bargaining among government, industry and labour. But the record is not a straightforward one. Corporatist solutions were more solid and fared better in countries with strong centralised unions and long periods of social democratic presence in government (Sweden and Austria are the prime examples). They proved almost impossible in countries with a divided or decentralised labour movement. In this respect, the socialists' role in the Italian coalition cabinets was ineffectual and labour's major advance towards political influence came only at the end of the decade, when a massive, direct mobilisation of workers imposed in an adversarial manner those claims (wage rises, workers' rights legislation, pension reform) that the socialist ministers could not achieve by means of political negotiation. In Britain, the Labour government's attempt to engineer an income policy as part of a pact for productivity growth enjoyed only an ephemeral success, and then ended in political failure with an increasing cleavage developing between the unions and the party leadership.

In Germany, on the other hand, economic policy co-ordination was the hallmark of the Great-Coalition government; the '*Konzertierte Aktion*' brought about a durable and relatively effective pattern of tripartite accommodation; and the SPD managed to extend the scope of the co-determination procedures. The French case is different. Ever since the postwar settlement, the country was characterised by a tight, robust government–business axis that left labour on the side. De Gaulle's regime then reinforced this dirigiste but unilateral pattern of political economy. In the European context it did not stand out as an exception in terms of large government involvement in economic regulation, but it did clearly highlight, by default, the role played elsewhere by the social democracies in assuring that corporatist arrangements were socially balanced by a full inclusion of labour interests (Crouch, 1979; Flanagan *et al.*, 1983; Markovits, 1986).

All these political issues and solutions, however, are only part of the explanation for the partial left-ward shift of European polities in the 1960s. Deeper changes were taking place in societies and it is to these that we must now turn.

New voters for renewed parties

In most countries of Western Europe the period we are now considering coincided with the maximum historical expansion of industrialisation, with the culmination of the specific form of productive organisation now commonly labelled as 'fordism', and with the massive urbanisation of millions of small farmers and peasants transformed by immigration into industrial wage earners. It is against this demographic and structural background that we can make better sense of the partial shift in voting patterns.

The long postwar boom itself can be explained as the result, among other factors, of the intensification and extension into new regions of a century-long process of industrialisation. For most West European countries – notably Austria, Denmark, Finland, France, Italy, the Netherlands, Norway, Portugal, Spain, and Sweden – the reorganisation of economic activities around a highly productive industrial core culminated in the 1960s, when the spread of the factory system of mass manufacturing production reached its peak. In Germany and Italy employment in industry, as a percentage of total employment, kept growing until it reached its historical ceiling in the late 1960s. In France the same record level was achieved just a few years earlier, in the first half of the decade.

For Western Europe as a whole the ratio of the workforce employed in industry had undergone a strong, continuous growth from 1945, and such a trend culminated at around 42 per cent of total active population precisely between 1960 and 1970. It should be noted that this historical peak was reached in spite of a pronounced counter-trend in Belgium and above all in Britain: two nations where industrialisation was already receding. And it should further be emphasised that this represented the highest level of industrialisation ever reached by any society in history: neither the US nor Japan was so densely an industrial society at any moment of its history (Kaelble, 1989; Milward, 1993).

It would certainly be inaccurate to infer a direct, mechanistic correlation between such an enlargement of the industrial workforce and the concomitant electoral growth of the social democratic parties. In the 1950s the rapid expansion of the industrial labour force had not exactly translated into an ascendancy of socialism. Besides, many of those who joined the widening ranks of the industrial workforce were educated white-collar workers who had nothing to do with the socialist culture of the working class. And many of the semi-skilled and unskilled manual workers who filled the new fordist factories came directly from a rural background with a persistently traditionalist, often Catholic, culture.

However, a few, partial correlations are clearly visible and indeed inescapable. By the 1960s, the persistent, prolonged transfer of population from rural to urban areas, and from under-employment in the farming sector to relatively secure jobs in urban factories, had indeed involved many of the earlier immigrants in a cumulative cultural transformation that eventually overcame their rural identity. Now turned permanently into urban dwellers and workers, many of them developed a new sense of collective identity, as mass producers and consumers, that gave new life to working-class solidarity, labour union militancy and leftist political leanings. That such a process favoured the electoral fortunes of the left is a fact most clearly visible in the

Italian case, where the uprooting experience of migration and urbanisation was particularly extensive (Ginsborg, 1989: chap 9).

But a good indicator that a culture of collective action, and to a certain extent even a refashioned working-class identity, were indeed growing also in other nations is given by the increasing rate of unionisation. In the 1960s the ranks of labour unions and the overall rate of unionisation swelled quite markedly in Belgium, Denmark, Finland, Great Britain, Italy and Sweden. It remained stable in Germany and France, where most of the industrial labour force's growth was represented by new foreign immigrants, who would only become unionised at a later stage and even then just partially (Kaelble, 1990: 94). There is little doubt that the growing strength of labour unions provided the social democracies with enhanced political clout and electoral influence, at least until the overheating of the economy at the end of the decade. On the one hand the socialist parties appealed to working-class voters as the natural representatives, in the political sphere, of labour's new assertiveness; on the other hand their role as mediators obviously appeared more valuable to conservative politicians, business leaders and opinion makers.

Specific studies on voting patterns show that in the 1960s the German SPD further increased its majority among working-class voters, particularly unskilled manual operatives and labourers. The British Labour Party, on the other hand, experienced a slight decrease of its overwhelming share of manual workers' votes. Both parties, however, enjoyed remarkable gains among the expanding ranks of white-collar employees, technicians and civil servants, and they advanced rather visibly among the young voters. In Britain, the Labour Party was also able to appeal to some of the middle-class self-employed (Koelble, 1991: 20).

It is this twin strategy combined that explains the expansion of the social democrats' electoral appeal. While retaining and often widening their representation of an industrial working-class, that had reached its maximum historical extension, the most successful of the social democracies were also able to reach out for crucial portions of the fast-growing urban middle class. It was precisely the type of electoral strategy inherent in the late 1950s revision of the social democratic parties' programme, profile and image. One of the common threads that ran through the SPD discussion at 'Bad Godesberg', the concomitant debate within the Scandinavian parties, the modernising refashioning of British Labour and the Italian Socialist approach to government, was an analysis of social trends focused on the new salience of non-manual employees. Theoretical and policy revision was finalised with a redefinition of social democracy as the 'people's party': a policy formation capable of diluting its strictly blue-collar heritage within a widened concept of the working classes that now encompassed the swelling ranks of white-collar salary earners (Esping-Andersen, 1985; Padgett and Paterson, 1991: 35–40).

In industry no less than in the public and private service sector the new middle class of technicians, administrators, clerks, teachers and social workers was indeed growing into a core electoral constituency as well as a crucial, if not dominant, element of society's self-representation. Among them, those who worked in large, hierarchically-organised units were beginning to develop their own forms of collective action and union organisation. Many also perceived a direct self-interest in the expansion of the welfare state administrations that gave them jobs and standing. And, no less than manual workers, most of them valued the improved and extended provision of public services – like health, transport or culture – that appeared vital to their lifestyle, or of income transfers – like pensions – that guaranteed the economic security of their own families and of their often poorer, working-class parents. Perhaps most importantly, this vast new middle class naturally viewed with keen interest, and eagerly supported, the growth of free, public education, since it was the key to their own and their children's enhanced income and status. The massive increase of higher education – in the 1960s it more than doubled in size in almost every nation of Western Europe – can be taken as key evidence not only of the enlargement of the white-collar middle class, but of its political clout as well (Flora *et al.*, 1987: chap 10).

Finally, to this set of issues, which made the social-democratic policy posture palatable to the white-collar workers, we should add a broader cultural consideration. Throughout Western Europe – and perhaps more markedly in its Catholic South – the urban middle-class of the 1950s and 1960s underwent a process of modernisation and secularisation. In Italy, for instance, the percentage of the population that were regular churchgoers fell, between 1956 and 1973, from 69 per cent to 35 per cent (Ginsborg, 1989: 586). Traditional and religious values, rooted in rural or small-town self-contained life, were overcome by the experience and expectation of affluence, by new hopes of social and individual mobility, by a productivist culture of rationalism and materialism. In its eager embrace of modernity the educated middle-class, and especially the younger generation, thus became more receptive to the renovated social-democratic message of economic rationalisation, social advancement and cultural improvement.

Conclusion

To sum it all up, we can view the 1960s ascendancy of social democracy, its access to government and its full inclusion in centre-left coalitions, as the result of several intertwined processes of historical change. The unprecedented extension of a densely urban and industrial society based on large-scale serial production endowed the political representation of labour with a uniquely large constituency of homogeneous workers to which to appeal. The social democrats' ability to reach out for new strata of the technical and bureaucratic middle-class further underscores the historical salience of mass-organised work. How relevant this was to the social-democratic success soon became apparent in the light of its unravelling, in the following decades, with the incipient disaggregation of the 'fordist' society.

The long postwar boom had created the possibility, and indeed the necessity, for an enlarged social citizenship. Both social pressures from below and concerns for a stable polity propelled the social democracies into a pivotal role as mediators of more inclusive economic and political arrangements. With their co-management of the mixed economy, long-standing demands for income growth, economic security and welfare provisions were given the most ambitious and comprehensive response since the 1930s. It is now clear that the 1960s represented a peak in the attempt to reduce social inequalities and narrow the range of poverty in modern capitalist societies. The comparison with America's concomitant 'Great Society' highlights both the similarity of such attempts throughout highly industrialised societies and the relative success of the European experience (Osberg, 1991).

If we can base these conclusions on reasonably good evidence – on the political history of the social democracies, on the extension of welfare state services and on the establishment of neo-corporatist arrangements – we are still at a loss on a few equally important subjects that define our period. We still know very little, especially in a comparative framework, about liberal and conservative parties, and on the process that brought most of them, and their constituencies, to an unprecedented degree of convergence with the left in the technocratic management of a high-employment mixed economy and a full-fledged welfare state (van Kersbergen, 1995). And it is painfully clear that we cannot match our knowledge of welfare state spending with an equally crucial analysis of the concomitant process of public revenues' extension. We can discuss this and that social groups' propensity towards public consumption and income transfer, but we are still in the dark about those same groups' attitudes towards increasing taxation. Our view of the political economy of public taxing and spending is thus seriously incomplete and deeply inadequate.

One final point worth mentioning, even though it cannot be thoroughly addressed here, concerns the institutional framework of social democracy's ascendancy in the 1960s. Insofar as it took shape as a technocratic co-manage of the mixed economy, it obviously relied on the extensive ability of national governments to manipulate the very foundations of their fiscal, monetary and, to a lesser extent, even trade policies. We know how these capabilities were thereafter increasingly reduced, especially in Western Europe. And we know how the various trends that we usually group together under the label of 'globalisation' have deeply affected, indeed disabled, the role and policies of the social democracies (Sassoon, 1996: chap 16). It seems, then, necessary that we should relate the 1960s politics of centre-left coalitions also to a peculiar, very brief stage in the development of interdependence. That is to say, to a period during which the growth accelerating effects of an already highly liberalised commercial regime (at least for industrial output) were still coexisting with relatively intact national prerogatives on fiscal and monetary matters. The advantages of trade interdependence were not yet balanced, or perhaps outweighed, by substantial losses of sovereign control on capital movements, currency exchange and interest rates. Without such a highly temporary mix of national prerogatives and interdependent product markets, the social democratic co-management of full-employment economies would have certainly had a much rougher time and we would not look back to the 1960s as a decade of Keynesian prosperity, full-fledged welfarism and political convergence.

References

Armstrong, P., A. Glyn and J. Harrison (1984) *Capitalism since World War II. The Making and Breakup of the Great Boom*, London.

Bell, D. (1960) *The End of Ideology*, Glencoe.

Childs, D. (1992) *Britain since 1945. A Political History*, London.

Crosland, A. (1956) *The Future of Socialism*, London.

Crouch, C. (ed.) (1979) *State and Economy in Contemporary Capitalism*, London.

Crouch, C. and A. Pizzorno (eds) (1978) *The Resurgence of Class Conflict in Western Europe after 1968*, London.

Esping-Andersen, G. (1985) *Politics Against Markets. The Social Democratic Road to Power*, Princeton.

Flanagan, R., D.W. Soskice and L. Ulman (1983) *Unionism, Economic Stabilization, and Income Policies. The European Experience*, Washington D.C.

Flora, P. and A.J. Heidenheimer (eds) (1981) *The Development of Welfare States in Europe and America*, London.

Flora, P., F. Kraus and W. Pfenning (1987) *State, Economy, and Society in Western Europe. A Data Handbook in Two Volumes*, London.

Galbraith, J.K. (1958) *The Affluent Society*, London.

Ginsborg, P. (1989) *Storia d'Italia dal dopoguerra a oggi*, Torino.

Hobsbawm E. (1994) *Age of Extremes. The Short Twentieth Century, 1914–1991*, London.

Howell, D. (1979) *British Social Democracy*, London.

Kaelble, H. (1989) 'Was Prometheus Most Unbound in Europe?' *Journal of European Economic History*, 18, 1, 70–80.

Kaelble, H. (1990) *Verso una societé europea. Storia sociale dell'Europa 1880–1980*, Roma (original edition München 1987).

Kersbergen, K. van (1995) *Social Capitalism: a study of Christian Democracy and the Welfare State*, London.

Klotzbach, K. (1982) *Der Weg Zur Staaspartei*, Berlin.

Koelble, T. (1991) *The Left Unravelled. Social Democracy and the New Left Challenge in Britain and West Germany*, Durham.

Lieberman, S. (1977) *The Growth of European Mixed Economies 1945–1970*, Cambridge.

Maier, C.S. (1993) 'I fondamenti politici del dopoguerra,' in Perry Anderson *et al.* (eds) *Storia d'Europa*, Vol. 1, Torino, 313–74.

Markovits, A.S. (1986) *The Politics of the West German Trade Unions*, Cambridge.

Milward, A.S. (1993) 'L'Europa in formazione,' in P. Anderson *et al.* (eds) *Storia d'Europa*, Vol. 1, Torino, 161–222.

Osberg, L. (ed.) (1991), *Economic Inequality and Poverty. International Perspectives*, Armonk.

Padgett, S. and W.E. Paterson (1991) *A History of Social Democracy in Postwar Europe*, London.

Sassoon, D. (1996) *One Hundred years of Socialism. The West European Left in the Twentieth Century*, London.

Shonfield, A. (1969) *Modern Capitalism. The Changing Balance of Public and Private Power*, Oxford.

Stephanson, A. (1994) 'The United States', in D. Reynolds (ed.), *The Origins of the Cold War in Europe*, New Haven.

Tamburrano, G. (1990) *Storia e cronaca del centro-sinistra*, Milano.

Van der Wee, H. (1983) *Prosperity and Upheaval. The World Economy 1945–1980*, London.

Wegs, R.J. (1994) *Europe Since 1945. A Coincise History*, New York.

9
The Realisation of Affluence and Stability through the Shifting Political Climate: a Comparison of Postwar Japan and West Germany

Hideo Otake

Japan and West Germany have shared many historical experiences: a latecomer in industrialisation and imperialism, the totalitarian political regime during the 1930s and the 1940s, aggression and defeat in the Second World War, occupation by the Allied Powers, and spectacular postwar economic reconstruction and growth. Postwar political developments in both countries also showed an interesting parallel. In this chapter, I will analyse their common pattern in terms of whether laissez-faire liberalism or social democracy (or conservative mass democracy) was the dominant ideology in the respective periods during the postwar era, and examine how these two nations achieved the transition from austerity to affluence. In this framework, their postwar histories can be presented as follows:

- First stage: 1945 to 1948/49, dominance by social democracy in alliance with conservative mass democracy in terms of social catholicism/revised capitalism.
- Second stage: 1948/49, 'reaction' by conservative laissez-faire and individualistic liberalism. (In this chapter, the term liberalism will be used in this sense, unless otherwise qualified.)
- Third stage: 1950 to mid-1960s, gradual emergence of conservative mass democracy in the field of economic and social policies under government by the conservative party: the Liberal Democratic Party (LDP) in Japan and the Christian Democratic Union (CDU)/the Christian Social Union (CSU) in the Federal Republic.
- Fourth stage: 1967/69 to 1979, further shift toward the left, under the government joined by (1966–69), or dominated by (1969–), the Social Democratic Party (SPD) in the FRG, and under the weakened conservative rule in Japan.
- Fifth stage: 1980 to the present, resurgence of neo-liberalism.

This chapter focuses on the period up to the early third stage in the two nations during which they consolidated the foundation for political stability and economic prosperity.

The predominance of social democracy in the immediate postwar period

In the immediate postwar period, leftist groups, particularly their radical wings, gained prestige and influence, which is quite understandable in view of their strenuous and sometimes heroic resistance against the respective totalitarian regimes. Their popularity was raised also by the world-wide political climate at that time; American reform fervour of New Deal idealism strengthened by wartime solidarity, the British Labour Party's resurgence and its victory in the general election of 1945, the vivid memory of wartime alliance with the Soviet Union, to mention a few examples. On the other hand, the prestige and influence of big business had sharply degenerated due to their collaboration with the fascist regimes. Moreover, people had not recovered from the dreadful experiences of the depression of 1929 and its aftermath, which shattered their trust in the market economy.

The Communists joined the mainstream left with increased influence, particularly among youth organisations, and occupied a legitimate position in Japan as well as in Germany. Even within the conservative parties in both nations, leftists were predominant. In postwar Germany, Christian Socialists, consisting of Catholic clergymen and Christian unionists, initiated the founding of the Christian Democratic Union in many localities and socialist ideals such as the socialisation (nationalisation) of basic industries, participation in management (co-determination), welfare policies and spirit of mutual help continued to be the main slogans of the conservative party. Leaders of Christian Socialism also advocated 'the third road' between the United States and the Soviet Union (Rupp, 1982; Groseer, 1980; Becker, 1979; Eschenburg, 1983; Uertz, 1981).

The Japanese political climate in the postwar era was not different. The slogan of 'revised capitalism' was widely accepted by many Conservative Party leaders, including Ashida Hitoshi and Miki Takeo, who joined the Socialists to form a coalition government in 1947. Revised capitalism was espoused by the influential circle of younger business leaders as well. They organised themselves in 1946 as the Japanese Council for Economic Development (Keizai Doyuukai), one of the most powerful business organisations in Japanese politics (Otake, 1987).

In this circumstance, it is no wonder that socialists gained power in the two nations. In the western part of Germany where the central government was disbanded, the SPD controlled most of the Land (State) administrations, often by alliances with Christian Socialists within the conservative parties. In Nordrhein-Westfalen, the largest Land, for example, Christian Socialist Karl Arnold became the first Prime Minister in April 1947 in the coalition government with the SPD. His government attempted to socialise major industries in the Ruhr area, and advocated co-determination in industries and land reform in agriculture. It also drafted and adopted the Land Constitution with many social democratic ideals. Its contents were in many respects similar to the new Japanese Constitution directly drafted and imposed by American New Dealers. Moreover, the British Government, ruled by Labour, who occupied the largest and the most important area including Nordrhein-Westfalen, supported and encouraged these policies. It, for example, attempted the nationalisation of coal and steel industries (Hüwel, 1980).

Meanwhile, the Japanese Government was governed by the similar coalition of Socialists and Left Liberals who espoused revised capitalism. And they were actively supported by the GHQ (the Allied Occupation in Japan), who was suspicious of 'bourgeois' democracy and favoured socialists. It is well-known that many reforms introduced in the occupied Japan, which were radically egalitarian and idealistic, were planned and imposed by American New Deal Liberals, who shared basic ideology with social democrats. In political terms, these social democratic ideals included radical democratisation, reflecting idealism toward democracy and expressing naive attachment to the 'will' of the people. They were manifested in the institutional devices such as referendums and initiatives in the new Constitution. Article 9, the renouncement of war and military power, was one of the prime expressions of these social democratic ideals. (Pacifism and anti-militarism has been an important element in social democratic tradition) (Kozeki, 1989).

In economic respects, the occupation authority in the (British–American) unified zone in Germany, Bizone, was forced to tighten economic control in the face of enduring acute shortages of food and crucial industrial materials. Not only in order to increase production of coal and steel but also to avoid famine and social disorder, governmental allocations and regulation was believed inevitable and was considered as the only measure. It was under these circumstances that the newly established West German Economic Council adopted 'the Emergency Bill for Economic Control'. This bill was supported both by the CDU and the SPD, and implemented in autumn 1947. Only by these measures was the German economy able to survive the winter of 1947/48. Thus, West Germany seemed to be moving toward socialism at least in the economic sphere.

With respect to Japanese economic policy, the coalition government reinforced regulatory control over economic activities, which had been introduced during the war. It also started comprehensive economic planning. The GHQ suggested and encouraged the formation of a powerful agency, the Economic Stability Board, for overall planning and regulatory control. The Japanese economy during 1947/48 also seemed to be moving toward socialist planning and control.

Swing toward laissez-faire liberalism

Konrad Adenauer, one of the most powerful leaders within the CDU, belonged to the minority group of classical liberals (both in economic and political aspects). On the basis of his conviction in individual freedom and private property, he began his endeavour to shift party ideology from socialism as early as 1946 (Schwarz, 1995). His attack aimed particularly at socialisation. His attempt, however, encountered severe resistance and the CDU adopted in 1947 the so-called 'Alhen Program'. This programme included the socialisation of coal and steel, which Britain had made its intention public to implement. Since the SPD and the Communists supported the socialisation, there existed bipartisan agreement on this socialist policy. But Adenauer and his followers within the CDU, many of whom came from the managerial class, continued his criticism on socialisation and adopted a series of delaying tactics in the Land Parliament. They expected the US would eventually intervene on their side. Their expectation was realised and socialisation was finally suspended in 1948 by American pressure. This was the first sign of the turning of the tide, and it was followed by a dramatic turn in economic policy by the occupation authorities namely the Currency Reform.

In Japan, a similar swing was first detected in the shift of labour policy during the occupation. Although the GHQ initially encouraged the labour movement, it eventually faced its unexpected radicalisation and was forced to suppress its radical wing, with the threat of arrests by military forces, when necessary. At the same time, it encouraged moderate union leaders behind the scenes. They also uplifted the suspension and encouraged employers to organise themselves nationally so as to counterbalance the enduring labour offensive. Thus, revised capitalism and its compromising stance quickly lost its popularity among business leaders. In its place militant liberalism emerged as a dominant ideology within the business elite. In addition, small businesses, who had felt betrayed and exploited by the wartime practices of a controlled economy, supported economic liberalism in terms of economic activities and warmly welcomed the Liberal Party's slogan of freedom from governmental control. These factors all led to the severe electoral defeat of the Socialist and Left-Liberal Parties in January 1949 (Masamichi, 1949), and paved the way to the implementation of the Dodge Plan in 1949, the Japanese counterpart to the German Currency Reform.

Both the Currency Reform and the Dodge Plan were implemented by the occupation authorities; this practically meant by the US, which had become the dominant power also in West Germany. The cold war already started with the Truman Doctrine and the Marshall Plan and wielded strong influence upon American occupation policies, shifting priority from democratisation to reconstruction of Japan and Germany as its own partners. The new economic policies toward Japan and West Germany were planned by almost identical people, including William Draper and Joseph Dodge, and most of them were staunch economic liberals who came from Wall Street and committed themselves to balanced budgets, the stability of currency and a self-help (anti-welfare) stance (Schonbereger, 1989).

Three months before the Currency Reform was introduced in June 1948, the German (neo-)liberal economist Ludwig Erhard was elected to be President of the Economic Council, with support from the CDU. This was at the time when the severe winter of 1947/48 had been overcome by the tightening of economic control and the period of re-examination came. Erhard played a critical role in preparing liberalisation measures and persuading General Lucious Clay, the senior leader of Bizone, to adopt these measures against opposition by his own staff, while American laissez-faire liberals were preparing a drastic currency reform. (Clay himself favoured to economic liberalism, although he was a lay in economics (Smith, 1990).) With the liberalisation measure, the Currency Reform proved to be a great success, and the 'Miracle of June 20' revived among German people trust in the market economy and rehabilitated the German business elite politically as well as economically (Müller, 1982; Wallich, 1955).

Deeply impressed by this success and having recognised its electoral potential, the CDU abandoned its original socialist ideology and shifted toward economic liberalism under the forcible leadership of Adenauer. 'The Free Market Economy' was formulated in the CDU's Dusseldorf Program in the summer of 1949, just before the first general election. The election was fought over general principles of economic policy: free market or socialism. The slogan of '*Marktwirtschaft*' led to the electoral victory of the CDU in September 1949 and to the formation of the Adenauer Cabinet, which would rule for 14 years thereafter. The Adenauer administration was in this sense the product of economic liberalism. And it continued to use this popular slogan, 'Sozialmarktwirtschaft', as its official ideology for many years to come (Schwarz, 1981).

Not only at the above-mentioned economic front but also at the political front, social democracy experienced a severe setback. In Germany, it was a direct consequence of East–West confrontation over its own territory. Soviet mobilisation of the youth and other mass organisations against 'bourgeois elements' in East Germany revived the memory of Nazism and had shaken trust in mass participation and direct democracy. This was reinforced by the continuous flood of voluntary or forced immigration from East Germany, who brought with them news of political persecution. By this time, the sort of spiritual renaissance manifested as the 'revival of religion' or enthusiasm for spiritual reconstruction of Germany in the immediate postwar period had faded away. Adenauer's fear of mass democracy now seemed warranted and his conservative liberalism gained wider support.

It is in this anti-totalitarian context that the West German Constitution, Grundgesetz, was formulated in the Parliamentary Council in 1949. The founders of the West German Constitution thus shared a basic mistrust of the masses with the American Federalists, and hence the Grundgesetz showed conservative–liberal principles similar to the American Constitution. The former also excludes the so-called social right clause except a vague phrase 'Sozialstaat' (social state). (However, the Sozialstaat clause proved to be a powerful weapon for the subsequent development of the West German welfare state through the decisions of the Constitutional Court.) Adenauer was proud of its classical liberalism as a symbol of the victory of seventeenth-century liberalism over nineteenth-century nationalism and statism. It represented in fact a new militant liberalism of the postwar type, re-examined through the experience of Nazi totalitarianism and in view of the acute threat from Soviet totalitarianism (Adenauer, 1965; Poppinga, 1975). In sum, the political ideology had shifted by 1949 in West Germany from the anti-fascist coalition of Catholic left liberalism, social democracy and communism (the second as dominant) to the anti-communist coalition of militant liberalism and social democracy (the former as dominant).

The ideological swing in the economic field in Japan was essentially the same as that in West Germany. The political elite with business backgrounds in Washington became increasingly impatient with the staggering or even deteriorating Japanese economy and were alarmed by idealistic reforms against the Japanese 'free enterprise system'. Using American financial aid to Japan as a lever, they took the initiative from GHQ and succeeded in changing occupation policies in Japan. Joseph Dodge, a Detroit banker, who had worked for the German Currency Reform half a year before, was sent to Japan to impose tough economic policies. He rejected GHQ's previous policy of planning and control and in its place implemented liberalisation. He also introduced a tight balanced budget, bringing an abrupt stop to inflation (Schonberger, 1989).

Yoshida Shigeru had returned to the Prime Ministership three months before Dodge's arrival and gained a stable majority in the Diet in the general election. As was mentioned earlier, in this election Yoshida's Liberal Party appealed to the electorate, particularly to owners and workers in small business, with the slogan of liberalisation and tax reduction. Like Adenauer, Yoshida himself was an 'instinctive' economic liberal. He did not understand the economy well and relied upon his Finance Minister, Ikeda Hayato, a Japanese Erhard, who would become Prime Minister ten years later. Yoshida and Ikeda staked their political fortune, and Japan's, on Dodge's decision, and faithfully implemented his policies. Inflation quickly stopped and severe deflation followed. It was only with the outbreak of the Korean War invJune 1950, more than a year later, that the correctness of the Dodge Plan was proved to the eyes of the Japanese general public. The war gave momentum to economic recovery and the liberal position was strengthened, the government enlarged liberalisation and continued the tight budget.

In the political field, the direction of ideological change in Japan was similar to that in West Germany, but more extensive. That is, it swung from the anti-fascist coalition between left liberalism and social democracy to the anti-communist coalition between militant liberalism and traditional authoritarianism. There were, at least, two reasons for this 'going too far'. First, while West German labour leaders tacitly accepted the logic of the market economy and did not seriously try to mobilise union workers against the Erhard policies, Japanese union leaders were divided, and the majority of them intensified their opposition against the government and management when the Dodge Plan was implemented. This was in part because of ideological differences between the unionists in each country. But it is also because deflation caused by the Dodge Plan resulted in large-scale lay-off of workers and sharply increased unemployment rates, while the main victims of the Currency Reform were pensioners and those living on savings. In any case, mass demands for securing employment, instigated by radical or communist agitation, often led to riots in Japanese cities.

In the face of the increased radicalisation of labour movement, the GHQ and the Japanese government relied upon high-handed measures; reinforcement of control over Communist activities, the revision of the Police Law and Labour Union Law, and increasing the number of police officers. These measures understandably created fear among leftists that Japan was returning to prewar authoritarianism. While high-handed measures and the reliance upon police power, which is certainly a shift from the compromising and tolerant stance of social democracy, does not necessarily contradict with liberalism, rather it is a logical result of militant liberalism, as the Reagan and the Thatcher administrations recently showed. The essentially liberal administration of Kanzler Adenauer also showed a similar militancy in its dealing with communism.

Yoshida's confrontation against labour and his attack on vested interests achieved by social democratic revolution could be justified in terms of liberalism. However, unlike Adenauer, Yoshida did not, or could not, justify his policies in this manner; he relied upon traditional authoritarian rhetoric, regarding any opposition, including social democratic ones, as rebellious. Statements made by party politicians and public officials responsible for public order, including Yoshida, reflected, consciously or unconsciously, deep-rooted traditional values and ways of thinking and manifested their cultural identity, symbolised in the House of Emperor. They also showed aversion towards the postwar regime imposed by foreign powers.

Besides, in part to cope with radical movements, but also reflecting their own value system, Yoshida's government resorted to appeals for national pride and Imperial tradition when the issues of moral education and rearmament surfaced after 1950. These political leaders were better compared with the nationalistic German political elite of the era immediately after the First World War, such as Gustav Stresemann, than those following the Second World War. Here lies the second reason for the difference with West Germany. The Kanzler himself was deeply apprehensive at the possible resurgence of the German tradition of nationalism and statism. He and his followers had learned much more tragic lessons from fascist rule and total war than his Japanese counterpart (Dawer, 1979; Otake, 1985).

In addition, while education in West Germany lies essentially in the Land jurisdiction and is insulated from party competition at the national level, educational policies in Japan, particularly the issue of how to teach children morality and national history to foster national pride and solidarity, has been one of the most hotly debated issues between the party in power and the opposition at the national level. The conservative parties have utilised this issue in order to mobilise mass electoral support (Dore, 1959). This is in part due to the fact that moral and nationalistic education costs far less than armament build-up. Furthermore, the Japanese leaders, when forced to increase the military budget by American pressure, relied upon nationalistic appeal instead of military necessity to justify costly rearmament. They themselves simply did not feel threatened by the Soviet Union and did not believe that the argument based on military necessity was convincing at all for the ordinary Japanese (Otake, 1990).

Political confrontation in Japan thus appeared more as traditional authoritarianism versus civil liberty (represented by left liberalism) than militant neo-liberalism versus social democracy. However, notwithstanding such traditional rightist rhetoric mobilised by the Japanese political elite, it should be emphasised that militant liberalism played the dominant role at least in labour management confrontations. Unlike prewar managers, postwar managers did not challenge workers' right for collective action. Instead of suppressing through police power workers' endeavour to improve their working conditions, the managers resorted to the slogan and practice of 'high productivity and high wage' and thereby fostered labour's voluntary collaboration. Union leaders, often after severe labour disputes, accepted the argument of economic liberalism by the management and positively co-operated in higher productivity. In the economy, at least, traditional authoritarianism played little, if any, role in the confrontation with social democratic forces (Price, 1997). This is why I prefer the term 'liberal reactionism' to characterise the period of 1948/49, to the commonly used term 'reverse course' which implies a return toward traditional authoritarianism.

By handicapping social democratic forces, the ascendancy of liberalism thus created in both countries the first condition for long, stable conservative rule, as well as for economic reconstruction and prosperity.

Increasing democratic pressure: West Germany

Both the Currency Reform and the Dodge Plan were planned and implemented by the Occupation Authorities largely on the basis of economic considerations, that is, without democratic consent by the governed. Soon after these drastic reforms accomplished the initial momentum toward economic recovery and growth, domestic political forces began to make their voices heard. This happened particularly because both nations were expected to regain their sovereignties in a few years (in fact, Japan achieved full independence in 1952, West Germany in 1955). From the beginning, in 1949, the West German government did not follow liberal economic policies as faithfully as is often considered (Abelshauser, 1983; Shonfield, 1965). It relied on Dirigismus in some important respects. Tax exemptions, for example, were used for stimulating investments in such strategically important industrial sectors as shipbuilding and the construction industry. And the tax burden remained high during these years. In addition, the US intervened forcefully, ensuring the implementation of economic and planning controls in preparation for the rearmament of the new West German State. The Marshall Plan was thus administered through investment planning, and business associations were mobilised to co-ordinate the private sector plans. Nevertheless, it is undeniable that economic liberalism remained as one of the basic guidelines for West German economic policies. For example, the Government rejected the SPD's proposal for Keynesian deficit spending to attain full employment, and continued a deflationary policy and deliberately forced exports by restricting domestic demand. It also restrained wage increases to maintain the international competitiveness of German commodities. Top labour leaders tacitly collaborated with this policy of Lohndiziplin (wage discipline). Furthermore, the Government liberalised international trade, in marked contrast to the autarchic practice of the Third Reich. These economic policies were pursued under the leadership of Economic Minister Erhard and Finance Minister Fritz Schaffer, two committed liberalists.

As was mentioned earlier, domestic political forces reacted against liberal policies step by step (for the following paragraphs see Schwarz, 1981). The first concession made by the Adenauer Government toward social democratic forces was its enactment of the co-determination bill for the iron and steel industry in 1951. Adenauer gave his consent through meeting with Hans Bockler, the Chairman of the German Trade Union Federation. A more serious and substantial concession was made to the demand for compensation for wartime and postwar damages caused by such political acts as the deportation of Germans from the East of the Oder-Neisse border, now a Polish territory. So-called 'Lastenausgleich' (Equalisation of Burden Act) was demanded particularly by the Federation of German Refugees. Representing half-a-million unemployed and 400 000 governmental relief receivers among the refugees, the FGR organised massive demonstrations in the spring of 1952. It threatened to shift its political support from the CDU to the BHE, a minor rightist party. Adenauer, presumably in consideration of the coming 1953 general election, overcame the opposition by the Finance Minister and gave support for generous budgetary allocations to their causes. Economic recovery appeared to have been secured by the time the second general election was held (the recovery was at least a few years earlier than in Japan). Therefore, the most prominent campaign issue in this election was social policy toward the socially weak. And the majority of refugees gave their electoral support to the CDU.

Yet, serious discussions on social policy did not start until the spring of 1954, when Labour Minister Anton Storch with the support from the 'Sozialausschusse' (social committee) within the CDU argued for comprehensive social security policy. This was his response to widely publicised parliamentary debates, but he encountered strong opposition from the Economic and Finance Ministers as well as from employers' associations. Although welfare spending gradually increased thereafter, no comprehensive plan for social policies materialised, partly because of such opposition. Meanwhile, Catholic Socialists in the CDU demanded 'Kindergeld' (child allowance). Supported by the Family Minister, they also argued for the regulation of movie films and the restriction of divorce. Moreover, they pushed for greater Catholic influence on education, particularly through teacher training. However, in contrast to Japanese politics, these social and religious issues were not intermingled with controversies over rearmament and foreign policy, and did not lead to severe politico–cultural confrontation between the right and the left. On the contrary, conflicts in these two issue areas cross-cut. For example, the CDU's coalition partner, the Free Democratic Party, was an essentially Protestant social-liberal party at the time, and staunchly opposed to these policies. Adenauer, unlike Yoshida, was not sympathetic toward traditional Catholic claims, and tried to avoid these potentially inflammatory issues. Thus, their attempts all failed and these issues had faded away by the end of 1954.

As the third general election of 1957 approached, political pressures for wider governmental responsibility began to make themselves heard more loudly. First, agricultural groups argued for tax reductions and subsidies in order to rectify imbalances between industry and agriculture. Small business also demanded tax reductions. And tax reform became a big issue. Secondly, leftists within the CDU clamoured for higher relief measures for war victims and pensioners. In response to these claims by interest groups inside and outside the CDU, the party in power established a 'Programmkomission', while the government

markedly increased the size of the total budget and introduced a substantial tax cut. The reserved fund for costly rearmament had to be
diverted to this Programme; fortunately the planning and implementation of the defence build-up was far behind schedule. Nevertheless, it
was only because of the unexpected and unprecedented rapid growth of
national income that deficit spending was avoided; the annual budget
increased 40 per cent during 1954–57, while the GNP increased 37 per
cent in the same years.

Within the expansion of social welfare, no programme was more
important than the pension reform of 1957, undoubtedly aimed at
the 1957 election. Adenauer himself had a keen interest in this programme and actively engaged his leadership for its realisation. He relied
upon the advice of favoured scholars and encouraged his Labour Minister
to formulate the concept of the 'dynamic pension' pushing through
this programme, while overcoming the opposition from the Economic
and the Finance ministers. He was competing with the SPD in presenting an attractive welfare programme and wooing voters, and the pension reform was implemented in May 1957, several months before
election day. One of the reasons for the SPD's defeat in 1957 was that
the party could not present a more attractive social security programme
to voters, although foreign policy was a major campaign issue, at least
at mass media level.

The generous tax reductions and subsidies of the mid-1950s were
the beginning of interest group politics in West Germany, while the
massive distribution of welfare benefits in 1956–57 contributed to the
consolidation of a welfare state. Both were the government's accommodation of the pressure from democratic (mass) politics. By returning to
Bismarckian paternalistic tradition, the Conservative government
incorporated some of the basic social democratic ideals (Bartholomai,
1977; Hartwich, 1978). The CDU thus consolidated its government and
maintained its political ascendancy through adaptation to the changing political climate.

Increasing democratic pressure: Japan

Since the Dodge Plan directly affected various aspects of the Japanese
economic and political system, the repercussions were also many-sided.
First, planning and control of the economy began to be resumed soon
after the Dodge Plan was implemented, although in differing forms.
Under the Dodge Plan, the Economic Stability Board was severely
reduced in budget, personnel and competence, and was reorganised

as the Economic Planning Agency, specialising in economic analysis and forecasting. The Ministry of Commerce and Industry was also reorganised as the Ministry of International Trade and Industry (MITI). The reorganisation was ordered directly by Prime Minister Yoshida, who had been critical of its autarchic orientation, namely the tradition inherited from the experience of Manchurian development in prewar years. Yoshida, Ichimanda Hisato, President of Bank of Japan, and many other top leaders at that time believed it was unrealistic and unfruitful to attempt to make Japan a nation of heavy industry; their conceptualisation of the future Japan was an export nation of light industrial products similar to that of prewar Japan. On the other hand, officials of MITI pursued the road to heavy industrialisation, overcoming the reluctance and resistance of those such as Yoshida and Ichimanda (Otake, 1986; Kono, 1992).

In part to mitigate the deflationary Dodge policy, but also to rehabilitate and further develop heavy industry, MITI, with the support of some senior officials in the Finance Ministry, resorted to monetary policy in place of previous fiscal policy. The adoption of the 'tight budget, easy money' policy thus became a major governmental tool in economic guidance. And following the mid-1950s when the governmental budget was balanced, more active developmental policies were pursued, and yearly budget-making processes became the focal arena between MITI and the Finance Ministry. This gradual, silent turning might be better interpreted as the revival of a statist, rather than of a social democratic tradition. It should, however, be remembered that the postwar planning and control by the Economic Stability Board and the Ministry of Commerce and Industry was introduced by a Socialist government, and that the prewar statist technocrats, who had been often accused of being 'red' were, in fact, sympathetic to the principles of socialism, or at least to those of 'revised capitalism'. It is, however, also to be noted that socialist planning and control was never fully rehabilitated. MITI, whose organisation and personnel were drastically circumscribed by Dodge and Yoshida, had to rely upon indirect, rather than direct control, and any attempt to introduce more comprehensive planning in the 1950s and the 1960s has been frustrated by liberal forces in the government and business community. Their indirect control based on the manipulation of the market, however, proved to be more effective in the long run and contributed by making the most of the dynamics of the market mechanism, instead of restricting it, to unprecedented high economic development of the Japanese economy. Japanese economic policy is not so different from that of West Germany, as it appears at first glance. In any case, Japanese economic policy shifted toward a (neo-)liberal direction in the few years after the Dodge Plan.

The second political arena in which reactions against liberal policies also took place was central–local relations (Kawanaka, 1957). Traditionally, the Japanese government had been extremely centralised and the occupation reforms only remedied this 'authoritarian' structure to a limited degree. In the postwar period, the local government's dependency is particularly evident in the financial structure. While the national government had a lion's share of the tax revenue, many social services indispensable to the people's lives were the responsibility of the local governments. In addition, the local governments were required by law to administer the policies and business of the national ministries. Thus, they are heavily dependent upon subsidies and grants-in-aid, and as local government is closer to the people they are more susceptible to democratic pressures.

Along the line of the Dodge Plan, the Finance Ministry substantially reduced subsidies and grants-in-aid to local government. By these measures, the ministry intended to force the local governments to rationalise administration by curtailing personnel and administrative costs as well as by cancelling some welfare projects. However, this led many local governments to the brink of bankruptcy after 1951. Hence, local government reacted against the implementation of the Dodge Plan, representing the interests of their constituencies as well as their own institutional interests. Faced with such resistance, Yoshida and his ministers made various reform proposals, including making the Governorship subject to appointment by the national government, instead of through popular election; this was, or at least was suspected to be, one of the proposals to revive the authoritarian prewar system, and naturally alarmed the left as well as the local government Conservatives. Yoshida, however, counterargued that the present leaders of local government, who were subject to electoral pressure, were too much concerned with popularity in seeking re-election and irresponsibly reacting to the whims of the people (Yoshida was also dissatisfied by their lukewarm collaboration in reinforcing police control over the Communists and the radical labour movement). Statements such as this further stimulated the opposition of local leaders.

Local government resorted to several institutional channels in their opposition. For example they engaged, through the National Governors Association or the National Mayors Association, in activities such as publicising their opinions through the mass media, appealing to their constituencies and pushing from behind the scenes the Diet members from their prefectures. They also tried to strengthen the newly created

Local Autonomy Agency. This Agency was the outcome of strenuous efforts by former officials of the Home Ministry, which had been regarded as responsible for the undemocratic centralisation and wartime mobilisation, and hence was disbanded by the Occupation. Those officials saw, in the predicament of the local government lacking in powerful representation within the national government, new opportunities to argue for the creation (or revival) of a Ministry to represent local interests. The Agency, now in the guise of promoting local autonomy, intervened in the tug-of-war between local government and their representatives in the party in power on the one hand, and the top national leadership and the Finance Ministry on the other.

The Agency's first clear victory was achieved in the autumn of 1952 by the increase in grants-in-aid in the revised budget for FY1952. This was accomplished also by very energetic activities of the National Governors Association. The coming general election of April 1953 was certainly an important factor in their success. Thereafter, the budget-making on grants-in-aid and subsidies to the local governments became subject to tough negotiations between the Agency and the Ministry. And during the 1950s, particularly after Japan's recovery of its sovereignty, the position of the liberals was getting weaker as party influence increased (the Agency was upgraded to the status of a fully fledged ministry in 1960).

When Hatoyama Ichiro replaced Yoshida as Prime Minister in late 1954, the Finance Ministry desperately tried to retain a balanced budget. Hatoyama, in his mobilisation of Conservative rank and file members, appealed for more positive fiscal policy as well as bolder rearmament, and criticised Yoshida as being undemocratic and bureaucratic in neglecting local interests. And when he came to power, the general election was expected to take place soon (actually held in February 1955) and the regular unified local elections of April 1955 were approaching. Pressure for larger grants-in-aid was untenable to the government leadership. The Finance Ministry was isolated politically and even threatened, by a series of reorganisation proposals, for budget-making decisions to be taken from the Ministry and placed in the jurisdiction of the Cabinet secretariat. Meanwhile, by the mid-1950s, Japan was achieving economic recovery and stable growth. As in West Germany, the budgetary surplus made it possible and at the same time inevitable to increase the size of the budget and push Japan to a wider government. It was under these circumstances, of an increasing representation of local interests, that the conservative parties merged and established 'the 1955 Political System'.

The third arena of conflict between economic liberalism and mass democracy was agriculture (Imamura, 1978); it was again fought within the conservatives, not between the left and right. The Dodge Plan was a serious blow to farming households. It drastically reduced subsidies to agricultural production and substantially raised taxes on agriculture, while keeping the price of rice artificially low. As a result, the farmer's incomes were markedly lower. When the Korean War gave momentum to economic recovery in the industrial sector and improved the financial conditions of the government in the later half of 1950, farmers' discontents surfaced on the political agenda. First, farmers demanded the reduction of agricultural income taxes. Second, they asked for a raising of the price of rice. Third, they clamoured for the restoration of previous subsidies and the establishment of new ones. Needless to say, they were energetically engaged in pressure group activities through the agricultural co-operatives and the Diet members from their districts. Soon they organised the most powerful political network in Japanese interest group politics; Nokyo.

It was quite understandable in view of the fact that the farming population constituted at that time nearly 50 per cent of the total Japanese population. Besides, their influence was felt all the more strongly under the Conservative government, particularly because the agricultural areas were the power base of the Conservative parties. The Socialists as well were quite sympathetic to farmers' interests and were competing with the Conservatives in their proposal for larger, more comprehensive subsidies. The agricultural income taxes were gradually reduced after 1951 and the government purchase price of rice was gradually raised at the same time. The greatest success of the farmers' lobby was, however, in attaining subsidies. The passage of the Bill for Extraordinary Measures to Promote Snowy and Cold Areas in March 1951 was marked as the beginning of a long list of laws to give a greater variety of financial aids to agriculture in the 1950s. By departing sharply from economic liberalism, Japanese politics had created one of the most protected agricultural sectors in the world.

Miscellaneous interest groups joined the farm lobbies, and their pressure group activities further pushed the government toward a bigger budget. As a result, Japanese politics had a new wave of interest group formations during the early 1950s. In contrast to the immediate postwar period when the organisations of labourers and other 'progressive' forces mushroomed, there emerged in this period a number of groups oriented toward the Conservative parties such as associations of small businesses, ex-landlords or ex-soldiers. And the Conservative parties, particularly their rank and file Diet members, were responsive to the claims made by such groups.

The most prominent, or at least the most visible, example was pressure group activities for the restoration of ex-soldiers' pensions (Izokukai, 1962; Goyurenmei, 1967). After the war, the Soldiers' Protection Society was disbanded. Attempts to re-establish such an organisation were made immediately in many localities and in 1947 the Japan Federation for the Welfare of the Bereaved was organised. The Occupation authorities watched this association with some suspicion and its campaign for relief had to be conducted with caution. After 1949 when the Diet discussed this issue and proclaimed its declaration on this subject, the Federation intensified its public campaigns. The government, however, resisted because of financial difficulties. In early 1952, the government made concessions and gave the bereaved a small amount of relief in the budget of FY1952. Subsequently, the Law to Protect the War Wounded and the War Bereaved was promulgated just before the Peace Treaty became effective. After that, the Conservative parties increased governmental aid for the war wounded and bereaved step-by-step, responding to their strenuous pressure group activities. Other interest groups followed a similar pattern and pressures accumulated for a budget increase (Taguchi, 1969).

The Yoshida Cabinet persistently tried to keep a tight budget, being committed to the philosophy of economic liberalism. Yoshida himself intervened in the FY1954 budget process, the last budget by his government, and barely overcame the pressure from his own party to expand the total budget. After FY1955, the budget surplus made it unnecessary to keep a tight budget and the interest groups began to enjoy generous financial aid. As in West Germany, the party in power thereafter consolidated its rule through budget allocations. Besides, again as was the case in West Germany, the government in Japan also contributed to defusing potentially anti-democratic tendencies in conservative social groups by giving them immediate material benefits, and integrating them into the parliamentary system. Moreover, the cumulative demands for budget allocations made full-scale rearmament difficult, even following the greatly improved financial conditions of the late 1950s, and thus minimised the potential risk of the remilitarization of the Japanese economy. All of these in turn further consolidated the stable government by the Conservative Party.

Concluding remarks

Both West German and Japanese politics gradually shifted from the (neo-)liberal reaction to mass democracy during the early half of the 1950s. It should be noted, however, that the two economies have remained as a liberal system in one important respect. After the drastic rationalisation of the economy in both countries (and through the harsh political suppression of the left in Japan), economic recoveries were steadily achieved. Labour unions now co-operated in increasing productivity and claimed their legitimate share within the existing arrangement, rather than attempting to change it. Partly due to favourable international conditions, their strategy was rewarded: real wages increased and employment was secure. Labour–management relations were thus depoliticised and basically settled without government intervention. Consequently, liberalism remained intact in this respect.

Meanwhile, as the financial conditions of the government were improved, the party in power in each country became responsive to voters' potential, as well as manifested, demands. As a result, a wider government based on mass democracy emerged gradually. And it was realised under a conservative status quo oriented atmosphere. This coincided with labour's above mentioned conservatism. This gradual shift was in sharp contrast to the abrupt change brought by the liberal 'reaction' in 1948/49. The latter process was characterised by an acute sense of crisis resulting from cumulating and chronic problems. In contrast, the gradual shift which took place in the 1950s in West Germany and Japan was achieved with a sense of relief and relaxation. Besides, its dominant Zeitgeist was individualism and orientation toward private life, particularly consumption. In this respect, this age inherited a crucial element of economic liberalism, namely individualism while the militant, aggressive aspect of economic liberalism substantially waned. This also meant the continuing retreat of humanitarian idealism and solidarity. Such a Zeitgeist re-emerged only in the late 1960s both in West Germany and Japan.

As this characterisation of each decade suggests, a similar politico–economic cycle can be detected in other advanced capitalist nations including the UK and the US. In fact, this author took as an initial clue for this historical and comparative framework, the almost simultaneous restoration of economic liberalism and traditional conservatism (nationalism, 'the Moral Majority' and so on) of the late 1970s and the 1980s in Great Britain (Thatcher), the United States (Reagan), France (Chirac) and Japan (Nakasone). Policy outcomes and their consequences have been quite different when comparing these nations, probably due to differences in institutional settings, as recent institutionalists argue. But ideological configurations show unmistakable similarities and the patterns of conflict also show basic similarities.

One axis is conflict between laissez faire liberalism and social democracy (and conservative mass democracy), concerned mostly with economic policies including welfare, which seems to emerge from conflict between economic rationality (logic of capitalism) and political rationality (logic of democracy). The other axis is conflict between traditionalism and libertarianism. Also involved is the rise and fall of political idealism, and political aspirations for direct democracy (Hirschman, 1982). These two (or three) cycles seem to synchronise and have created a basic condition for class and party alignment/dealignment. These cycles also seem to synchronise internationally and give a roughly simultaneous political development in major advanced nations.

This chapter is an attempt to sketch a cycle in this historical and comparative context in postwar Japan and West Germany and to examine the processes through which postwar prosperity and political stability were established in these two nations.

References

Abelshauser, W. (1983) *Wirtschaftsgeschichte der Bundesrepublik Deutschland 1945–1980*, Frankfurt am Main.

Adenauer, K. (1965) *Erinnerungen 1945–1953*, Stuttgart.

Bartholomai, R. (1977) *Sozialpolitik nach 1945*, Bonn.

Becker, J. (1979) *Vorgeschichte der Bundesrepublik Deutschland*, München.

Dawer, J. (1979) *Empire and Aftermath: Yoshida Shigereu and the Japanese Experience, 1878–1954*, Cambridge.

Dore, R.P. (1959) *Land Reform in Japan*, Oxford.

Eschenburg, T. (1983) *Jahre der Besatzung 1954–1949*, Stuttgart.

Groseer, A. (1980), *Western Alliance: European-American Relations since 1945*, New York.

Hartwich, H.H. (1978) *Sozialstaatspostulat und gesellschaftlicher status quo*, Wiesbaden.

Hirschman, A.O. (1982) *Shifting Involvements : Private Interest and Public Action*, Princeton.

Hüwel, D. (1980) *Karl Arnold : Eine politische Biographie*, Wuppertal.

Imamura, N. (1978) *Hojokin to Nogyo*, Noson, Tokyo.

Kawanaka, N. (1957) 'Chiho Zaisei Saiken Seisaku no Keiseikatei (1)–(6),' *Jichikenkyu*, Tokyo.

Kono, Y. (1992) 'Yoshida Gaiko to Kokunai Seiji', in N.S. Gakkai (ed.), *Sengo Kokka no Keisei to Keizai Hatten*, Tokyo.

Kozeki, S. (1989) *Shinkenpo no Tanjo*, Tokyo.

Lukomski, J.M. (1965) *Ludwig Erhard. Der Mensch und der Politiker*, Düsseldorf/Wien.

Masamichi, R. (1949) *Seijiishiki no Kaibo*, Tokyo.

Müller, G. (1982) *Die Grundlegung der westdeutschen Wirtschaftsordnung im Frankfurter Wirtschaftsrat 1947–1949*, München.

Otake, H. (1985) *Adenauer und to Yoshida Shigeru: Die Wiedergeburt des Liberalismus als Konservative Ideologie*, Tokyo.

Otake, H. (1987) 'The Zaikai under the Occupation: The Formation and Transformation of Managerial Councils', in R.E. Ward and S. Yoshikazu (eds), *Democratizing Japan: The Allied Occupation*, Honolulu.

Otake, H. (1990) 'Defense Controversies and One-Party Dominance: The Opposition in Japan and West Germany,' in T. J. Pempel (ed.), *Uncommon Democracies: The One Party Dominant Regimes*, Ithaca.

Otake, H. (1985), *Konrad Adenauer und Shigeru Yoshida: Die Wiedergeburt des Liberalismus als konservative Ideologie*, Tokyo.

Poppinga, A., (1975) *Konrad Adenauer: Geschichtsverständnis, Weltanschauung und politische Praxis*, Stuttgart.

Price, J. (1997) *Japan Works: Power and Paradox in Postwar Industrial Relations*, Ithaca.

Rupp, H.K. (1982) *Politische Geschichte der Bundesrepublik Deutschland, zweite Auflage*, Stuttgart.

Schonbereger, H.B. (1989) *Aftermath of War: Americans and the Remaking of Japan, 1945–1952*, Kent, Ohio.

Schwarz, H.P. (1981) *Die Ära Adenauer: Gründerjahre der Republik 1949–1957*, Stuttgart.

Schwarz, H.P. (1995) *Konrad Adenauer: A German Politician and Statesman in a Period of War, Revolution and Reconstruction*, Oxford.

Shonfield, A. (1965) *Modern Capitalism: The Changing Balance of Public and Private Power*, Oxford.

Smith, J.E. (1990) *Lucius D. Clay: An American Life*, New York.

Taguchi, F. (1969) *Shakaishudan no Seijikino*, Tokyo.

Uertz, R. (1981) *Christentum und Sozialismus in der frühen CDU : Grundlagen und Wirkungen der christlich-sozialen Ideen in der Union 1945–1949*, Stuttgart.

Wallich, H.C. (1955) *Mainsprings of the German Revival*, New Haven.

10
The Politics of Collective Consumption in Western Europe

Bo Stråth

The expansion of the politics of collective consumption in Western Europe in the 1950s and 1960s within the framework of economic growth and affluence was rooted in the Great Depression of the 1930s. The 1930s brought two kinds of responses to mass unemployment: Fascism/Nazism on the one hand and social democratic liberalism on the other. The latter made concessions to the working class, which, in the long run created the prerequisites for mass consumption. This, in turn, provided the basis for mass production, in a mutually reinforcing process. In the democratic case, the symbiosis of mass production and mass consumption provided a basis for political participation of the masses in the distribution of welfare. In the Fascist/Nazi countries this democratic phase did not occur until after the Second World War.

The organisational expression of the transformation in the wake of the crisis was the accumulation of hierarchical structures for tripartite central bargaining and trade-offs. The emerging neo-corporatist organisation of interests was the culmination of Keynesian strategies. This emerging model of economic regulation based on increased public intervention and centralised bargaining was diffused and consolidated in Western Europe during the 1950s and 1960s. Keynesian economies provided a theoretical legitimation.

The dynamics in this transformation varied from society to society in Western Europe. In Sweden a Keynesian model of social bargaining already existed in 1956–57; in the Federal Republic of Germany it only arrived ten years later. Even if the timing varied considerably, two essential elements can be identified: the maintenance of the balance between supply and demand through policies to support demand, and the use of public expenditure as the primary component of such policies, and also as a tool to produce compromise. This arrangement was

173

accompanied by an increasing importance of the macro-economic level and a progressive growth of the regulative role of the 'centre'. Especially where workers' movements were strong and left-wing parties had access to government, the Keynesian welfare state was sustained by tendencies leading towards the centralised co-ordination of the economic and social policies of the government and the largest interest groups.

There was a substantial continuity between Keynesian policies and centralised concerted action, where the primary aim was to control aggregate demand. Concerted action was the tool for the maintenance of this objective in a situation of increased power for the trade unions. Neo-corporatism, in the sense in which Schmitter introduced the concept in relation to democratic societies in his article in 1974, not only meant state intervention in the economy but also tripartite negotiation and hierarchical organisations with disciplined members, so that the agreements could be guaranteed (Stråth, 1996; Schmitter, 1974; Trigilia, 1991).

The emergence of welfare politics within a public framework was the matter of a long process of increasing government intervention through social politics in order to maintain internal peace and to integrate the working classes into society as a whole. The first comprehensive steps in this direction were taken during the decades before the First World War when class conflict in most European societies intensified. A second decisive step was the response to mass unemployment in the wake of the Great Depression. This development was general, but it varied in intensity over Europe. It is justified to talk about historically developed north–south and west–east divisions concerning welfare state developments and politics of collective consumption, meaning that until recently – when the performance of the welfare state has become problematic, and the politics of its deconstruction has become topical – the core of the welfare state pattern of collective consumption was northwestern Europe: France, Germany, Britain, Benelux and Scandinavia.

This north–south/west–east difference has to do with the industrialisation process. The proletarian working class emerged in Europe during the end of the 19th and early 20th centuries more unified and in some respect stronger than, for example, in Japan and the US. Especially in northwestern Europe the working-class milieu developed a network of associations that mobilised the workers for the labour movement and the trade unions. In this sense, the working-class consisted of a labour-movement culture rather than a working-class culture and was split into political camps: social democratic, catholic and communist

(Kaelble, 1994). The confrontation between the ruling classes and organised labour varied in form and content, as did the ways in which the working class was socially integrated. There was a mixture of patterns of upside down and downside up integration processes. The relative importance of parliament varied in social democratic strategies, as did their estimation of the state apparatus and to what extent it could be used for political purposes. The opportunities for the social democrats and the labour movements to find coalition partners also varied, which resulted in a subsequent difference in welfare politics between working-class concentration or more universal ambitions. Because of these historically determined differences, the role of the state and public and private associations of social insurance varied, over the European continent.

These European differences increased during the immediate postwar years. The war had not affected all countries to the same degree. Some countries were much more affected by hunger, by scarcity of housing and fuel, by epidemic diseases, by the breakdown of the provision of basic needs, public administration and schooling. Contrasts in everyday life were very strong, especially between the small part of Europe which did not participate in the war, that is Sweden, Switzerland, Spain, Portugal and Ireland on the one hand, and the regions most affected by the war: Britain, France, Germany, Italy, Benelux, Poland, Yugoslavia, Finland and the Soviet Union. In addition, governments and societies drew various lessons from the war.

The continuity of élites, the political role of former resistance movements and social reforms in a wide sense, varied enormously from one country to another as a direct consequence of the war. In Britain, for example, the war led to a fundamentally new concept of social policy, the Beveridge plan, which inspired the immediate postwar reforms of the British welfare state. In Germany, the war and the Nazi regime strengthened the position of the opponents of any reform of public social security. In France, the war contributed to an awareness of the backwardness of the French economy and to a vigorous modernisation policy by planification (Kaelble, 1995). In neutral Sweden, the politics of war economy provided the social democratic leadership with new insights in the opportunities to use the state for political regulation and economic redistribution under maintained legitimacy. In this respect there was a high degree of continuity. The war was a bridge between state intervention to stabilise collapsing markets in the 1930s and welfare politics in the social arena in the 1950s.

Besides this national variation there was a much more fundamental division within Europe; the split between Eastern and Western Europe.

This difference was not simply a phenomenon in the wake of the cold war but also had substantial long-term historical roots. The degree of industrialisation and modernisation was much lower in Eastern Europe. However, the cold war not only produced differences, but it also stimulated integration and economic development in Western as well as Eastern Europe. The role of the cold war as an integrative force and promoter of economic growth is difficult to exaggerate. The 1950s and the 1960s was a period of unique rise in the standard of living without any parallel in Europe's past. The timing and intensity of the rise in the standard of living was not the same in all European countries but the basic trend can be found everywhere, in the west as well as in the east, in the north as well as in the south. The industrialisation, as well as the rise in the standard of living, was reinforced, though not fully explained, by the new international economic order established in the West by the US and by different but highly purposeful national economic policies (Kaelble, 1995).

For a long time the emergence of a European free trade regime was seen as the motor of this development. Recent research indicates rather the opposite causative chain. Economic growth and increasing living standards started in the early 1950s, whereas free trade was introduced only in the 1960s. The rising standard of living was an important framework condition when governments dismantled trade obstacles under political legitimacy (Milward, 1992). This development occurred in the framework of a changing Zeitgeist. Until the mid-1950s, there was considerable uncertainty about whether the postwar recovery could be maintained. At the end of the 1950s, insight grew in Western Europe, that the economic expansion was to continue and that economic theory provided intellectual tools for political guidance of economies with persistent growth. There was a growing belief that a solution had at last been found to the age-old problem of unemployment and slow growth that had bedevilled the earlier history of capitalism. It seemed unlikely that there would be a major set-back in Western growth. Economic growth was seen as the norm (Shonfield, 1965; Galbraith, 1958; Galbraith, 1967).

Government commitment to growth based on full employment was the most important feature of this development within the framework of the cold war. In the early 1960s, there emerged a common assumption that government policy, with the state budget as a key instrument, could be constructed in a way that ensured that the economy would continue to grow. Governments increased their intervention in the economy, not only in the form of public spending as a growing share of the GNP, but also through responsibilities for new polity areas such as health, environment and leisure. There was a changing balance between public and private in most economies, although this change was not uncontested. Concomitantly with government expansion, the 1960s witnessed criticism of ever-higher taxes. Sweden as a high-tax state was used as both a warning example and an example worth following in the European debate.

Within the general trend in a Keynesian direction of an increasing role for governments, European variation was great. However, the increasing mentality of a new normalcy, in the framework of economies which were considered to be politically governable, growth and security constituted a key element of a general cultural change and transformation of life styles. The precise shape of this development has been very little investigated in a comparative European perspective. To what extent it is justifiable to call this process Americanisation, how penetrative the process was in different European societies, the degree of continuity and the variations between different countries are highly relevant questions for a future research agenda. Furthermore, these questions of cultural change must be referred to the questions of political and economic change in terms of growth and governance.

When the interpretative frameworks of this development were constructed through theoretisation in economics and social sciences, historical legitimatising was looked for in the 1930s, when a worldwide depression with mass unemployment had last occurred and had ended in a world-wide conflagration. The 1930s were constructed as a watershed in the 1960s. In retrospect the years of affluence have often erroneously been seen as a long era of prosperity and political confidence lasting from the 1930s to the erosion in the 1970s and 1980s. Erroneously in the sense that the consistency between economic performance, political governance and cultural belief in a new order of growth lasted for only a very short period in the late 1950s–early 1960s. Before this period uncertainty predominated. After 1965, new challenges to the sense of security and the belief in political governance were waiting around the corner, as we know today. What was, for a short period, believed to be the ultimate realisation of the industrial society in a Keynesian middle way between planned and market economies, was in fact also the beginning of its transformation into an information society based on less and less need for labour.

The epoch of the welfare state based on the convention of full employment was conspicuously short. Instead of quite a stable period of half a century or so of prosperity following on from the Great

Depression and the war, and based on comprehensive governance of the economies, the emergence of the affluent society was a much more fumbling and tentative process of problem resolution, where the sense of security and the belief in the ability to master the future only lasted a decade or so. During this short period, several phenomena, originating in the organisation of society around 1900 (for example the workers' struggle for justice and the integration of their protests) came to an end, while others, deriving from the social and economic implications of the emerging information society in a transnational order, began. What looked, in the first years of the 1960s, like great stability contained many severe tensions under the surface, which made themselves apparent in the 1970s.

One of the cornerstones of the politics of collective consumption was the social insurance system. In a long historical perspective social insurance can be seen in three phases:

I   worker insurance;
II   social insurance;
III social security.

Worker insurance dominated before the First World War. The number of people insured as well as the number of risks covered was limited to the working class and the most prominent goal was to integrate the workers politically and socially into society (Alber, 1982; Stråth, 1996).

Basically, four risks were covered when the social insurance systems emerged during the 30-year period 1885–1915: occupational injuries, sickness, old-age pension and unemployment. The introduction in most countries was in this order. The development was a mixture of general patterns and trends, and national variations concerning time of introduction, scope, financing, and so on. The interwar years brought a general wave of expansion, embracing new population groups and covering more risks. Except for Finland, Iceland and Switzerland, all European countries offered their workers virtually complete protection against the standard risks of income losses.

After the Second World War, a new wave of expansion started. The restriction of insurance to the working class, as described above, definitely ceased. Only a few countries, such as Sweden, had used a universal principle from the beginning. The system not only expanded to include more social groups, but also grew from covering basic social needs towards the maintenance of the normal income level in case of accident, sickness, old age and unemployment. This expansion meant that in 1975 sickness insurance and old-age pensions in Western

Europe covered more than 90 per cent of the active population, that is of the population under 65 years of age. Occupational injury insurance covered 80 per cent of the population and unemployment insurance 65 per cent. The nature of the publicly guaranteed insurance changed from compulsory insurance, which guaranteed the maintenance of a certain basic level of living, to the public subsidising of voluntary insurance schemes with the ambition of guaranteeing the income level. Such voluntary schemes were introduced early in the Mediterranean countries, Scandinavia and Switzerland.

Two early driving forces of this expansive development were the solidarity established around the resistance movements during the war and the impetus for social integration provoked by the cold war. At the end of the 1950s, economic growth provided a basis for expansion towards income security. The prerequisites for the social insurance system's guaranteeing the maintenance of the normal income standard were full employment and economic growth. When both these preconditions disappeared in the 1970s (the first signs of erosion were already visible in the late 1960s), the basis of the whole system was destroyed, although this was not fully politically clear until ten or twenty years later, when finance and budget crises hit the governments. When this occurred, governments were much more vulnerable than when the expansion began after the war, because of the increasing share of the GNPs used for public expenditure. In 1930, the average share of GNP for social insurance was 2.8 per cent. Germany had the largest share with 8 per cent. In 1950, the average figure in Western Europe had increased to 5 per cent. At the end of the 1950s, the figure was 7 per cent. In the 1960s, the expansion accelerated. In 1970, 10.7 per cent of the national resources went to social insurance. In 1974, the figure was 13 per cent, almost twice as much as in 1960. The share in Sweden and the Netherlands was more than 17 per cent by 1974.

The UK was the only country where the expansion of the social insurance expenditures in relative terms stagnated rather than accelerated. In Germany and Austria, which in 1950, together with the UK, had the highest level among the European nations, the dynamic development was maintained. The fastest development was in Finland, Norway, Sweden, the Netherlands and Italy, countries which, except for Sweden, had positions below the average in 1950. In reality government expenditures for social security included more than just social insurance, raising the total share of the GNP shown in Table 10.1 by about one third again. In Sweden and the Netherlands, which had the largest share, the figure was 25 per cent by 1974.

Table 10.1 The development of social insurance expenditures as a share of GNP, 1930–74

	1930	1950	1960	1970	1974
Austria	4.4	6.5	8.6	11.7	12.2
Belgium	–	6.1	8.7	11.2	14.0
Denmark	2.6	5.2	7.5	10.2	11.3
Finland	0.7	1.9	4.6	8.5	10.1
France	–	4.8	6.0	10.5	13.2
Germany	7.8	7.3	10.0	12.0	14.9
Ireland	2.8	4.9	6.4	7.6	10.7
Italy	–	3.3	6.1	10.6	13.9
Netherlands	1.5	3.7	7.3	13.9	17.3
Norway	1.0	3.9	6.5	11.7	14.1
Sweden	1.1	5.4	7.8	13.9	17.8
Switzerland	1.4	3.9	5.4	8.2	11.3
United Kingdom	4.6	6.7	5.3	8.7	8.8
Average	2.8	4.9	6.9	10.7	13.0
Standard Deviation	2.1	1.5	1.5	2.0	2.6

Source: Alber, 1982: 60.

The general European pattern in the field of collective consumption was a coincidence of government penetration and bureaucratisation with a weakening of the control mechanisms, owing to the increasing complexity of the insurance systems in the wake of the expansion. Increasing generosity was one of the ingredients of the expansion and the fight for votes among the political parties a driving force of the whole development. Government penetration meant that the subsidising of voluntary insurance totally disappeared as a method. Compulsory government schemes became the exclusive order. This expansion of the public sector cannot be immediately translated in terms of financing, however. There was considerable variation among Western European societies concerning the distribution of the insurance costs between taxes and compulsory contributions.

This variation notwithstanding, the political capacity to impose increasing obligations on growing sectors of the population meant a considerable government expansion of power, a general pattern in the booming economies of the 1950s and 1960s. Paradoxically, because of the tax implications of the government expansion, probably the most important driving force of this development was the fight for votes on tightening political markets (Stråth, 1987).

Once guided by Bismarck's ambitions to substitute social for political reform, welfare policy in the 1950s was informed by a widespread agreement that social rights should complete, and not sidetrack, the process of emancipation. Previously, social policy had sprung from the hopes of society's élites for stability. Now there emerged a broad agreement behind the welfare state. Britain led this development after the Second World War with the Beveridge proposal for a uniform and universal system of social insurance. All citizens were included, classified by groups in relation to the causes of economic insecurity and the protection required to meet them. A National Health Service and universal family allowances were assumptions of his recommendations. Pensions were to be flat rate, subject to no means test and sufficient for subsistence. Financing was provided by the system's members and employers, with the state covering 15–20 per cent of most insurance benefits, the lion's share of the NHS and the sum of family allowances. Within each category everyone paid uniform contributions regardless of income. Benefits were to be universal, flat rate, subsistence and not conditional on need (Baldwin, 1990).

How European welfare systems achieved universalist reform varied in accordance with the manner that social policy had first been implemented in the 19th century. The continental approach was opposed to the Scandinavian one with its early universalist, means-tested and tax-financed benefits. Germany and France had begun with legislation that – limited to certain classes defined by their employment – was related to need only insofar as some social groups were less fortunate than others. In Scandinavia, on the contrary, the first measures covered all classes, but only the poor within each. British development vacillated between these two poles. Postwar universalist reform as embodied in pensions, for instance, was therefore a goal arrived at by separate paths from at least two distinct starting points. Along the route followed on the continent, it meant expanding measures previously restricted to workers laterally so as to include other classes. Such horizontal universalism was important in France and Germany, where the self-employed and salaried employees were now also to be enrolled in social insurance. By contrast, to the north and across the Channel, horizontal universalism was scarcely an issue since the needy of most classes were already covered by statutory pensions. Universalist reform in Britain and Scandinavia involved a vertical movement that drew in those who had not formerly been the object of statutory attention. There universalism meant giving what had previously been reserved for the poor alone also to the better-off. Need was eliminated as a prerequisite for entitlement by abolishing the means tests and relaxing the earning rules that otherwise disqualified the well-off from measures targeted at the poor (Baldwin, 1990: 113–14).

Different explanations have been advanced to account for the emergence of universalism. The war and its political aftermath allowed greater influence for the working class in Britain and Scandinavia and thereby social policy of a solidaristic cast. Conversely, in this interpretive framework, the defeat of the left in France, Italy and Germany during the first postwar years explains equally why egalitarian reforms failed there.

A somewhat different explanatory approach considers the parties of the right and the centre rather than the social democrats as the key of social reform and asks why these parties were associated with reform. This approach finds the answer in the general unanimity fostered by the war, that made necessary a greater scope for state intervention (Baldwin, 1990: 109).

The common denominator of both perspectives is the co-operation/coalition between moderate socialists and reforming liberals in both Britain and Scandinavia. In the Scandinavian case the farmers' parties were involved in this coalition, too. This lab-lib co-operation had started already in the 1930s or even earlier. Citizenship meant that all were granted a moral equality of status if not of income. Conservatives, too, were moved to accept a larger role for the state either by neo-corporatist inclinations or traditions or paternalism. In Sweden, Liberals proceeded steadily forward in their acceptance of increased statutory intervention, hailing Keynes and Beveridge as the examples.

During this period in Scandinavia and, less successfully, in Britain there was constructed what has been called the social citizenship state; the realisation of Alfred Marshall's vision which aimed to give all an equal social right to basic security and welfare regardless of their class or status position (Esping-Andersen, 1985). Social democratic parties built a broad social contract based on redistributive policies, forging a coalition of workers and the middle classes that gave their welfare states firmer political foundation than more residual and conservative ones, aimed primarily at the poor.

Its universality and all-inclusive scope was a crucial feature of the Anglo–Scandinavian Welfare State but not the only one. Even more important was universalism in the sense of not conditional on need which resulted in demand-oriented economic politics. Keynes provided theoretical legitimation for a distributive economic policy with sustained demand as the crucial variable and goal for government politics. Demand produced mass consumption which, in turn, produced mass production in a mutually reinforcing process.

A driving force of this development was not only social democratic strength but paradoxically enough in their weakness, namely their need to build coalitions and extend the basis of voters beyond the proper working class in order to maintain parliamentary power. This feature was particularly obvious in Scandinavia, where the farmers constituted the basis of the coalition from the 1930s. When the farmers rapidly declined as a social group in the 1950s, the social democrats looked for new coalition opportunities among the middle classes.

This was particularly the case in the Swedish struggle about supplementary pensions in 1957–58 where the social democrats came out as the great victors. In this battle they solidly established the basis of their power position which had been conquered in the 1930s with the support of the farmers and which was to last to the mid-1970s. The supplementary pension system, which was introduced, meant a change from basic security, as in the coalition with the farmers, to income security, which attracted the middle-class voters.

In contrast to the increasing taxes and duties was the growing social expenditures from which more and more social groups benefited, which meant an expansion of state functions as opposed to markets and voluntary associations. The increased role of collective consumption diminished the impact of personal risk, especially in the fields of health care, unemployment insurance and pension provision, and provided a cornerstone for the growing affluence experienced in Western Europe.

The growth of the welfare state was as much a reaction to the change in political culture accompanying the emergence of affluence as a contribution to it. The politics of affluence meant that expectations rose. These expectations required a political response in the form of welfare schemes. The role of expectations is demonstrated in Table 10.1. The expansion of welfare expenditures continued in the 1970s, when the economy of growth had been stagnating for half-a-decade or so, and the economic preconditions for the politics of collective consumption were about to change dramatically.

The increasing spread of taxation, directly or through employers' levies on wages, was spent on collective consumption, and gave a broader section of the population a stake in the political process. A new coalition emerged that demanded, in addition to a consolidation of welfare, a continuation of rising incomes and employment opportunities. Employment security became particularly expensive in the era of mass unemployment from the 1970s onwards, when labour in the emerging information society was increasingly replaced by robots and computers, and when labour could no longer be automatically exchanged, as in the industrial society. The politics of collective consumption faced its limits, although this was only barely being realised at the time.

The desire to guarantee a certain level of income security meant a tension in relation to a redistributive ambition in insurance schemes. This contradiction between basic security guarantee and the maintenance of status differentiation indicated long-term structural problems as early as in the 1960s. The expansion of the Welfare State promoted social and party political polarisation at the end of the 1960s. Several Western European governments appointed commissions to analyse the future of their programmes. Increasing political uncertainty about the future direction of welfare and social insurance emerged (Alber, 1982: 67) (see Table 10.2).

Expansion of government taxation has accelerated dramatically twice in Europe during the 20th century: during the First World War and the 10–15 years after the mid-1960s, that is when the economy of exceptional growth in the wake of the Second World War had already stagnated. During the First World War government income increased

Table 10.2   The financing of social insurance in 1950 and 1974. Sources of finance in the European OECD countries (%)

	Insured		*Government*		*Employers*	
	1950	*1974*	*1950*	*1974*	*1950*	*1974*
Austria	40.5	45.0	13.0	37.2	36.8	22.7
Belgium	28.9	31.6	34.3	26.8	40.5	28.3
Denmark	21.9	5.6	71.2	2.5	6.0	88.3
Finland	33.1	43.2	8.3	19.0	61.3	10.3
France	30.3	62.1	6.9	26.9	60.6	10.0
Germany	42.4	47.1	9.5	40.9	41.9	13.4
Ireland	11.1	22.0	63.9	17.5	28.0	53.4
Italy	3.2	87.8	4.2	14.9	55.9	23.1
Netherlands	48.0	19.1	29.6	31.4	50.0	18.0
Norway	19.6	45.6	28.5	51.0	34.4	9.5
Sweden	22.4	10.0	61.5	18.5	34.6	71.5
Switzerland	47.1	26.3	19.8	46.5	22.0	25.4
United Kingdom	37.4	30.7	27.6	38.4	45.4	13.8
Average	29.7	36.6	29.1	28.6	40.1	26.7
Standard Deviation	13.2	21.4	19.4	13.4	14.8	21.2

Source: Alber, 1982: 65.

dramatically and never returned to the prewar levels; often referred to as the displacement effect. From the mid-1920s to the mid-1930s the tax share of GNP accounted for by taxes increased very little from some 15 per cent to somewhat above 17 per cent. The Second World War had a similar although smaller displacement effect. In 1955 the tax share was 22.9 per cent, in 1960 23.4 per cent and in 1965 25.4 per cent. Then there was an accelerating increase to 29.6 per cent in 1970 and 31.3 per cent in 1975. This development is even more remarkable if we consider the proportions of the GNP accounted for by income taxes and employers' and employees' social insurance fees. This figure was 13.7 per cent in 1955, 15.2 per cent in 1960, 18.0 per cent in 1965, 21.1 per cent in 1970 and 27.4 per cent in 1975. In 20 years, the share had doubled (Flora, 1979).

At this point the limits of the expansion of government expenditures were discerned even with the expectations of lasting economic growth. These limits can hardly be defined empirically, although they are much easier to discern in principle and theory. They are situated where the economic foundation of the taxation state is in a process of long-term erosion and where capital escapes across the frontiers, and parliamentary democracy loses its political support. Tax protests and a kind of tax-welfare backlash became an increasing government problem in the 1970s and more so in the 1980s, with Thatcherism and neo-liberal monetarism (Wilensky, 1976).

The social theory of the welfare state was very much related to the theory of the growing pie, where two spheres, distribution and production are considered as two separate and autonomous units. The point of departure is economic growth in the sphere of production. In a second and separate phase, there is rational bargaining about the distribution in the framework of a social convention. This theory for the affluent society based on Keynesianism and neo-corporatism was called into question in the 1970s with decreasing growth rates and increasing social protests, at the same time as governments accelerated Keynesian strategies to ride out the storm, and political scientists invented the concept of neo-corporatism to describe an order, which was more deeply eroded than they realised. Economic growth was combined with income distribution, but the belief that both developed at the same pace, was undermined in the 1970s. It seems as if social solidarity and equality improved with economic growth to a certain limit, beyond which this growth became nervous and began to produce social inequalities (Jobert, 1979) (see Table 10.3).

Table 10.3 The growth of the GNP and of transfers in the European OECD countries 1951–75 (%)

	Annual growth of transfers	Annual GNP growth	Transfers as a percentage of GNP
1951	17.3	17.9	7.2
1952	19.0	10.7	7.7
1953	9.9	5.9	8.1
1954	5.7	6.7	8.1
1955	10.5	8.6	8.3
1956	10.2	8.2	8.4
1957	14.6	7.3	8.9
1958	11.1	4.4	9.2
1959	8.5	6.7	9.3
1960	7.1	12.4	8.7
1961	11.1	9.1	8.8
1962	13.5	8.6	9.3
1963	13.7	8.6	9.7
1964	12.7	11.7	9.7
1965	17.4	9.4	10.4
1966	11.9	7.9	10.8
1967	13.2	7.6	11.3
1968	13.2	8.7	11.8
1969	13.8	11.2	12.0
1970	12.0	11.5	12.5
1971	15.1	11.0	13.0
1972	16.0	12.3	13.5
1973	17.0	14.7	13.7
1974	20.9	14.1	14.4
1975	23.7	12.5	16.1

Source: Flora, 1979: 127.

References

Alber, J. (1982) *Vom Armenhaus zum Wohlfahrtsstaat. Analysen zur Entwicklung der Sozialversicherung in Westeuropa*, Frankfurt/Main.

Baldwin, P. (1990) *Politics of Social Solidarity*, Cambridge.

Esping-Andersen, G. (1985) *Politics against Markets: the Social Democratic Road to Power*, Princeton.

Flora, P. (1979) 'Krisenbeweltigung oder Krisenerzeugung? Der Wohlfahrtsstaat in historischer Perspektive' in: J. Matthes (ed.), *Sozialer Wandel in Westeuropa. Verhandlungen des 19. Deutschen Soziologentages, 17–19 April 1979*, Frankfurt/Main.

Gailbraith, J.K. (1958) *The Affluent Society*, London.

Galbraith, J.K. (1967) *The New Industrial State*, London.

Jobert, B. (1979) 'Die liberale kritik des Wohlfahrtsstaates in Frankreich', in: J. Matthes (ed.) *Sozialer Wandel in Westeuropa*. Verhandlungen des 19 Deutschen Soziologentages, Frankfurt/Main.

Kaelble, H. (1994) 'European Integration and Social History since 1950', in P.M. Lhtzeler (ed.), *Europe after Maastricht*, Oxford.

Kaelble, H. (1995) 'The Social History of European Integration' in C. Wurm (ed.), *Western Europe and Germany. The Beginning of European Integration, 1945–1960*, Oxford.

Milward, A.S. (1992) *The European Rescue of the Nation-State*, London.

Schmitter, P.C. (1974) 'Still the Century of Corporatism?', *Review of Politics*, Vol. 36.

Shonfield, A. (1965) *Modern Capitalism. The Changing Balance of Public and Private Power*, Oxford.

Stråth, B. (1987) *The Politics of Deindustrialisation*, London.

Stråth, B. (1996) *The Organisation of Labour Markets. Modernity, Culture and Governance in Germany, Sweden, Britain and Japan*, London.

Trigilia, C. (1991) 'The Paradox of the Region: Economic Regulation and the Representation of Interests', *Economy and Society 20*, 3.

Wilensky, H.L. (1976) *The New Corporatism, Centralization and the Welfare State*, London.

11
Japan Was Not A Welfare State, But ...

Toshiaki Tachibanaki

The purpose of this chapter is to evaluate whether, during the transition period from pre-rapid growth economy to post-rapid growth economy, Japan was or was not a welfare state. There are three views on the subject. The first is that the notion that Japan is indeed a 'welfare superpower', though this is decidedly a minority standpoint (Nakagawa, 1979). The second view does not necessarily state that Japan is a welfare state, but suggests that there is a Japanese-style welfare model. There is much support for this notion. The third is that Japan lags far behind in welfare aspects in comparison with the European welfare states (see, for example Yokoyama (1988)).

Overall, this chapter leans towards the third view. However, it suggests that this does not necessarily imply that the welfare level was so much lower in Japan than that in Europe. An important point in support of this is that the state, in the form of the Japanese government, did not play an important role in providing income support and welfare services such as medical care, public health, livelihood support, and so on. In other words, a large part of the cost of welfare services and income support was covered privately within families and firms, and equivalently was not paid by government transfers. Another important characteristic in Japan is that, because the role of the government was not crucial, there was no sense of a 'national minimum', which formed an important philosophical background for welfare states in Europe. If the government had acted as an anchor of the welfare state, it would have been necessary to establish a universal rule or framework (such as national minimum, mini–max principles, or other rules and principles) in order to have a comprehensive system welfare state with the consent of the people.

Since this chapter is primarily concerned with the period from pre-rapid growth economy to post-rapid economic growth economy, it will examine the relationship between the working of the private economy and the contribution of the government in both non-welfare fields and welfare fields. Put more simply, we examine the extent to which the minor role of the government in welfare provision was a contributory factor in attaining higher economic growth and in the efficient working of society and economy. This subject is interesting because welfare states are often criticised as a system that harms the achievement of such goals.

Objectives of the welfare state and Japanese interpretations

The welfare state in this study has two faces. The first corresponds to a narrow definition of the welfare state in which the public sector (at both national and local levels) administers the plan of welfare programmes and the actual daily operations. The government sector collects funds through taxation and/or social security contributions from both individual people and firms, and provides social services and various income support programmes such as medical care, old-age pensions, unemployment compensation, supplementary benefit for disabled and low income people and so on. There is one important distinction in this daily operation of the system. In some countries the public sector directly owns and manages institutions (typically hospitals and nursing homes) while in others the public sector bears the financial cost of these services, which are however operated through the private sector. In the latter case, employees are not civil servants, but they are private employees.

The second face of the welfare state corresponds to a broad definition, concerned with public policies in general, aimed at providing services such as education, public goods, merit goods, even military and diplomatic services and including, of course, social welfare programmes in a narrow sense as defined above. This definition embraces all services provided by the public sector and paid for through tax revenues and social security contributions. In other words, all revenues collected by the public sector are the financial source for these activities and services.

The distinction between narrow and broad definitions of the welfare state gives one insight into the contrast between small government and big government. Big government exists when various public services are generous, and thus when the ratio of the sum of social security contributions and tax revenues over national income or GNP is high. By contrast, one can speak of small government when various public services are not generous, and thus the ratio of the sum over national income is low. Since the level of social welfare services is able to indicate the degree of the welfare state, the degree of the welfare state can indicate the difference between a small government and a big government. It is noted that the distinction becomes complicated if we have to take into consideration the government's budget deficits. Since there is an argument about whether or not a big government reduces the efficiency and incentive aspect of economic activities performed by private citizens and firms, it is interesting also to inquire whether or not the welfare state reduces them as well.

When the efficiency aspect enters the argument of the welfare state, equity (or equality) must also be evaluated since there is a famous trade-off between efficiency and equity. The economic and social effect of the welfare state is directly related to this trade-off, and there are a large number of national and comparative studies that investigate this issue both theoretically and empirically. This trade-off is particularly important for Japan because of the role usually attributed to efficiency during the transition period between the low growth economy and the high growth economy. The social welfare aspect was not emphasised during that period. A more interesting observation on Japan is that the degree of equity and/or equality was considerably higher despite the low degree of welfare provision characteristic of a small government. This chapter attempts to explain this later, implying that a high degree of equality was achieved despite a lower degree of welfare provision.

In summarising the above, I prefer the wider view of the welfare state to the narrower view, and thus understand that the welfare state implies those economic and social policies of a country which emphasise the importance of equality and individual protection against social hazards.

If we turn now to consider why welfare states emerged, four main objectives and three main economic reasons can be supplied (Barr, 1992). The objectives were:

- efficiency;
- supporting living conditions;
- the reduction in inequality;
- social integration.

The economic reasons to explain its emergence were:

- traditional market failures such as imperfect competition, external effects, increasing returns to scale, public goods, and some others;
- information failures such as imperfect information about quality and price of goods, information asymmetry in insurances (i.e., adverse selection and moral hazard);
- public choice school, which emphasises the role of the electorate, and proposes that distortions and inefficiencies caused and led by both bureaucrats and politicians are likely to occur, when the government activity is big.

It is useful to discuss the Japanese perception of these objectives and economic reasons of the welfare state with emphasis on the examination of how the Japanese people and government assessed them and coped with the welfare programme.

The objective of *efficiency* has not been considered as an important element that should be pursued by the welfare state. In other words, better resource allocation and higher economic growth cannot be pursued by the welfare state, in particular the welfare programme, although a wider range of public policies such as tax policies, public expenditure policies and public investments, can seek efficiency in terms of better resource allocation and higher economic growth.

The Japanese discussion on efficiency has always been centred on the proposition that the welfare programme, or the welfare state, is harmful for achieving better resource allocation and higher economic growth because both firms and individual people have to contribute significantly through taxation and social security contributions. Such charges are likely to have negative effects on individual labour supply and savings, and firms' profits and investment activity. Of course, welfare payments also entail negative effects. This kind of argument is usually advocated by industrialists and the relatively rich, but it is one frequently made without presenting any quantitative evidence which supports such propositions empirically. It is true that no reliable statistical source exists in Japan, which allows an investigation into the effect on labour supply and personal savings. Moreover, no serious field work is available either. In sum, the argument is based only on causal impression.

There are, nevertheless, several studies that investigated whether or not the negative effects on work incentive, labour supply and savings can be supported empirically. Surveying these studies, I dismissed the likelihood of negative effects on work incentive, labour supply and savings, although a minor negative effect on labour supply for married women could not be ignored. A similar conclusion is available also for investment and profit of firms. Therefore, one should view the stress on negative effects proposed by industrial employers and the rich as elements in a campaign of political propaganda, lacking in serious empirical support (Tachibanaki, 1996b).

The objective of *supporting living conditions* has a long history in the welfare state argument. Barr raised three components in the form of poverty relief, the protection of accustomed living standards and income smoothing (Barr, 1992). Obviously, when we are interested in examining the welfare state, poverty relief is the most important component of the three because the other two can be managed through private insurances or citizens' own effort without necessarily receiving any government help.

Poverty is strictly related to the concept of the national minimum, which states that every citizen has the right to a minimum standard of living whose level is above the poverty line. The famous Beveridge Plan (1942), one of the classic writings in the history of the welfare state, proposed the importance of 'Freedom from wants' (poverty), and raised about eight different areas for which a society as a whole should be responsible. The fundamental proposition of the Beveridge Report recommended that the principal method to support a national minimum was the social insurance system through social insurance contributions collected from all citizens. Both the voluntary insurance system and the public assistance system, which does not require any social insurance contribution but is supported by the general tax revenue, should work only as supplementary systems to the social insurance system.

Looking at the objective of *reducing inequality*, there are two concepts of inequality. The first is concerned with vertical equity, which postulates redistributive policies from individuals and families advantaged in economic status to disadvantaged ones. The degree of redistribution differs from country to country. Japan belonged to a group of countries where in the past relatively strong redistributional measures in social security system and taxation were adopted (Tachibanaki, 1981: 92). Recently, there has been some demand for weakening such strong redistributional policies and I will return to this issue later.

The second concept is concerned with horizontal equity, which postulates that equal capability should be taxed equally, or pay the equal amount of social security contribution as well as social security benefit.

Unlike vertical equity this kind of horizontal equity has been managed badly in Japan. For example, the degree of under-reporting of income for tax purposes is considerably different by occupation even if their annual before-tax income is the same. This obviously violates horizontal equity.

Dignity, no stigma and social solidarity are the main concepts which represent *social integration* and are goals of the welfare state. Although these subjects are important, this study does not discuss them fully partly because it is hard to verify these issues by data, and partly because the discussion encompasses various subjects such as sociology, philosophy, ethics, and so on. These concepts, however, will be used later from place-to-place when the Japanese way of welfare is discussed.

At this stage, it is useful to look briefly at several characteristics of social welfare in Japan, before undertaking a detailed examination of the chronology of developments in social welfare, and the relationship between social welfare and general economic conditions. Such an overview can serve as an introduction to a detailed examination.

First, there has been always a feeling that generous social welfare, or in a more general term a big government, is detrimental to better private resource allocation and higher economic growth. As described above, this attitude has been dominant among industrial employers and is even shared within government circles.

Second, much emphasis is placed on the family as the site of social welfare and service delivery. For example, it is suggested that 'East Asian Social Welfare Regimes' distinguish themselves from a 'Western pattern' because Confucian family ethics and the feudal class system in the Edo period encouraged mutual aid and obligation among families (Dore, 1987; Goodman and Peng, 1995; Gould, 1993; Jones, 1993). This characteristic obviously reduces the role of the public sector as an institution to provide fellow citizens with welfare services. Although I do not deny the importance of family ties in Japan, it is not unique to Asia. Such feelings and obligations were common earlier even in Europe and North America. Moreover, this feature exhibits a decreasing trend even in Japan. I will argue this issue later again.

Third, enterprise welfare is frequently cited as a system which substituted for a welfare state because generous welfare services provided by large enterprises in Japan reduced the role of the public sector (Taira, 1970; Koyama, 1983; Fujita, 1984; Gordon, 1985). I have three comments on this. First, it is not unique to Japan; we can cite a not insignificant number of British, American and European companies that initiated generous company welfare programmes before the Second World War and that have continued to today. Second, it is possible to suspect that enterprise welfare in Japan was established to improve industrial relations between employers and employees in the firm rather than to supplement inadequate welfare programmes provided by the public sector. Third, enterprise welfare is observed only among large enterprises. Thus, employees in smaller firms (the great majority), the self-employed and farmers are excluded from this programme. This is a crucial problem.

Finally, there is one school that suggests that there exists an 'American–Pacific social welfare regime' (Rose and Shiratori, 1986). It questions the validity of conventional assumptions about the universal convergence of social welfare along the line of European-type welfare regimes and takes as its point of departure the small government, low social welfare expenditure models in the USA, Japan, Canada and Australia. This interpretation is sceptical of the so-called convergence theory, which suggests that modernisation and industrialisation lead to common features of social security systems in the form of the welfare state (Flora and Heidenheimer, 1981; Tominaga, 1987; Wilensky, 1975; Wilensky and Lebeaux, 1965). Since several American–Pacific countries are highly industrialised and developed, but are not welfare states in the sense of the European tradition, they can be the counter-examples against the convergence theory. Although it is somewhat questionable to regard Japan and the US as one group, the idea of the American–Pacific regime is interesting because these countries are different from the traditional European countries in the sense that self-help or self-reliance based on the preference of individualism is highly regarded.

Chronological development in social welfare in Japan and its interpretations

The *Meiji* and *Taisho period* (from 1860s to 1910s) can be characterised as providing no significant social welfare programmes through the public sector because families or households and local communities were responsible for health care and retirement incomes. Part of the explanation for this situation lies in the fact that the majority of people were employed in farming, retail trades and family-oriented industrial production. Unless some outside effort, for example by the government, was made to organise the system of social insurances, it is hard to expect a grassroot effort. Although some authors have pointed to the Gonin Gumi Seido (Group-of-Five System in Tokugawa Japan (1600–1867)), and the Rinpo Sofu (a system of neighbourhood watch and mutual aid associations) in the Meiji State (1868–1912)

(Dore, 1967; Goodman and Peng, 1995), their capabilities were quite limited and an expansion to the national scale took place only after the Second World War.

Second, there was no significant social mobility or regional labour mobility, implying that parents and children engaged in common occupations (for example farmers and traders) and that people remained in common communities from generation to generation. In these circumstances it was natural for aid in the field of economic support and health care to be provided mainly within families and, to a limited extent, by local communities.

Third, it is important to note that aid within families was not entirely motivated by altruism – gift exchange or strategic purposes also played a role. Parents left land, shops, workshops and financial assets as bequests and gifts for their children (usually the eldest son) who, in turn, were responsible for continuing the parents' business and, in exchange, for taking care of their aged parents. If no son was available, a comparable arrangement was made elsewhere within the family. This type of intergenerational transfer was common in Asia and is not unknown in Europe and North America (Tachibinaki, 1994a).

Fourth, one could argue whether such familial aid, which can be a substitute for social welfare programmes, satisfied family members. My understanding is that, willingly or unwillingly, most people were obliged to obey such a tradition partly because it had been a social norm and partly because there were no alternatives. The pre-industrial period, when the majority of people were poor and less educated, produced such a social norm naturally. I tend to believe that people accepted such an arrangement unwillingly, because once the country had industrialised, people preferred more social welfare programmes and less familial aids. In other words, children no longer followed their parents' occupations, but wanted the freedom to decide careers for themselves and to move freely to other locations and regions. Industrialisation encourages this preference and movement.

Three laws related to social security were implemented *before and during the Second World War,* aimed at implementing a social security system in the field of health and pensions. Since they were deeply flawed both in the coverage of people and the amount of payments, they should not be regarded as the birth of social security. In particular, the right to live was not universally approved, allowing Fukutake to brand the reforms as only a pre-history social security system (Fukutake, 1983).

The new constitution after the war, in particular article 25, officially approved the right to live. Thus, it is possible to describe the postwar period as the beginning of the social security system in Japan. Democratisation, reconstruction, land reform and some other important reforms, recommended by the American occupation force, were proposed and implemented – as was reform in social security. At the same time, several laws covering unemployment compensation and labour accidents were prepared. However two major fields in social security, namely medical care and retirement pension, escaped reform partly because of the prevailing social and economic chaos after the war and partly because these areas were extremely underdeveloped.

In 1950 the *post-war reform* of social security was proposed by the Committee for the Social Security System, and it officially approved the right to live as its main underlying principle. The fundamental rule of social security was recommended. In the first half of the 1950s, however, the damage of war was enormous. People were poor, and thus the most urgent goal of the social security system was the alleviation of poverty. Despite the strong policy measures adopted, it is impossible to judge the policies as successful. Everybody was poor in that period.

Besides the war against poverty, there are several important characteristics in this 1950 reform, which determined the future course of social security in Japan. Some of them can be regarded as representing the origin of the Japanese-type social welfare and it is worthwhile discussing them. First, the principle of social insurance was recommended as a fundamental and central governing rule in medical care and retirement pension programmes for two reasons. First, there was the influence of the Beveridge Report. Second, since everybody was poor, the state was at the time obliged to form voluntary social security systems. In other words, those who were too poor and unable to participate in social insurances and pay the contributions were excluded from these schemes.

Second, private enterprises were recognised as institutions sharing some of the responsibility for developing social security systems. For example, each large firm formed and managed its own medical insurance programme financed from contributions by both employers and employees, with 20 per cent contribution from the general government tax revenue. By contrast, the government managed medical care insurance for employees in smaller firms (that is the number of employees is over five) but funded in a similar way to those of large enterprises. These examples clearly suggest that firms played a major role in forming and managing medical insurance programmes. Civil servants also formed their own programme. The remaining people (employees in extremely small firms, self-employed, farmers and retired people) were covered by a web of local authorities that together made up the national health insurance programme.

Third, the above description clearly demonstrates that health insurance programmes were organised and managed by an extremely large number of institutions. These comprised individual firms, government agencies, various occupational groups such as teachers, medical doctors, nurses and other professions. This gave rise to several difficulties. First, since the management of a medical insurance programme comprised numerous small segments operating separately, the financial condition of health insurance programmes differed considerably from segment to segment. Second, there were no benefits of economies of scale to be enjoyed. Only with a truly national health programme, such as that of the UK, can there be a considerable saving in administrative costs. These two difficulties lay behind the appearance of many financially troubled health insurance programmes at a later stage. Integration is a major policy issue and is still under debate even today. The main reason for approving such an extremely large number of separated health insurance programmes at that time lay in the fact that people demonstrated too little solidarity to accept integration, arguing that the existence of several financially sound health insurance programmes disapproved the need. At the bottom line, they refused to transfer their surplus to troubled programmes.

Last, a transfer from the general government tax revenue to social security systems was proposed. As we saw, it had been accepted that 20 per cent of social security payment should be covered by the general tax revenue. Since the first priority of the government expenditure at that time was for reconstruction and industrialisation, no resource transfer was made at the time. It was postponed until the 1960s, by which time rapid economic growth had considerably increased the amount of tax revenue. This example suggests that a transfer of the general tax revenue to social security is feasible only when the amount of tax revenue is considerably large.

The late 1950s marked the beginning of the rapid economic growth that changed the whole structure of Japanese society and economy. The growth rate of the economy was already 9.1 per cent in the late 1950s. Strong industrialisation and higher productivity growth led by high exports and prosperous domestic investment activity strengthened the economy. Since the causes of this development have already generated a large literature (Kosai and Ogino, 1984; Minami, 1986) I do not discuss them in detail here. Nonetheless, it is necessary to observe two characteristics during the rapid economic growth, which are strictly related to social welfare programmes and social security.

First, the personal saving rate was quite high. This high rate was one of the most important causes of the rapid economic growth, which provided the entire economy with a sufficient financial source for investment activity. When the high rate of personal savings is evaluated from the suppliers' viewpoint (that is, households), it reflects the inadequacy of the social security system since households felt obliged to save a lot to accumulate sufficient wealth for uncertainty and consumption after retirement. Indeed several economic studies consider the insufficiency of the system as one of the causes for the high personal savings rate in that period. In my personal judgement, the story can better be viewed from the other side of the coin, whereby the high personal savings rate lowered the government's incentive to provide a sufficient and generous level of social security in Japan. If individual people or households have enough savings, it is not necessary for the government to worry about their citizens' uncertainty, future income or welfare. This form of the chicken and egg problem requires further investigation to confirm which relationship is the more realistic.

Second, although the social security system was further refined, it was still underdeveloped because there were large numbers who were not covered by any welfare programmes. For example, it is reported that in the late 1950s about 3 million people (about 10 million people, if their family members are included) remained outside all medical care insurance – particularly employees in extremely small firms (employing five or less) and the self-employed. A similar situation prevailed for retirement pension programmes again because small firms and the self-employed lacked the financial and administrative means to undertake such programmes on their own. After the initial stage of the rapid economic growth (that is, the late 1950s) the Japanese economy took-off into the *full-scale rapid economic growth* at the beginning of the 1960s. The famous 'Income-doubling Plan' of the Ikeda Cabinet, aspiring to a doubling of per capita income in ten years was launched in December 1960. This was surpassed in practice.

In 1961 the principle of social security for all people was achieved. The social security system was extended to cover all citizens, including now employees in extremely small firms, farmers and self-employed. Part of the reason was that, since Japan had attained economic prosperity, the people and the government felt that the next task was to develop the system to the level prevailing in Europe. This formed part of a wider objective of 'catching up' to the Western industrialised nations

(Goodman and Peng, 1995). National statistics in 1960, for example, showed that Japan devoted 5.6 per cent of national income to social security expenditure, compared to over 13.0 per cent in many European countries and about 20 per cent in West Germany. This performance was regarded as miserable, implying that Japan was welfare-backward or a welfare-underdeveloped country. The need to catch-up seemed indisputable. However, the low Japanese figure does not necessarily imply that the country was so underdeveloped. First, since the age distribution was biased toward younger generations, the level of social security payments (both pensions and medical care) was consequently lower. Second, as emphasised earlier, families and enterprises played an important role in welfare provision, thus reducing the proportion of expenditure through governmental transfer. These two factors combined meant that Japanese welfare provision was not as inferior as it seemed, although it still lagged behind the European levels to which the government now aspired.

A second reason behind the extension of the system was that inequities now became apparent. In Medicare insurance the distinction between the enterprise-based health insurance system and the non-enterprise-based equivalent (for self-employed, farmers, retired people and employees in extremely small enterprises) was obvious because the former received an employer contribution (that is, 50–50 contributions rate between employers and employees) whereas the latter was largely self-funded. Therefore, the budget of the former was healthier and the benefit provisions more generous than the latter, which frequently required subsidies from both central and local government. A similar situation prevailed for retirement pension programmes. In both cases the financial weakness of non-enterprise-based schemes prevented them from providing better services for their members. This distinction reflects the traditional dual structure in Japanese industries, which suggests that larger firms have an enormous lead over smaller firms in productivity, wages and working conditions. This distinction was even more obvious for social security, although the wealthy farmers and small businesses did not suffer much. One can speak of a dual structure in social security, and it was accentuated, and made more visible, by the economic divergence caused by the persistence of rapid economic growth.

Third, it is important to bear in mind that the dual structure did not create large social problems because large transfers from central and local government buoyed-up disadvantaged non-enterprise schemes. This, in turn, was possible because the rapid economic growth generated extremely large and unexpected increases in tax revenues. The media called this 'scattering social welfare', and it was characterised as an almost endless extension and expansion of the system.

Fourth, an important improvement was achieved in another field. That was a significant increase in the level of income support or supplementary benefit for extremely poor people. In 1961, the level was increased by 20 per cent. More important was the change in the rule for determination of the amount. Previously it had been based on the criterion of absolute poverty. This was now altered by the introduction of the so-called 'relative concept' aimed at reducing the gap in living standard between ordinary households and those receiving assistance. This brought Japanese practice in line with that of most developed countries. One important feature of income support is the low take-up rate in Japan. A comparison between Japan and the UK, presented in Table 11.1, reveals that while the take-up rate in the UK increased considerably from 1950 to 1970, that of Japan showed a gradual decline. In 1970 almost six times as many people claimed benefit in the UK than in Japan – an amazingly large difference. The recent study by Atkinson shows that the UK, the Netherlands and Germany have incomplete take-ups, while France has a high rate of take-up (Atkinson, 1995a,b). Since the UK is listed as a country with a low take-up rate, then Japan's case is much lower by international standards.

It is possible to raise several reasons for this low take-up rate in Japan. First, the means test is very strict and this discourages many potential claimants. Second, the government sector did not make much effort to find eligible people and to persuade them to claim assistance. Third, people were complacent about the rights given them by law. Fourth, there was a feeling of stigma, shyness, shame or other psychological reluctance in receiving the assistance. Finally, even if a person were eligible, he or she would be unable to receive benefit if close relatives

Table 11.1 Take-up rates of income support in Japan and the UK 1950–70

	UK (1) (%)	Japan (2) (%)	(1)/(2)
1950	3.9	2.30	1.70
1955	4.4	2.16	2.04
1960	5.3	1.74	3.05
1965	5.4	1.63	3.31
1970	7.7	1.30	5.92

Source: Soeda (1988).

could support him or her financially. A higher take-up rate in the future will only be possible if such barriers are reduced.

Fifth, the rapid economic growth helped one area of the social pro-gramme, namely unemployment. The unemployment rate was consid-erably lower during the period and it has continued to be so until the 1990s, despite several serious recessions and an overall slow-down of growth (Tachibanaki, 1966a, 1996b). If the number of unemployed were relatively small, the role of unemployment compensation, which is one of the most important social insurances, should also have been small. According to Atkinson the most important reason for poverty in the UK is unemployment (Atkinson, 1995a) and this is probably also true of other European countries which have considerably higher rates of unemployment. Unemployment plays an important role in the social security system and reducing the number of unemployed should be an important goal of social policy.

It is true that Europe's experience in the 1960s also exhibited low rates of unemployment. Therefore, the case of both Japan and Europe suggests one doctrine, namely that the necessity of social welfare pro-grammes is reduced during periods of economic strength. The growth economy also benefited the financial condition of social insurances in medical care and retirement income enormously, because of the growth of the level of social insurance contributions. The growth economy itself is probably the most crucial remedy for the social disease, which calls for a welfare state provision. Alternatively, a strong economy enables us to have generous welfare programmes. The period of rapid eco-nomic growth in the 1960s in Japan rigorously supported this view.

Sixth, it is remarkable that inequality in income distribution was also lower during the period of rapid economic growth. Since many writers believe that there is a trade-off between efficiency and equity (that is the degree of efficiency would entail the sacrifice of a degree of equity) income distribution and/or wealth distribution should have been more unequal. However an international comparison by Sawyer demon-strates that the degree of inequality in income distribution in Japan was much lower than the average figure of all OECD countries, and was almost equivalent to the lowest level prevalent in the Scandinavian countries (Sawyer, 1976). Several studies have shown that income distribution data in Japan have two serious deficiencies. First, the data excludes households with only one member, whose income level is usually lower than average. Second, it excludes income figures for farmers and retired people (Tachibanaki and Yagi, 1997). These two deficiencies are likely to a certain extent to reduce the degree of inequality in income distribution and this should lead us to treat Sawyer's conclusions for Japan cautiously.

It is true, nevertheless, that the degree of inequality in income distribution in Japan was lower than in other advanced countries, although it was not at the lowest level. Japan seemingly provides a counter example against a popular trade-off between efficiency and equity. Although I can only answer the question briefly, it is interesting to inquire into the cause of a lower inequality in income distribution and a higher economic growth in Japan. First, wage distribution was fairly equal owing largely to the seniority payment rule for many employees. Second, partly because of the low interest-rate policy during the rapid growth period, the share of property incomes in total income was relatively small, and property incomes are a notorious contributor to a skewed distribution. Third, the period of rapid growth in Japan corresponds to the period of a lower degree of inequality in terms of the Kuznets' inverse U-shaped curve that postulates the following. At the initial stage of industrialisation or economic development the degree of inequality in income distribution is low and then it increases with economic development. After reaching the highest degree of inequality, it starts to decrease. Thus, the most advanced countries have normally had low degrees of inequality in income distribution and I guess that Japan in the 1960s and early 1970s was at the end point of the Kuznets hypothesis. Incidentally, Tachibanaki and Yagi showed that the degree of inequality in income distribution was considerably higher in the late 1980s and early 1990s (Tachibanaki 1996b; Tachibanaki and Yagi, 1997). Thus, the Kuznets inverse U-curve showed an increase again. In sum, it would be useful to adopt the Kuznets thesis to explain the relatively low degree of inequality in income distribution based on the history of Japanese economic development rather than seeking the cause of the counter example against a trade-off between efficiency and equity.

The Japanese economy reached *the final stage of rapid economic growth* in the early 1970s when per capita GNP was close to the average of the OECD countries. Such rapid economic development enabled the government and the Japanese people to think about social welfare programmes much further. In particular, the issue of living conditions became an important policy matter.

The year 1973 has been dubbed by the media as the 'first year of social welfare' because several crucial reforms in social welfare were implemented. Both the government and the people felt that, in addition to experiencing strong economic development, Japan had also become an advanced country in social welfare. The declaration that Japan is now a welfare state was frequently made. Two immediate comments and subsequent outcomes, which will be argued later, are possible. The first is that the statement that Japan had become an advanced country in social welfare is misleading. It is an overstatement stemming from overconfidence. The second is that for Japan the oil crisis ended the age of rapid economic growth in the early 1970s and Japan became a more stable economy for the next 20 years. This feature changed public opinion towards social welfare programmes. Before examining these two comments, it is necessary to explain why the year 1973 was the first year of social welfare. First, the amount of income support for the poor was increased considerably. Second, both the coverage and the payments for health insurance and pension programmes were improved. Third, a price indexation system was introduced for public pensions. Fourth, family allowances and child allowances were introduced. Fifth, free health care was introduced for those aged over 70 years of age (Yokoyama, 1988). Specialists proclaim that the last two features were epoch-making in the history of Japanese social welfare programmes. All these reforms were made possible by the abundant tax revenues received by both central and local governments thanks again to the previous rapid economic growth. Now I will argue the above two comments in detail.

I interpret the first comment, that Japan now is a welfare state, as an overstatement. First, international comparison shows that the rate of social security contribution, the rate of tax burden and their combination over national income in Japan were lower than those in other industrialised countries, as is given in Table 11.2. In 1970, as a percentage of national income, the rate of social security contribution and the tax burden in Japan were by far the lowest, and lower by about 10 percentage points compared with other countries. Even the more recent figures in Table 11.2 do not drastically alter this impression. On the basis of such statistical comparison Japan cannot be said to be a welfare state. However, as emphasised before, this does not necessarily imply that the level of welfare was so much lower than that in other countries. Part of the contribution of both families and enterprises does not appear in this table. More importantly, the increase in the payment level of both medical care and retirement income was not based on a very rigorous and plausible actuarial calculation. The government was optimistic about the future course of the economy, predicting that the growth economy would persist into the 1970s and 1980s, and with it a continuing increase in both tax revenues and social security contributions. The two oil crises turned this prediction into a nightmare. While

Table 11.2   The rate of tax burden, social security contribution and their combination over national income in 1970 and 1991

Country %	Tax burden		Social security contribution		Total	
	1970	*1991*	*1970*	*1991*	*1970*	*1991*
Japan	19.4	27.4	5.4	11.8	24.8	39.2
US	29.3	25.6	7.4	10.7	36.8	36.3
UK	40.6	39.4	7.9	10.6	48.5	50.0
France	29.1	33.7	18.9	28.1	48.0	61.8
		(1989)		(1989)		(1989)
West Germany	30.3	29.2	15.3	21.8	45.3	51.0
		(1990)		(1990)		(1990)
Sweden	42.2	42.0	11.5	13.5	53.7	55.5
		(1988)		(1988)		(1988)

Source: OECD National Accounts of OECD Countries.

the failure of many economists to anticipate these events relieve the government of some blame, it does not absolve it altogether, since the government committed itself to too high social security payments without paying serious attention to the revenue side.

Let us now turn to the second comment and outcome: that Japan had become a stable economy, with lower rates of growth than previously. It is an irony that the declaration of the welfare state, albeit exaggerated, and the end of the growth economy coincided. One important phenomenon, namely a trend towards an ageing population structure, was also predicted at that time. Several improvements in social welfare programmes in 1973 increased public expenditure considerably and it was one of the causes of the budget deficit in the public sector. These pessimistic stories and predictions – slower economic growth, a ballooning public sector deficit and an ageing population – altered the view toward welfare programmes. One group of people and politicians suggested that the generous social security system was responsible for the budget deficit and that it harmed economic growth. This kind of opinion was explained in the first half of this chapter and is not repeated here again. A new characteristic was that this kind of proposition gained ground not only in Japan but also in many other advanced countries. More precisely, the world became dominated by new liberalism and conservatism. Their philosophical background was provided by Hayek, Friedman and some others (Friedman, 1962; Hayek, 1960). In the real world political power also shifted to the so-called

Reagan–Thatcher–Nakasone line, which preferred lower government involvement, less generous welfare programmes, more respect for freedom and responsibility, and higher expectations from the private sector. This inspired some reforms in social welfare programmes and their influence even extended to the Scandinavian countries, where traditionally a national consensus on the welfare state had prevailed.

Another group of people and politicians stress the importance of social welfare programmes. However, the power of this group was relatively weak both in Japan and elsewhere and so it was the opinion of the first that dominated political decisions and directed welfare reforms. The debate between the two groups was so intense that social security became one of the most important policy issues in several elections of congressmen and governors in Japan in the 1970s. In most cases, political parties or candidates who objected to social security in their electoral campaigns were defeated, leading most candidates to either support the importance of social welfare programmes or at least keep silent for the duration of the campaign. This does not necessarily imply that the winning parties or candidates were particularly eager to develop social welfare programmes further, because they were also aware of the constraints already described above.

The Japanese electorate is immature in the field of social security, in that they do not fully recognise that social welfare provision requires somebody to contribute to the system, or sound financial resources to enable the system to operate well. In other words, they still think that social security payment is covered by somebody who is 'unknown', or even by God, or that it comes from heaven. Put more scientifically, people are much interested in the payment side but are not concerned with the contribution side. As described previously, this characteristic was also true to a certain extent in government circles in its optimism about the budgetary consequences of the 1973 programmes. This kind of immaturity must disappear if social welfare programmes are to work well.

Still on the topic of the second comment and outcome, it has been suggested by governments and industrialists in many countries that generous social welfare provision is harmful for economic growth. The Reagan–Thatcher–Nakasone line believed it rigorously. As already emphasised, the Japanese case lacks any strong evidence for this contention. I concluded previously that it is only a political campaign. It is true that several studies by eminent economists support the claimed harmful effects of welfare programmes on efficiency and economic growth in Europe (see Lindbeck *et al.*, 1993 for Sweden, and Dréze and Malinvaud, 1994 for Europe). Atkinson (1995b), however, concludes after reviewing many studies that the results are mixed and that it is too early to yield conclusive evidence about it. He called for more studies and Japan is no exception to this call.

The path toward reform

By way of conclusion on this section, I suggest three important elements, which determine the future course of social welfare programmes in Japan. The first is that the role of families, which substituted for the public sector in the past, is a decreasing trend. Individuals can support themselves financially to a considerable extent without much help from their families, and at the same time they love to be independent and want to live without outside interference. Typical evidence is the decline of the extended family. This popular preference will lead to the demand for much higher levels of social welfare provisions and transfer payments. I only hope that Japanese people will also recognise the necessity for a higher level of contributions.

Second, the role of enterprises, in particular larger enterprises, which also substitute for the public sector, must be reduced. There has been a discrepancy in treatment in the Japanese welfare programmes between employees in larger firms and those in extremely small firms, farmers and the self-employed. When Japan was an underdeveloped economy, it was obliged to rely on the social welfare role of larger enterprises at least for employees in those enterprises because the country could not care for all the people. Japan is no longer an underdeveloped country. Moreover, society allowed large enterprises to save on the cost of corporate taxes by committing to enterprise-based welfare programmes and by employees in larger firms also enjoying lower personal income taxes. It is unfair to favour both large firms and their employees through taxation. It is time to eliminate this feature in Japanese social security, for example, by modifying what I called 'the dual structure in social security', by reducing non-wage fringe benefits and forcing larger firms to compensate for them as wages (Tachibanaki, 1994b, 1997).

Third, the above point supports the integration of the social security system and the tax system, including the disparate and separate medical insurance programmes and retirement income programmes into a single national health insurance system and national retirement pension scheme. This would allow us to throw away the so-called dual structure in social security, and to eliminate some discriminatory treatment by sex, occupation, size of firm and industry in social welfare programmes (Tachibanaki and Shimono, 1994).

References

Atkinson A.B. (1995a) *Incomes and the Welfare State*, Cambridge.

Atkinson, A.B. (1995b) 'The Welfare State and Economic Performance', *LSE Welfare State Programme Working Paper No. 106*, London.

Barr, N. (1992) 'Economic Theory and the Welfare State: A Survey and Reinterpretation', *Journal of Economic Literature*, Vol. XXX, pp. 741–803.

Beveridge, Sir William (1942) *Social Insurance and Allied Services*, Cmd. 6404, London.

Dore, R.P. (1967) *Aspects of Social Change in Japan*, Princeton.

Dore, R.P. (1987) *Taking Japan Seriously: A Confucian Perspective on Leading Economic Issues*, London.

Dreze, J. and E. Malinvaud (1994) 'Growth and Employment: The Scope for a European Initiative', *European Economic Review*, Vol. 38, pp. 489–504.

Flora, P. and A. Heidenheimer (1981) (eds) *The Development of Welfare States in Europe and America*, New Brunswick and London.

Friedman, M. (1962) *Capitalism and Freedoms*, Chicago.

Fujita, Y. (1984) *Employee Benefits and Industrial Relations*, (in Japanese).

Fukutake, N. (1983) 'Fundamental Problems in Social Security', in Social Security Research Institute. Chapter 1.

Goodman, R. and I. Peng (1995) 'Japanese, South Korean and Taiwanese Social Welfare in Comparative Perspective', *LSE Welfare State Programme*, Working Paper No. 112. London

Gordon, A. (1985) *The Evolution of Labour Relations in Japan*, Cambridge.

Gould, A. (1993) *Capitalist Welfare Systems: A Comparison of Japan, Britain and Sweden*, London.

Hayek, F.A. (1960) *The Constitution of Liberty*, Chicago.

Jones, C. (1993) 'The Pacific Challenge: Confucian Welfare States', in C. Jones (ed.), *New Perspectives on the Welfare Stated in Europe*, London.

Kosai, Y. and Y. Ogino (1984) *The Contemporary Japanese Economy*, London.

Koyama, M. (1983) 'Social Security as a Policy System', in Research Institute for Social Security, *Fundamental Problems in Social Security*, Chapter 4, Tokyo (in Japanese).

Lindbeck, A., P. Molander, T. Persson, O. Petersson, A. Sandmo, B. Swedenborg, and N. Thygesen (1993) 'Options for Economic and Political Reform in Sweden,' *Economic Policy*, Vol. 17, pp. 219–64.

Minami, R. (1986) *The Economic Development of Japan*, London.

Nakagawa, Y. (1979) 'Japan, the Welfare Super-Power', *The Journal of Japanese Studies*, Vol. 5, pp. 5–51.

Rose, R. and R. Shiratori (1986) (eds) *The Welfare States East and West*, Oxford.

Sawyer, M. (1976) 'Income Distribution in OECD Countries', *OECD Occasional Studies*, Paris.

Tachibanaki, T. (1981) 'A Note on the Impact of Tax on Income Redistribution', *Review of Income and Wealth*, Vol. 27, pp. 327–32.

Tachibanaki, T. (1992) 'Japanese Tax Reform: Equity versus Efficiency', *Public Finance*, Vol. 47, pp. 271–85.

Tachibanaki, T. (1994a) (ed.) *Savings and Bequests*, Ann Arbor.

Tachibanaki, T. (1994b) (ed.) *Life-cycle and Income Support*, Tokyo (in Japanese).

Tachibanaki, T. (1996a) *Wage Determination and Distribution in Japan*, Oxford.

Tachibanaki, T. (1996b) *Public Policies and the Japanese Economy: Savings, Investment, Unemployment and Inequality*, London.

Tachibanaki, T. (1997) 'Transformation from Non-wage Fringe Benefits to Wage Payments', in N. Yashiro, (ed.), *Income Support and Aging Society*, Tokyo (in Japanese).

Tachibanaki, T. and K. Shimono (1994) *Personal Savings and the Life-Cycle*, Tokyo (in Japanese).

Tachibanaki, T. and T. Yagi (1997) 'Distribution of Well-Being in Japan: Towards a More Unequal Society', in P. Gottschalk, B. Gustafsson and E. Palmer, (eds), *Changing Patterns in the Distribution of Economic Welfare*, Cambridge.

Taira, K. (1970) *Economic Development and the Labor Market in Japan*, New York.

Tominaga, K. (1987) 'The Determination of Social Security: Formation of the Welfare State and Its Universal Interpretation', *The Quarterly of Social Security Research*, Vol. 23, no. 1 (in Japanese).

Wilensky, H.L. (1975) *The Welfare State and Equality: Structural and Ideological Roots of Public Expenditure*, Berkeley.

Wilensky, H.L. and C.N. Lebeaux (1965) *Industrial Society and Social Welfare*, New York.

Yokoyama, K. (1988) 'Social Security After the First Year of Social Welfare', in University of Tokyo Institute of Social Sciences, *Welfare State in Transition*, pp. 3–78 (in Japanese).

12
The Transformation of the European Countryside

Wendy Asbeek Brusse

Economic and historical studies on Europe's postwar 'Golden Era' have usually paid little attention to its impact on the countryside. Many analysts saw this growth spurt as a predominantly industrial and urban phenomenon. Moreover, while Keynesian economic and political analysis prevailed among contemporary observers, the main unit of analysis tended to be the country as a whole rather than its regional components. Be that as it may, this contribution assumes that even in the broadly similar industrialised societies of Western Europe, the transformation from austerity to affluence in the rural community is worth examining in its own right.

Europe's countryside provides a unique and very profound focus on transformation. Although one can easily dispute the logic of using this unit of analysis, the 1950s and 1960s brought a set of similar challenges to rural areas distinct from those in urban settlements. This article examines the nature of this transformation by considering how and to what extent the change from austerity to affluence affected Europe's rural communities.

Before surveying these issues, the concept of countryside requires clarification because it can be approached either from an occupational, economic, demographic, socio-cultural or ecological perspective or from a combination of these (Robinson, 1990: 12). Here, 'countryside' and 'rural area' are used interchangeably. The words rural community refer to those sections of the population living outside cities, towns and large villages, whereas agricultural community refers only to those people in the countryside employed in farming (Bandini, 1971: 44).

Many European governments adopt different definitional criteria, which serve to complicate international comparisons. For instance, the official Swiss definition of a rural settlement is that of a community of

10 000 inhabitants or less, the French and German that of fewer than 2000 inhabitants whereas the Danish authorities only consider a population of under 250 as rural (see Table 12.1).

This problem also occurs if we compare the official rural population statistics (based on the UN's classification using the national criteria described in Table 12.1) with agricultural employment in European countries. This shows that Switzerland and Greece both had more than 60 per cent of their total population officially classified as rural in 1951. However, their rural economic and social circumstances could hardly have differed more; 16 per cent of the Swiss population depended for a livelihood on agriculture (including forestry) compared to 49 per cent of the Greek.

Clearly, the drawback of employing just the official definitions is that they underscore the complex historical, economic, social and cultural differences between rural areas in Europe. Countries whose shares of rural population were more or less similar during the transformation period may have had entirely different rural economies and societies as a result of diverging rates of population growth, agricultural structures and patterns of land use or government policies. Moreover, rapidly changing patterns of settlement and land use further complicate the analysis of the countryside. Historical processes of urbanisation, rural industrialisation and suburbanisation in Europe have tended to blur the distinction between sparsely and densely populated areas and between occupational activities in rural and urban areas. Over time, therefore, determining where urban areas begin and where the countryside ends has become an increasingly arbitrary business. Nevertheless, even though official definitions vary, at least they have in common that the urban side of the equation may incorporate some rural components while the rural segment excludes urban elements. Given the large weight of population living in urban areas, these official definitions of rurality are unlikely greatly to distort a broad comparative analysis. This study of Europe's countryside therefore begins by looking at the wider picture using official definitions. In subsequent sections a more nuanced analysis will emerge from three national case studies of economic and social transformation in Europe's countryside.

The choice of these national cases is guided by Robinson's definition of rurality, based on a total of 15 different demographic, economic, social and physical variables (such as: population density, shares of arable land, permanent crops and forest, tractors and fertiliser consumption per head of the population, GDP per capita, and food imports and exports as a share of total imports and exports). These were recorded

Table 12.1 Comparison of agriculturally active populations in Western Europe at various times of the population census

Country	Year	A %	B %	Official definition of rural areas
40–50 per cent				
Spain	1950	49	63	Communities of less than 10 000 inhabitants
Greece	1951	49	63	Agglomerations of less than 2000 inhabitants
Portugal	1959	48	69	Agglomerations and other administrative areas of less than 2000 inhabitants
Ireland	1951	40	58	Settlements of under 1500 inhabitants
30–40 per cent				
Austria	1951	32	51	Communities of less than 5000 inhabitants
Italy	1961	30	41	Communities of more than 50 per cent of the economically active population working in agriculture
20–30 per cent				
France	1954	27	43	Communities with less than 2000 inhabitants in the administrative centre
Luxembourg	1947	26	42	Communities with less than 2000 inhabitants in the administrative centre
Norway	1950	26	50	Clusters of less than 20 houses
Denmark	1950	25	31	Agglomerations of less than 250 inhabitants
West Germany	1950	23	25	Communities of less than 2000 inhabitants
Sweden	1950	20	34	Sparsely populated area with less than 200 inhabitants
Netherlands	1947	20	40	Municipalities with a population of less than 10 000 inhabitants
10–20 per cent				
Switzerland	1950	64	64	Communities with less than 10 000 inhabitants
Belgium	1947	37	37	Communities with less than 5000 inhabitants
10 per cent				
United Kingdom	1951	5	20	The area outside legally established boroughs and urban districts

A   Population engaged in agriculture, forestry, hunting and fishing.
B   Rural Population.
Source: UN ECE, 1962.

for 1970, when the transition from austerity to affluence can be considered completed even in more 'backward' parts of the countryside. What he did was to cluster these countries according to their rank–order correlation with respect to such indicators. The outcome of this statistical exercise is three different groups or clusters of countries, each with certain rural characteristics in common at the end of their transformation (see Table 12.2). If we limit ourselves to the major European countries under examination in this book, we can distinguish a first group of three, comprising Austria, Norway and Sweden. These shared relatively high per capita incomes, low shares of agriculture in GDP, forestry as an important part of their rural economies and the typical rural inhabitant living in isolated dwellings or hamlets in open countryside.

Within the second group, France and Italy still had relatively large agrarian populations whose contribution to GDP and exports remained

Table 12.2   A typology of the European countryside, 1990

Country groups	Group characteristics
Austria Norway Sweden	• high proportions of forest land • high GDP per capita • small share of agricultural production in GDP • low population density
France Italy	• large share of population economically active in agriculture • large share of agricultural production in GDP • large share of food exports in total exports • small share of purchased inputs • large share of permanent tree crops • large share of extensive agriculture • low levels of investment in agriculture
Belgium Luxembourg West Germany Netherlands UK	• small share of population officially classified as rural • small share of population economically active in agriculture • small share of agriculture production in GDP • high GDP per capita • high population density • large share of intensive, 'industrial' agriculture • high levels of investment in agriculture • food imports exceeding food exports
Denmark Switzerland	• high GDP per capita • large share of agricultural production in GDP • low population density

Source: Robinson, 1990.

substantial at the end of the transformation. In both countries there existed large regional differences between rural areas, such as those between modern capital intensive, small village-dominated regions in northeastern France and the Italian Po valley on the one hand, and extensive, low income regions with medium-size villages in southern France and southern Italy on the other. These relatively backward regions represented the last remainders of traditional peasant society.

A third group, comprising the Benelux countries, West Germany and the UK, combined high per capita GDPs with high levels of investment in an increasingly 'industrial' agricultural sector and a small share of the population working in agriculture. The rapid pace of urbanisation in these relatively densely populated areas resulted in growing urban and industrial pressure on the countryside throughout the 1950s and 1960s. A residual group to which also Denmark and Switzerland belong, consisted of countries that were too diverse to cluster on the basis of the variables chosen.

Although still subjective, this classification offers a method for selecting national case studies that cover different transformation experiences. For the purpose of this article, one country from each of the three clusters is chosen, that is, Sweden, France and the Netherlands. Where the empirical data allow this, their experiences are used to obtain details from different angles of the rural perspective. It should be stressed again, though, that the information available does not always allow for rigorous comparison of rural indicators across countries.

The economic transformation of the countryside

While the postwar move from austerity to affluence in the countryside involved broadly based social as well as economic changes that require attention, there are reasons for perceiving it first and foremost as associated with two interlinked and mutually reinforcing processes of economic change: urbanisation and agricultural modernisation. In many European countries the two postwar decades witnessed expanding industrial employment opportunities and relatively high wages and incomes in urban centres, which pulled labour away from the countryside and encouraged urbanisation (Robinson, 1990: 25). Reinforcing this process of industrial expansion and rural depopulation was the modernisation of agricultural production. In many areas a decline in agricultural labour promoted widespread mechanisation, specialisation and the use of industrial and biochemical inputs, thereby boosting land reforms and economies of scale. The resulting rapid increases in labour productivity further triggered rural out-migration of agricultural workers in search for industrial employment (Grigg, 1982).

Before tracing the impact of these changes, it is well worth stressing that neither urbanisation nor rural depopulation nor agricultural modernisation were specifically postwar phenomena. They formed part of a long-term process of rural economic development and change rooted in early industrialisation (Gavignaud, 1987). Moreover, these changes took place across a range of regional economies and societies, each with their own rural traditions and development trajectories. If we want to grasp the characteristics of the countryside's postwar transformation and its unprecedented impact on rural life, we should begin by examining very briefly the historical background of rural change in Europe.

Migration from rural to urban areas has been a continuous feature of European history. Around 1850, however, rural growth created such pressures that neither the widespread fragmentation of farms and plots nor the growth of off-farm employment (in crafts, services and proto-industries) could absorb all the rural labour. It was then that the 'normal' pace of migration from rural areas to towns made way for a continuous rural exodus that outpaced natural population growth in the countryside. Simultaneously, the upward trend in Western Europe's agricultural labour force was reversed (Grigg, 1992: 25–7; Zelinsky, 1963: 106–7; de Vries, 1984; Bairoch *et al.*, 1988). While in Western Europe as a whole the decline in absolute numbers employed in agriculture began fairly slowly around 1920, the timing and degree of this decline varied substantially across nations. At one extreme of the spectrum were the UK, Belgium and later also Switzerland, where rising employment in mining and manufacturing in the second-half of the 19th century had caused a gradual outflow of rural population into towns. At another extreme one can find the Netherlands and Austria, where the rural and agricultural population only reached their peak after the Second World War. Moreover, in each of these cases along the spectrum the share of agricultural labour in the total labour force differed a great deal (see Table 12.3).

In the second-half of the 19th century, industrialisation, rural out-migration and the growth of urban centres corresponded with major improvements in agriculture. Use of harvesting machinery and combines, introduction of guano and artificial fertilisers, soil improvements through drainage and fertilisation and, not least, concentration of production through consolidations of fragmented land all resulted in rapid increases in yields per hectare. In addition, exploitation of new land in the Americas and the advent of cheaper and improved means

Table 12.3 Timing of the decline in the agricultural labour (male and female) force for various Western European countries, 1851–1947

Country	First year of absolute decline in numbers	Percentage of labour force in numbers
United Kingdom	1851	21.9
Belgium	1866	44.4
Switzerland	1880	42.4
Germany	1907	36.8
Sweden	1920	40.2
France	1921	41.5
Denmark	1930	35.6
Norway	1931	35.3
Italy	1936	48.2
Austria	1939	39.0
Netherlands	1947	19.3

Source: Grigg, 1982: 109.

of transportation meant that arable farming in Europe faced increased competition from overseas (Bairoch, 1989; Tracy, 1982: 387).

The degree to which these innovations penetrated rural areas differed substantially across Europe. At the risk of simplifying, one can identify several broad typologies of rural transformation that developed in reaction to technological improvements and urbanisation (Hoggart *et al.*, 1995: 81). Central to these distinct models are differences in patterns of land settlement and tenure, farm size and agricultural policies. In many regions of continental Europe, population pressure and international competition initially failed to bring about a major overhaul of landholding patterns and farm structures.

In West Germany, France and Italy, where dominant classes of landowners lived alongside impoverished masses of mixed peasant smallholders, rural economic development was retarded by protectionism and insufficient innovations, land consolidations and infrastructural improvements (Tracy, 1982: 34). In Britain, the main form of land tenure became that of mercantile estates. Fairly low density of land occupation meant that ownership patterns were concentrated around landlord–tenant affiliations. Rural communities initially suffered from the challenges of cheap grain from overseas, concentration of land ownership and rural depopulation. By the turn of the century, however, these large farms had become well suited to large-scale mechanisation and efficient, capital intensive production methods (Tracy, 1982: 56).

Denmark experienced a rather different process of adaptation to broadly similar challenges. Early land reforms around 1800 had encouraged tenant purchases of landholding and had helped build a strong group of independent farmers. By the 1890s, faced with strong population pressure, emigration and growing numbers of landless, the Danish authorities had allowed several remaining large estates to be subdivided and sold to landless farmers. They had also successfully promoted farmers' co-operatives, which raised competitiveness in mixed small-scale farming and strengthened rural communities (Hoggart *et al.*, 1995: 82–3). Several features of this Danish model can also be found in the Netherlands, Sweden, Belgium and Switzerland, which also had fairly large groups of small- and medium-sized farms occupied by tenant farmers. However, only the Netherlands addressed the international competition and technological change of the late 19th century with an export-oriented agricultural policy similar to that of Denmark (Dovring, 1965: 246–7; Tracy, 1982: 387–8).

If rural outmigration and declines in agricultural labour in many European regions had commenced as early as the 19th century and if a technological revolution had begun even earlier, why should we isolate rural transformation in the postwar period? What was so revolutionary about the countryside's demographic and agricultural changes after 1945? The key determinant of Europe's postwar transformation is the sheer scale of revolutionary improvements in agricultural productivity in combination with, and reinforced by, an unprecedented pace of outmigration. Agricultural productivity increases in the 1950s, 1960s and 1970s even outpaced those in industry (Bairoch, 1989: 343–4). As we will see below, these intertwining economic and demographic developments in turn had unprecedented consequences for social life in rural areas.

The rural transformation of the 1950s and 1960s

Demographic trends in the countryside show that throughout Europe the rural population (defined by national criteria) fell drastically between 1950 and 1975 as a result of outmigration to expanding industrial centres. Whereas in 1950 around 48 per cent of the total European population (including Eastern Europe) could still be classified as rural, this percentage had dropped to 33 by 1975 (see Table 12.4). The drop was most pronounced in Southern Europe, which experienced a decline in rural population from 64 to 41 per cent and it was smallest in Northern Europe. Western Europe's rural population fell from 27 to 23 per cent.

Table 12.4 Changes in rural and urban population in European regions, 1950, 1960, 1970 and 1975

	Urban	Rural	Rural population as % of total
Northern Europe			
1950	–	–	32
1960	0.9	−0.2	30
1970	1.1	−0.8	26
1975	0.7	−0.5	25
Western Europe			
1950	–	–	37
1960	2.2	−1.0	30
1970	1.5	−1.0	25
1975	1.2	−1.4	23
Southern Europe			
1950	–	–	64
1960	2.3	−0.2	59
1970	2.5	−0.7	51
1975	1.7	−0.7	41
Europe			
1950	–	–	48
1960	1.9	−0.4	43
1970	1.6	−0.7	37
1975	1.4	−0.8	33

Source: UN ECE, 1979: 179.

Again, national and regional developments differed. Italy, for instance, provides a classic case of a country where rising urban employment pulled large numbers of agricultural workers away from their rural communities. In Belgium, the Netherlands and Denmark migratory movements within rural areas understated the degree of change in the countryside. These countries witnessed population movements away from remote rural areas to rural towns. In Sweden, where a relatively modest agricultural labour force held small-size, uneconomic plots, a similar but larger outmigration took place (see Table 12.5).

Britain formed the major exception in the 1950s. Although it also harboured many regions with significant outmigration, such as Scotland and some part of Wales, its total rural population actually grew slightly, because improved public transport facilities in prosperous towns and increased car ownership began to enable urban, white-collar workers to settle in less remote rural villages. As we will discuss later, in other European countries this 'suburbanisation' process, in which rural villages

Table 12.5 Rural and urban population developments in Western European countries, 1950–70

	Rates of change (%)								
	1950s			1960s			1970s*		
	T	U	R	T	U	R	T	U	R
Austria	0.2	0.4	–	0.5	0.9	0.1	0.2	0.8	−0.4
Belgium	0.5	1.0 D	−0.2	0.6	4.6	−11.9	0.3	0.4	−0.1
Denmark	0.7	0.3	1.1	0.7	D	D	0.4	1.0	−2.0
France	1.1	2.1	−0.5	1.1	2.8	−2.2	0.8	1.0	0.1
West Germany	1.1	1.8	−0.9	0.9	1.4	−1.1	0.3	0.8	−2.0
Italy	0.6	2.1	−0.5	0.7	1.6	−0.3	0.5	1.3	−0.9
Netherlands	1.3	1.6	0.5	1.3	1.0	2.3	1.0	0.7	1.9
Norway	0.9	0.9	0.9	0.8	3.6	−0.9	0.7	2.1	−0.4
Sweden	0.6	D	D	0.8	1.9	−3.0	0.6	1.2	2.3
Switzerland	1.4	4.9	1.2	1.5	2.1	0.7	0.8	1.9	−0.4
UK:									
England and Wales	0.5	0.4	1.0	0.6	1.5	1.5	0.4	0.2	1.1
Scotland	0.2	0.2	–	0.1	−0.1	0.4	−0.1	−0.4	0.9
Northern Ireland	0.2	0.6	0.2	0.7	0.9	0.5	0.6	0.3	1.0

T = Total population
U = Urban population
R = Rural population
D = change in definition of rural and urban between two succesive censuses
* = early 1970s
Source: UN ECE, 1979: 182.

and areas function as extensions of suburbs for young, middle-class families escaping from the undesirable aspects of urban life, did not occur until the 1960s.

Apart from overall population movements, rural participation rates are another demographic characteristic worth examining. Male participation rates in rural areas followed the general decline at the extreme end of the age groups (that is, 15–24 and over 54) taking place in advanced industrial states. In 1970, early entry and late withdrawal from the labour market were still characteristic for this rural male workforce, but by then improved education opportunities and expanding social security had narrowed down the difference in most countries. In Sweden, for instance, the rural male activity rate (defined as all economically active males aged between 15 and 59 per 100 of the population aged 15–59) dropped from 88 to 80 between 1960 and 1970.

Female participation rates increased in most urban areas, but it is not clear whether this trend also occurred in the countryside. The evidence from Sweden and Switzerland (two Western European industrialised countries for which age and sex specific data are available in this period) points in different directions. In Sweden, female participation in the countryside followed the national trend; it went up in most age groups, although somewhat more slowly than in urban areas (see Table 12.6). One explanation for this slower pace is that rural women traditionally already tended to participate in work on the land, which they could combine relatively easily with raising a family. Moreover, since they would often work unpaid on a family farm, their participation would not usually be recorded in the censuses.

The Swedish case can be contrasted with that of Switzerland, where female participation in rural areas did not follow the national trend. In 1960, participation rates of Swiss women in the countryside were consistently higher than those of urban women, but while urban rates for women went up in all age groups except those under 24, rural rates declined quite significantly in all age groups. In this case, therefore, the unusually high female participation rate must reflect a more generous registration system.

Activity rates by age suggest that by 1960, the average age of rural inhabitants was rising significantly because young males and females began to leave the countryside. In France, the share of people living in rural areas aged over 55 rose by 2 per cent between the two census dates 1962 and 1965, whereas their share in total urban population remained constant. The Swedish countryside witnessed a more pronounced population ageing. Between 1960 and 1970, the percentage of the over 55 increased from 28 to 35 per cent in the countryside. By comparison, in urban areas the proportion of the aged went up from 21 to 24 per cent (see Table 12.7).

As observed earlier, the unprecedented drop in agricultural population represents the main component of depopulation in Europe's countryside. The interwar period had seen only small changes in numbers employed in agriculture; rural outmigration had been dominated by non-agricultural village workers such as shopkeepers, builders and artisans (Mendras, 1971: 226). The 1950s formed the turning point when the exodus of agricultural labour accelerated. In France, Austria and Germany, though, the decline in absolute numbers active in agriculture was even larger in the 1960s (see Table 12.8). Outmigration initially affected males and females more or less equally, but it began to be more female-dominated once agricultural migration reached its peak (Dovring, 1965: 383). The explanation for this is that men tended to lead the rural exodus as seasonal or permanent migrants while

Table 12.6 Female activity rates in Sweden and Switzerland, 1950–70

Country	Rates per 100 females of given age																				
	15–19			20–24			24–34			35–44			45–54			55–59			>60		
	N	U	R	N	U	R	N	U	R	N	U	R	N	U	R	N	U	R	N	U	R
Sweden																					
1950	54	–	–	57	–	–	32	–	–	27	–	–	30	–	–	26	–	–	27	–	–
1960	47	49	49	39	61	43	39	61	2	36	41	19	36	43	43	32	38	18	27	30	17
1970	23	31	23	47	55	42	47	55	36	53	55	40	53	56	56	41	44	29	29	31	21
Switzerland																					
1950																					
1960	64	63	66	46	73	74	46	73	49	41	36	49	42	36	36	39	34	45	46	39	54
1970	59	56	53	48	73	69	48	73	43	44	46	41	45	47	47	40	41	38	40	40	40

N = national
U = urban
R = rural
Source: ECE UN, 1979.

Table 12.7 Rural and urban population older than 55 years of age, in France and Sweden (various census years)

Country	Census year	Rural %	Urban %
France	1962	27	23
	1968	29	23
Sweden	1960	28	21
	1965	32	23
	1970	35	24

Source: UN, 1979.

women stayed behind in the traditional social environment of the village and the family. With rising opportunities for urban employment in services, however, young women increasingly began to leave the countryside while at that stage in the migration flow young men tried to settle in their own villages as full-time farmers (Mendras, 1971).

The pull from fast growing, high income urban and industrial areas was a major cause of rural outmigration in Europe. However, in many regions the push from agricultural modernisation was even more forceful, particularly in those rural regions where farm structures underwent drastic changes. Improvements in size and spatial disposition of farmland proved fundamental for obtaining internal and external economies of scale. Since these advancements in farm structure, in turn, were main determinants of rural income levels and living standards it is worth examining these trends.

Historically, agricultural land fragmentation had been a major hindrance to agricultural prosperity in Europe. Many individual farmers owned plots that were small in size, of irregular shape and scattered across regions, and the average number of plots per farm could be as high as 30. As a result, labour and land productivity in these areas remained low, as did farm profitability. One estimate suggested that on the basis of 1950s technical standards, at least 30 per cent of agricultural land in Europe (including Eastern Europe) would require consolidation. In some countries this meant that 40 per cent or more of the nation's agricultural land needed restructuring (see Table 12.9).

Additional OECDs-estimates derived from national criteria indicate that this problem soared in the 1950s and 1960s. Farm tractors and combine harvesters had become the symbols of technical progress and capitalisation, in the same way that family automobiles symbolised modern consumerism in urban areas. They had conquered European

Table 12.8 Active population by economic sector in Western Europe, 1950, 1960 and 1970

	Agriculture	Industry	Services	Total changes in population active in agriculture		
				Year	000	%
Austria						
1951	33	37	30	1951–61	−310	−28.8
1961	23	47	30	1961–71	−342	−44.5
1971	14	43	43			
Belgium						
1947	13	50	37	1947–61	−169	−40.0
1961	8	48	45	1961–70	−92	−36.2
1971	5	45	51			
Denmark						
1950	25	34	41	1950–60	−151	−29.2
1960	18	37	45	1960–70	−123	−33.5
1970	11	36	53			
France						
1962	21	39	40	1962–68	−758	−19.4
1968	16	40	44	1968–75	−1040	−33.0
1975	10	39	51			
FRG						
1950	23	43	34	1950–61	−1549	−30.2
1961	13	49	38	1961–70	−1595	−44.5
1970	8	48	44			
Italy						
1951	42	32	26	1951–61	−2604	−31.5
1961	29	40	31	1961–71	−2415	−42.7
1971	17	44	38			
Netherlands						
1947	20	34	46	1947–60	−301	−40.2
1960	11	43	47	1960–70	−156	−34.9
1971	6	37	57			
Sweden						
1950	21	41	38	1950–60	−185	−29.3
1960	14	45	41	1960–70	−170	−38.0
1970	8	40	51			
Switzerland						
1950	17	47	37	1950–60	−75	−21.1
1960	11	51	38	1960–70	−50	−17.9
1970	8	48	44			

Table 12.8 (Continued)

	Agriculture	Industry	Services	Total changes inactive population in agriculture		
				Year	000	%
England and Wales						
1951	5	49	46	1951–61	225	23.7
1961	3	48	46	1961–71	178	24.5
1971	3	45	52			
Scotland						
1951	7	50	43	1951–61	−37	−22.4
1961	6	45	49	1961–71	−40	−31.3
1971	4	42	54			

Source: UN ECE, 1979.

Table 12.9 Land fragmentation and area in need of consolidation in Western Europe, 1950

	Average size of plots (ha)	Plots per ha	Plots per farm	Area in need of consolidation (assessments adapted for 1950)	
				100 of ha	as % of agricultural area
Country					
Denmark	–	–	–	150	5
Sweden	–	–	3.2	250	5
Netherlands	2.3	0.4	6.8	1000	43
Belgium	1.1	0.9	18	500	28
France	0.9	1.1	9.7	9000	30
Switzerland	0.5	2.0	9.7	450	38
West Germany	0.7	1.4	10	6000	50
Austria	–	–	–	1000	40
Italy	0.6	1.6	10.6	6500	40

Source: Dovring, 1965: 40.

farms to such an extent that by 1960 even the smallest French peasant could not be seen to work without them (Duby, 1976: 148–9). In all of Europe excluding Russia the number of tractors went up from 1.77 million to 4.58 million and the number of combine harvesters increased

Table 12.10   Uneconomically
viable units as a percentage of all
farms in Western Europe, 1971

Country	%
Sweden	62–84
Italy	64
Norway	58
France	53
Ireland	50
Netherlands	50
West Germany	50
Austria	26
Denmark	15–30

Source: Clout, 1971: 4.

from 96 500 to 557 000 over 1955–65 (Clout, 1988: 17). Ironically, though, changes in farm size, farm layout and rural settlement were too slow to allow for their optimal use (see Table 12.10). In all but a few countries examined more than 50 per cent of all farms were not considered viable by national standards. As one expert summed up the situation: 'The whole structure of the European countryside is becoming more inefficient as each year goes by and scientific and technical advances are applied to farming. The scale of agricultural activity demands dramatic enlargement' (Clout, 1988: 24). European governments thus tried to establish modern, efficient family farms, only to discover that their target was constantly moving (Bandini, 1971: 46).

After the rural exodus had started, in reaction to growing discontent among the remaining low-income smallholders, most governments adopted more rigorous reform policies to improve farm incomes by raising efficiency. One widely applied measure involved extending grant and credit schemes for farm improvements, co-operatives, and education and advisory services. More drastic measures for structural reform such as land consolidation and farmland enlargement usually followed, but their ambitions and results varied with the political economy of countries and regions (Clout, 1988: 42). The cases of France, the Netherlands and Sweden will illustrate this.

Traditionally, French governments saw agriculture as a vital component of social and political stability. During the Fourth Republic, farming interests benefited from a relative over-representation in electorally influential rural areas. The authorities gave lavish subsidies and credits and shunned large-scale reforms (Kolinsky, 1980: 140; Tuppen, 1983: 50–1). However, slow productivity improvements in marginal areas, growing discontent among small and medium-sized farmers and, above all, the requirements of industrial expansion and economic competitiveness within the EEC dictated drastic structural changes. By 1961, after mass demonstrations had left farmers internally divided, the traditional farmers' lobbies were outmanoeuvered by a coalition of the agricultural ministry and young, dynamic farmers united in the Cercle National des Jeunes Agriculteurs (CNJA), who represented the growing middle peasantry that was ready to accept structural change (Kolinsky, 1980: 142–4). In 1960 and 1962, two laws were passed to transform land holdings into efficient, viable units and to improve agricultural incomes and living standards (Clout, 1988: 89). Such measures were only the first in a long series of government sponsored welfare programmes to promote affluence in the countryside.

In the Netherlands, consensus on agricultural policies ruled throughout the 1950s and the larger part of the 1960s (Bauwens and de Groot, 1990: 146–54). The Dutch government's primary goal was to maximise agriculture's contribution to national income and exports by increasing productivity and reducing labour costs (Van den Brink, 1990: 113–14). Two major instruments of its structural policy were land reclamation and land consolidation for farm enlargement. Between 1954 and 1962, this resulted in a rise in the area under consolidation from 150 000 to 300 000 hectares. Paradoxically, though, despite this focus on increasing the size of farm enterprises, the inevitable need to reduce their numbers remained a taboo subject throughout the 1950s. Not until the 1960s did the ministry of agriculture explicitly recognise the need actively to reduce farm numbers. It was then, too, that a movement of so-called 'Free Farmers' (Vrije Boeren) became more vociferous in its criticism of the government and traditional farmers' organisations. This protest movement would eventually join the large farmers' protest actions against the EEC's Common Agricultural Policy (CAP) that swept across Europe in 1974 (Bauwens and de Groot, 1990: 152–6).

In Sweden, the first postwar policies for structural reform were also introduced earlier than in France, in the form of direct income support and rationalisation programmes. These measures intended to improve the size and quality of farm operations (by introducing better farm buildings and machinery) increase the size of arable or forestland and hence raise productivity and incomes. At the same time, the local physical planning institutions were charged with facilitating the transfer of redundant labour from rural areas to urban settlements (OECD, 1964: 398–403).

Clearly, the changes brought about by agricultural modernisation and structural reforms varied widely, as can be seen from Table 12.11. Generally, the outflow of labour was accompanied by a decline in the number of holdings and a rise in their average size. This resulted in drastic increases in the ratio of land to labour and labour productivity. Hired, non-family workers (who wanted to benefit from high wages outside agriculture) declined most in number, closely followed by family workers. However, there were several exceptions to this rule. In Italy and Denmark, the drop in family workers equalled that of hired farm labourers. France and the Netherlands, by contrast, witnessed by far the largest decline in the number of family workers, whereas for Sweden the number of farmers and family workers dropped almost by the same percentages.

Declining agricultural employment had a profound impact on economic activity in the countryside. Despite the lack of internationally comparable figures, it is clear that there has been a general trend towards rising shares of non-agricultural rural labour; employment 'industrialised' and part-time farming often became increasingly widespread (UN ECE, 1979: 269). The statistics for off-farm activities and income in rural areas close to urban centres, part-time employment in factories, public services, tourism and transport rose steadily (UN FAO, 1965: 61–2). In the 1950s, about half of the farmers in Austria and Norway, and 10 per cent of farmers in Denmark depended on off-farm payments, which sometimes amounted to 20 per cent of their total incomes. The Swedish trend was similar; farmers' shares of net income from off-farm work rose from 15 to 21 per cent between 1957 and 1961. For smallholders this share increased up to 40 per cent (UN FAO, 1965: 63).

Thus, behind the overall decline in agricultural employment a dual trend emerges. On the one hand there were rural communities where employment became even more agriculturally centred because hired farm labourers went to urban areas. In the less remote and more industrial 'open' rural communities, on the other hand, population influxes caused rises in secondary and tertiary employment. These benefited most from industrial growth, industrial decentralisation and rising mobility (Duby, 1976: 318, 359–60).

Incomes and living standards in the countryside

Now that the processes of urbanisation, rural depopulation and agricultural modernisation have been analysed, the next step is to map their influence on rural incomes and living standards. When and to what

Table 12.11 Change in active agricultural population by category of farm worker and change in the number and average size of holdings in Western Europe (%)

Country	Period	Farmers (i)	(i) + (ii)	Family workers (ii)	Non-family workers	Change in no. of holdings	Change in average size of holdings
Austria	1950–61	–	–25	–	–46	–46	+10
Belgium	1950–62	n.a.		n.a.	–36	–36	+21
Denmark	1950–61	–6		–44	–44	–44	+4
France	1954–62	–13		–35	–28	–28	n.a.
Germany	1950–60	–	–31	–	–56	–56	+19
Italy	1951–61	–14		–34	–34	–34	n.a.
Netherlands	1947–60	–8		–45	–39	–39	+22
Sweden	1950–60	–35		–37	–30	–30	+12
Switzerland	1950–60	–15	–	–21*	–	–	+10
UK	1950–60	–	–3	–33	–23	–23	n.a.

* = includes family and non-family workers.
Source: OECD, 1964: 28–29.

extent did the countryside share in the rise to affluence? To answer this question, the following social and economic indicators will be examined:

- wages, earnings and incomes
- private household consumption expenditure
- housing conditions
- rural community services

Wages, earnings and incomes

Since early rural earnings and income data are seldom comparable, agricultural statistics are used here as a proxy (UN ECE, 1967). An FAO study on wage rates and earnings in Europe for the period 1951–57 showed that rises in agricultural wages often lagged behind those in industry, which in many countries began to accelerate around 1952 (UN FAO, 1958). Other studies showed that in absolute terms agricultural workers' wages remained below those of industrial workers. Even so, agricultural wages did climb more steadily a few years later, and in some countries they improved more substantially than industrial wages.

Long run trends in relative agricultural earnings provide a less rosy picture, though. With the exception of West Germany, relative earnings in agriculture improved significantly in the first postwar years, but subsequently they stagnated or even declined. Between 1954 and 1964, only West German relative earnings experienced noticeable improvements (see Table 12.12) (Vriens, 1965: 17–19). Swedish and Danish male earnings rose modestly, the Dutch stayed the same, whereas Italian, Norwegian and British deteriorated somewhat. In most of these countries, this unfavourable development reflected falling profitability

Table 12.12 Male wage earnings in agriculture relative to male wage earnings in manufacturing in Western Europe, 1938–64

Country	1938 %	1948 %	1954 %	1964 %
Denmark	44	65	60	60
West Germany	64	66	67	67
Italy	43	58	60	60
Netherlands	61	83	88	88
Norway	42	76	71	71
Sweden	50	70	68	68
Switzerland	42	47	47	47
United Kingdom	481	72	69	69

Source: UN ECE, 1967: Chapter 5, 16.

due to the more rapid rise in the prices of agricultural inputs relative to those of agricultural output. This meant there existed little room for increases in agricultural wages and salaries.

Despite these relatively late and slow improvements in relative earnings, agricultural incomes did improve. Real incomes in Sweden rose by more than 70 per cent, whereas in Austria they almost doubled. With a 60 percent increase over the period, Norwegian per capita incomes grew somewhat slower and remained well below those in Sweden. France and Italy, which started off from low levels, also experienced very large income improvements. By the end of the 1960s, French average per capita incomes in agriculture had even surpassed those in Germany. In the Netherlands and Belgium, average agricultural incomes continued to rise throughout the period until they eventually surpassed British average income levels.

The upward trend in agricultural incomes was everywhere accompanied by a rise in consumption. To what extent not only farmers and agricultural workers but the entire population in the countryside managed to improve consumption levels is difficult to trace for the early period in the transition to affluence. Fortunately, for Denmark, France and Sweden the data offer some national trends in household and per capita consumption expenditures (see Table 12.13). Not surprisingly, these show that in the mid-1950s total consumption per household was substantially higher in urban than in rural areas. Per capita consumption differentials were larger still, since most rural households had to share lower incomes and levels of total expenditure with more household members than their urban counterparts.

National consumption trends show some other interesting developments. In Denmark, the gap between rural and urban total household expenditure levels was still intact in 1966, but per capita differences with more urbanised, less remote rural parts had more than disappeared. The Swedish statistics also point towards a convergence of expenditure levels; the 16 per cent difference in total consumption expenditure existing in 1958 had shrunk to 4 per cent in 1969. In per capita terms, however, the convergence was less complete, since the gap shrank from 22 to about 14 per cent.

The French census for 1956–57 suggests that rural household members dependent on agricultural employment were much worse off than members of an average French household. Interestingly, by 1972, rural inhabitants working outside agriculture had almost bridged the consumption expenditure gap with average household members; in per capita terms, the difference fell from 16 to less than 7 per cent.

Table 12.13   Indices of average total consumption expenditure per household in France, Denmark and Sweden, 1955–75

(Rural and urban in 1955 = 100)

Denmark	Salaried employees and wage earners	Indices of total consumption	Indices of per capita consumption	Size of household
1955	Rural and Urban	100	100	2.8
	Rural	85	71	3.2
1966	Rural and Urban	263	263	2.8
	Rural areas with urban populations	225	316	2.6–3.2

(Rural and urban 1958 = 100)

Sweden	All categories	Indices of total consumption	Indices of capita consumption	Size of household
1958	Rural and Urban	100	100	2.8
	Urban communities	97	105	2.6
	Large cities	126	98	3.6
	Rural communities	86	78	3.1
1969	Rural and Urban	191	198	2.7
	Large cities	213	220	2.7
	Rural communities	183	171	3.0

(Rural and urban in 1956–7 = 100)

France	Indices of total consumption	Indices of total consumption	Indices of per capita consumption	Size of household
1956–7	Rural and Urban	100	100	3.1
	Urban	109	116	2.9
	Rural non-agricultural	81	84	3.9
	Rural agricultural	98	78	3.0
1972	Rural and Urban	330	330	3.1
	Urban	324	279	3.1
	Rural non-agricultural	275	307	3.1
	Rural agricultural	265	249	3.3

Source: UN, 1967, 1977.

Moreover, again in per capita terms, these consumption levels had overtaken their urban counterparts. However, this contrasted sharply with agricultural households in the countryside, whose consumption had lagged still further behind. The 22 per cent disparity with overall (urban and rural) expenditure levels had risen by about 2.5 per cent between the two census dates.

Housing conditions

Changes in housing conditions provide another indicator of the timing of rural affluence. In the immediate postwar years, large parts of Europe's urban and rural population suffered from poor housing conditions, but since the war had inflicted much more damage upon towns than on rural settlements, it was obvious that government gave priority to rebuilding and renewing the urban housing stock. Urbanisation and agricultural depopulation added to this logic, especially if rural migrant flows into urban centres were causing acute housing shortages (UN, 1976: 47). However, surveys from the late 1950s indicate that this policy choice had begun to take its toll because rural housing had deteriorated substantially. Houses were on average much older than those in urban environments and often lacked basic facilities such as piped water inside, w.c.s, baths and sewerage system connections. In Northern Europe, piped water supplies in kitchens were more widespread, but even in remote rural parts of Sweden, Denmark and the UK, they were usually absent (UN ECE, 1962: 14).

By 1960, housing conditions in the Northern European countryside had improved considerably. In Sweden, almost 80 per cent of rural dwellings were equipped with piped water inside and sewerage system connections. In the Netherlands, more than 90 per cent of all houses had such a connection. In France and Italy progress was much slower but substantial nonetheless. Only 34 per cent of French rural dwellings in 1954 were equipped with piped water inside and only ten per cent possessed w.c.s. Eight years later, these percentages had risen to 59 and 21 respectively (UN, 1964 and 1968). As always, however, the statistics conceal large disparities. In various remote, poorly developed rural parts such as in Western Brittany, in Poitou-Charente or Aquitane in France, it was common practice until the late 1950s for farming families to live under the same roof as their animals and for farmworkers to be housed in barns (Rogers, 1983: 111). In the Netherlands, as late as 1956, 21 per cent of all these had to live, sleep and cook in houses with only one or two rooms. In the Northern provinces of Groningen and Friesland these percentages were as high as 35 and 41 (Maris and Rijneveld, 1963: 65).

Rural community services

The age of affluence brought more than improvements in basic amenities. The industrialisation and modernisation of agricultural production, the settlement of industrial enterprises in rural areas and the development of small, rural villages into centres with regional service functions all helped to promote economic and social well-being in the countryside. Technical and social infrastructures were improved, employment opportunities outside agriculture increased and economic, social and cultural differences between rural and urban communities began to fade. By 1960, 'automobilisation' and the growth of leisure activities added to this convergence process. Urban tourists flocked to the countryside in search of recreation whereas middle-class families with children settled in new, rural estates (Dyurand-Drouhin and Szwengrub, 1982: 4–5).

However, large parts of Europe's countryside never completely made the transition to affluence, even if they seasonally experienced urban tourist flows. These communities underwent a creeping process of decline and deprivation. The pattern of this phenomenon depended on a complex set of factors and circumstances that goes beyond the scope of this chapter. Clearly, it occurred most often in regions with small, dispersed rural settlements in peripheral and marginal areas, where there existed few alternatives to agricultural employment. In such communities, the outflow of young workers led to an ageing of the population and a decline in the level of local provisions such as shops, schools, bus and postal services and doctors, whose supply became increasingly uneconomical (Gilg, 1983: 94–5; Duby, 1976: 375). Other objective and subjective factors could strengthen this trend, such as the mechanisation of farming (which made traditional services provided by blacksmiths, builders or woodcutters redundant) and increased car, telephone and television ownership (which allowed rural consumers to shop in urban centres) (Groot, 1972: 89–90; Tonkens, 1963: 181–90). In the 1960s and 1970s, when the welfare state reached the height of its aspirations, European governments became increasingly concerned with the cumulative and cyclical process of rural deprivation. Existing national and European policies for agricultural price support and structural reform thus began to be supplemented by large-scale rural and regional development programmes.

Some concluding remarks

Europe's countryside profoundly altered during the 1950s and 1960s. Rural incomes and living standards had traditionally been lower than elsewhere, and rural communities had always changed in response to industrialisation and modernisation processes. However, the revolutionary transformation of postwar agriculture and the unprecedented urbanisation meant that prevailing small-scale labour intensive production methods made way for large-scale, capital intensive farming. As a result, agricultural workers left the countryside and farming lost its dominant role in rural economies (Dyurand-Drouhin and Szwengrub, 1982: 4–5). It was usually with substantial delay that rural communities began to share in the growth of prosperity. Rural earnings and incomes areas in general, and agricultural ones in particular, tended to remain below industrial, urban wages. However, they did improve considerably over time. Among the sparsely populated rural communities in Sweden, Norway and Austria, agricultural incomes rose steadily; Swedish household expenditure in rural areas for instance rapidly closed the gap with urban areas, also owing to extensive welfare state provisions. French and Italian agricultural incomes remained low throughout the 1950s but they improved quickly after 1960, at the peak of smallholders' rural exodus. If alternative rural employment was available, those who stayed behind often became much better off; in the 1960s, their incomes, life styles and expectations had become 'urbanised'. Those rural households that remained dependent on small plots of land, however, saw their living conditions decline relative to those in urban areas.

It cannot be stressed enough that behind these general trends one can find an immense variety of rural development patterns. Maybe it is safer to conclude that 'the European countryside' remains an academic invention that should be used with great caution. For instance, even in a small and densely populated country such as the Netherlands there existed remarkable differences in rural development trajectories. In the sandy regions in the East, where farming families had traditionally suffered from underemployment and low incomes, agricultural workers changed their professions and took on industrial jobs. They often stayed in their rural communities and became part-time farmers commuting to their work in town. It was a switch to part-time farming that also became still more common in many parts of Germany. In various rural areas in Groningen and Friesland, by contrast, where many salaried workers had been employed in agriculture and where alternative employment was almost non-existent, mechanisation and industrialisation led to a depopulation of the countryside. Several small villages there entered a vicious circle of depopulation, decline and deprivation and some even vanished.

References

Bairoch, P., J. Batou and P. Chèvre (1988) *The population of European cities, 800–1850: data bank and short summary of results*, Geneva.

Bairoch, P. (1989) 'Les trois révolutions agricoles du monde développé: rendements et productivité de 1800–1985', *Annales, Economies, societés, civilisations*, March–April, 2.

Bandini, M. (1971) 'National policies for rural development in advanced countries' in: R. Weitz (ed.), *Rural development in a changing world*, Cambridge.

Black, R., H. Buller and K. Hoggart (1995) *Rural Europe. Identity and Change*, London.

Bouwens, A.L. and M.N. de Groot (1990) 'Vijftig jaar landbouwbeleid in Nederland. Consensus en conflict' in: A.L. Bauwens, M.N. de Groot, and K.J Poppe (eds), *Agrarisch bestaan. Beschouwingen bij vijftig jaar Landbouw-Economisch Instituut*, Assen.

Brink, A., van den (1990) Structuur in beweging: het landbouwstructuurbeleid in Nederland 1945–1985, *Wageningse Economische Studies* 16, Wageningen.

Clout, H. (1971) 'Agriculture' *Studies in Contemporary Europe*, London and Basingstoke.

Clout, H. (1988) 'France', in: P.J. Cloke, (ed.), *Policies and plans for rural Europe. An international perspective*, London.

Dovring, F. (1965) *Land and labor in Europe in the twentieth century: a comparative survey of recent agrarian history*, The Hague.

Duby, G. (ed.) (1976) *Histoire de la France rurale, vol 4: La fin de France paysanne. De 1914, à nos jours*, Paris.

Dyurand-Drouhin, J.L and L. M. Szwengrub (eds) (1982) *Rural community studies in Europe. Trends, selected and annotated bibliographies, analyses: volume 2*, Oxford.

Gavignaud, G. (1987) 'De la révolution agricole, la révolution rurale', *Revue Historique* 277, 1.

Gilg, X. (1983) 'Population and employment' in: M. Pacione, (ed.), *Progress in rural geography*, London.

Grigg, D. (1982) *The dynamics of agricultural change. The historical experience*, London.

Grigg, D. (1992) *Transformation of agriculture in the West*, Oxford.

Groot, J.P (1972) 'Kleine plattelandskernen in de Nederlandse samenleving. Schaalvergroting en dorpsbinding', *Mededelingen Landbouwhogeschool Wageningen*, Vol. 72, Wageningen.

Hoggart, K., H. Buller and R. Black (1995). *Rural Europe. Identity and Change*, London/New York/Sydney.

ILO, *Labour force statistics*, various years

Kolinsky, M. (1980) 'Agriculture: problems of modernization' in: M. Vaughan, M. Kolinsky and P. Sheriff, *Social change in France*, Oxford.

Maddison, A. (1982) *Phases of capitalist development*, Oxford and New York.

Maris, A. and R. Rijneveld (1963) 'De Landarbeiders, een beroepsgroep in beweging' in: A. Maris and R. Rijneveld (eds), *Landbouw en platteland in een stroomversnelling*, Haarlem.

Mendras, H. (1971) 'Changing social patterns in rural communities in advanced countries' in: M. Weitz (ed.), *Rural development in a changing world*, Cambridge, Mass.

OECD (1964) *Low incomes in agriculture. Problems and policies*, Paris.

OECD (1969) *Agricultural statistics, 1955–1968*, Paris.

Robinson, G.M. (1990) *Conflict and change in the countryside. Rural society, economy and planning in the developed world*, Chichester.

Rogers, A.W. (1983) 'Housing' in: M. Pacione (ed.), *Progress in rural geography*, London.

Tonkens, E. (1963) 'De leefbaarheid van het platteland' in: A. Maris and R. Rijneveld. (eds), *Landbouw en platteland in een stroomversnelling*, Haarlem.

Tracy, M. (1982) *Agriculture in Western Europe. Challenge and response 1880–1890*, London.

Tuppen, J. (1983) *The economic geography of France*, London.

UN (1964) *Compendium of social statistics: 1963*, New York.

UN (1968) *Compendium of social statistics: 1967*, New York.

UN (1975) *Yearbook of national accounts statistics, Appendix A*, New York.

UN (1976) *Human settlements in Europe. Post-war trends and policies*, New York.

UN (1979) *Demographic yearbook, historical supplement*, New York.

UN ECE (1962) *The rural housing situation in Europe*, Geneva.

UN ECE (1967) *Incomes in postwar Europe: A study of policies, growth and distribution*, Geneva.

UN ECE (1979) *Labour supply and migration in Europe: Demographic dimensions 1950–1975 and prospects*, New York.

UN FAO (1958) *Output, expenses and income of agriculture in some European countries. Third report: 1952–1955*, Geneva.

UN FAO (1965) *The state of food and agriculture in 1965. Review of the second postwar decade*, Rome.

Vriens, J.A. (1965) 'De Westduitse landbouw in vergelijking met die van Nederland. Een beschrijving en analyse van de ontwikkelingen in de periode 1950–1963'. *Landbouw-Economisch Instituut Studie no. 25*, The Hague.

Vries, J. de (1984) *European urbanization, 1500–1800*, London.

Zelinsky, W. (1963) 'Rural population growth as an index to social and economc development: a geographic overview', *The Sociological Quarterly 1*.

13
Changes in Rural Society in Japan
Kamon Nitagai

Japanese agriculture before the war was rooted in a system in which most farming units were extremely small and worked by hand. Half of all cultivated land was controlled by landlords whose tenants did the actual farming. These two factors have been crucial in the agricultural system and also in the far-reaching changes that have occurred since the war.

Japan has been an agricultural country since ancient times and there has been little possibility of increasing the geographically limited area of cultivated land. The number of farm families, however, who tilled the land remained at an almost constant 5.5 million households from the Meiji Restoration to the Second World War, despite population growth. Capitalism in Japan grew rapidly, but it drew for its labour force upon only the younger sons of farm families, without stimulating entire families to leave agriculture. Consequently, as Table 13.1 shows, almost 70 per cent of farm families were farming one hectare or less, and over one-third of them had 0.5 hectare or less. This was a recipe for poverty. From the Meiji period onward tenant farming actually

Table 13.1 Distribution of farm families by size of area cultivated

	0.5 ha	−1.0	−2.0	−3.0	−5.0	5.−
1910	37.6	33.0	19.3	5.9	2.9	1.3
1920	35.3	33.3	20.7	6.1	2.8	1.6
1930	34.3	34.3	22.1	5.7	2.3	1.3
1940	33.4	32.8	24.5	5.7	2.2	1.4
1950	40.9	31.9	21.7	3.4	1.2	0.9
1960	38.0	31.8	23.6	3.8	1.6	1.0
1970	37.3	30.7	24.1	4.8	1.8	1.2

increased. A little over 40 per cent of farm families were part owner, part tenant farmers; almost 30 per cent were entirely tenant farmers. Owner-farmers never amounted to over one-third, thus leaving 70 per cent as tenants who had to pay high fees and who bore the added insecurity of impermanent rights of tenancy. Finally, they were forced to subordinate themselves to their landlords.

Because of poverty most farmers were unable to increase productivity through mechanisation. Instead they lived by the sweat of their labour, striving constantly to enhance productivity per unit area through plant breed improvement and increased use of fertilisers. In the lower classes in urban society there were groups even poorer, but it was the farmer who bore the image of the downtrodden; one who could never escape from poverty no matter how hard he or she worked. Agriculture served as the vital stepping stone to the development of capitalism, but it was left behind, never to benefit from the growth of a capitalist economy.

The postwar land reform freed agriculture from the second characteristic: the domination of tenant farming. With the development of a capitalist economy the influence of the landlord class in Japan began to decline, and from the Taishoh period (1912–26) into the early years of Shouwa (1926–89) it was replaced entirely by the newly dominant capitalist class. That is why, when production of foodstuffs and cheap rice was considered necessary for restoration of the economy after the war, the Japanese government conceived the idea of land reform. The American occupation spent a relatively large proportion of its time and energy in preparing even more thorough measures for a total reform of landholding rights and units of land, ultimately breaking up the landlord system and its ancient dominance over rural communities. Most farmers became owners of the land they cultivated.

After the land reform, agriculture witnessed higher productivity in rice, the main crop. Fruit and livestock production also registered remarkable increases. Machinery, which had been used by a few in the early years of Shouwa, was first used for tilling after the war, when small models of cultivators were introduced. At the present time Japan leads the world in mechanised power used per unit area. Mechanised agriculture also means excessive capital investment for the farm family. The rise in cost of production due to increased expenditures for the purchase of machines and agricultural chemicals has kept farm income low in spite of higher yields.

Until recently agricultural production rose steadily, but that increase never went beyond 3 or 4 per cent annually. By contrast, GNP continued to rise at an annual rate of 10 per cent or more. While the total economy was soaring, agriculture actually dropped. In 1955 it accounted for almost 20 per cent of the national income, but recently it has fallen to around 5 per cent. This productivity gap between agriculture and other industries has been steadily widening. Thus, farm families have become unable to live by agriculture alone, and this has resulted in the drain of farm population away from agriculture. The 1950 farm population of 18 million, or 6.2 million households, fell to about 13.9 million in 1960, and according to a labour force survey, it had dropped to 8.1 million by 1970, half what it was 20 years before. Its proportion in the overall employed population also dropped in this latter ten-year period from 30 to 15 per cent.

In spite of the sharp decrease in farm population, however, the number of farm households remains at over 5.2 million, not very different from the prewar level of 5.5 million. This is because farming is now carried on mainly by the aged and by women, while large numbers of the young adult male population have left agriculture. The spread of power cultivators has helped to compensate somewhat for the decrease in the farm labour force. For these and other reasons, the number of farm families engaging in other occupations is steadily and rapidly increasing. In 1950, when the economy had not yet recovered from the war, opportunities for employment were scarce and about half of all farm families were engaged exclusively in agriculture. But, as can be seen from Table 13.2, five years later this proportion had decreased to 35 per cent, ten years later to 21 per cent, and finally, in 1970, to 16 per cent. During the same period the proportion of farm families whose primary source of income was non-agricultural (type 2 part-time agricultural households) gradually increased from 25 per cent to more than half, where it stands at the present time. Also, at present 60 per cent of Japanese farm families have no male member exclusively engaged in agriculture, a telling symbol of the situation of agriculture in Japan today.

In 1961 the government undertook a basic reform of the structure of agriculture, beginning with the Basic Law on Agriculture (*Nougyo Kihonhou*). This law, however, did not affect the fundamental structure

Table 13.2   Percentages of full-time and part-time farm households

	1941	1950	1955	1960	1965	1970
Full-time	41.5	50.0	34.8	34.3	21.5	15.6
Part-time (Type 1)	37.3	28.4	37.7	33.6	36.8	33.7
Part-time (Type 2)	21.2	21.6	27.5	32.1	41.7	50.7

of agriculture, and it did not suffice to pull agriculture as an economic sector out of the precarious situation into which it had fallen. Waste, inefficiency and above all a self-destructive system were becoming more of a threat every year. Seeking an easy way to change the structure with only a small expenditure of funds, the government annually raised the price of rice in a makeshift effort to achieve some sort of balance. But government purchases of rice from farm families resulted in a rice surplus, which eventually had to reach a limit. In 1969, therefore, the price of rice was left unchanged, and planted acreage was reduced to curtail production. This truly marked a turning point for agriculture in Japan, a country known from ancient times as 'land of abundant rice' (*mizuho no kuni*) and a country where paddy cultivation formed the core of agriculture. For farmers, for whom increased production under the stable food rationing system had constituted the basic support, this brought on a serious crisis.

A rice surplus meant a conversion from rice culture to other crops, but further expansion of livestock raising or fruit is always accompanied by anxiety. Even if farmers switched to new kinds of products, increasing external pressure on Japan to liberalise imports raises the frightening possibility that Japan may have to compete with foreign agricultural products, a task of which it is incapable at present.

The only course open now is the rationalising of agriculture and the creation of a class of farmer who can catch up with the rise in the standard of living. At the present time, however, less than ten per cent of Japanese farmers are able to earn from farming alone an income equal to that of wage and salary earners to become 'independent' or self-supporting. After the enactment of the Basic Law on Agriculture, government authorities tried to encourage the growth of independent and self-supporting farm families, but the percentage of such farmers now comes to less than seven per cent. Further growth in the national income will, in all likelihood, only mean a smaller proportion of independent, self-supporting farm families. Thus it is necessary to begin all over again with structural reform of agriculture in the true sense of the term. According to most forecasts, in 1975 the farming population will have been about seven million, or 13 per cent of the total industrial population; in 1985 the figures will have been five million and 10 per cent, respectively. If the forecasts are accurate, it means that all farm families will of necessity become part-timers. Agriculture cannot be saved unless some measures are taken to enable large numbers to leave the farms and to develop a system, which will promote some form of co-operation among those families that remain in agriculture. It has been said that, given the current level of productivity, only one-twentieth of the present farm population would be sufficient to maintain Japan's agriculture. Though it may not be necessary to go to such an extreme, a radical structural reform of agriculture is necessary to resolve the present problem. It must include long-term, heavy capital investment in social overheads directed toward agriculture, and it must be carried out so that farmers can transfer to other occupations without being put out of work. Conservative party politics, however, are too closely linked with big business for this to be possible. The present Conservative government, though criticised for being pro-agrarian, is actually antiagrarian in the economic and welfare policies it supports.

Changing aspects of farm life

It has long been a fixed idea that life in the farm villages is one of poverty and that agricultural society is feudal and rigid. Before the war, certainly, farmers were often living in poverty. According to a report of the 1926–27 survey of family budgets carried out by the Cabinet Bureau of Statistics, the income of the farmer was 70 per cent that of the white-collar worker, and 95 per cent that of the labourer (whose wages were low enough to prompt international charges of 'social dumping' against Japanese products). Since the farmer's family was generally bigger than the labourer's family, per capita income was proportionately even lower. Half the household expenses of the farmer were for food. Efforts exerted were just to stay alive, much less 'make a living'. The proportion of household expenditures used for food (the Engel coefficient) was reported as 49 for the owner-farmer; 52 for the part owner, part tenant; and 57 for the tenant farmer. The low economic level of the farmer served to strengthen the hierarchical structure based on land ownership and to preserve the domination of landlord over tenant farmer. This status hierarchy naturally resulted in differences in the life styles of each class.

During the war production of the most essential item for human needs, food, gave the farmer an opportunity to approach the economic level of households engaged in other industries. Immediately after the war farmers' incomes surpassed those of waged and salaried workers. However, with the reconstruction of the economy, farm income once again dropped below other sectors. In 1960 the income of a farmer was 85 per cent that of the white-collar worker and 112 per cent that of the blue-collar worker. In per capita income the corresponding figures were 65 per cent and 87 per cent, and farm-family income did not exceed

73 per cent of the average income of all waged and salaried workers. The income of farm households began to increase thereafter, and at the present time it has reached a level about equal to that of a worker living in a city with a population of 50 000 or less. The Engel coefficient has dropped to almost 30. There is now almost no difference in this area between farm households and those of urban workers.

Thus the farm family, which before the war had to endure a life of poverty and suppress all cultural aspirations, has now been urbanised to the extent that it can spend two-thirds of its income on things other than food. A less concrete but important shift has also taken place in social attitudes. With a general changeover from tenant to owner as a result of the land reform and the consequent weakening of class distinctions, farmers no longer uncritically accept a different living standard for landlords and tenant farmers. The standard of living for all farm families has become equalised, but additional income stems largely from jobs in other industries as a supplement to inadequate farm income. The per capita share of the family budget is larger in families with small farms of 0.5 hectare or less, as less farmland means that they can devote relatively more time to earning non-farming income than can farmworkers with more land. By 1963 the practice of farm family members taking part-time jobs raised their outside income above the farming income. Moonlighting and working at non-farming jobs had been further encouraged by official reluctance to raise government payments to growers for rice and by the policy of discouraging rice production. Non-farming income is now greater than that from farming. For example, in 1970 the proportion of agricultural income in the total income of farm families dropped to 38 per cent; at present it amounts to only one-third.

Changing economic and social conditions have stimulated the 'urbanisation' of consumption patterns in farm families, particularly those with stable and substantial incomes from non-farming jobs. Ordinary farmers, who before the war might have resented the fact that the landlord could buy a radio while they themselves could not, have been quick to equip their homes with television sets. The rate of distribution of television sets among farmers is almost the same as in the big cities. Most farm families have refrigerators and washing machines, and there has been a sharp rise in the number who own automobiles; in 1970 the rate of car ownership surpassed that of urban workers. Table 13.3 shows the rise in levels of consumption during recent years. Taking 1965 as the base year, in 1970 total consumption was 127 for urban and 147 for rural areas. Relative rises in expenditure levels for clothing and

Table 13.3   1970 levels of consumption (1965 = 100)

	Total	Food	Housing	Utilities	Clothing	Misc.
Cities	126.7	111.7	145.3	137.4	122.2	137.6
Rural areas	146.9	116.4	143.6	133.6	151.7	182.5

miscellaneous expenses were far greater in rural areas than in urban; these were main factors in the rapid rise of consumption levels in farm areas.

While the Engel coefficient has dropped, there has also been a tendency to limit expenditure for food in order to buy consumer durables. While this tendency is not limited to rural families, they nevertheless spend a greater proportion of their food outlay for cereals than others do. There are still problems, but the life style of farm families, including types of clothing, food and shelter, has changed significantly. Farmers now wear Western-style clothes for going out, women go to beauty parlours just as city women do and children's clothing – something very different from even a generation ago – is indistinguishable from that of city children. Eating habits have also changed; seasoning is no longer limited to soy sauce and bean paste. There has been widespread improvement in dwellings, including kitchens and cooking facilities. Now 51 per cent of all rural communities have water systems, and there are very few hamlets without telephones.

In the old days opportunities for recreation in rural villages were limited to the annual Bon Festival folk dancing and Shinto festivals for the local guardian deity, an occasional village theatrical and relatively frequent gatherings of village fraternities. Now not only has television made recreation an everyday matter, but people also often go to nearby cities for diversion. Group excursions of farmers to other parts of Japan and sometimes even abroad have become common. As a result, there has been a striking increase in cultural and recreational expenditures compared with before the war. In the field of formal education the proportion of students who continue to high school exceeds 80 per cent, no different from that of urban youth. The time when an elementary school education was considered sufficient for farm children is now in the distant past.

Farmers once sought their *raison d'être* in an ideology that made agriculture the foundation for society and the system of social values in Japan; it was the life-giving occupation, unlike urban occupations, which corrupted and degraded man. Although agriculture was left in

the cold by modern industry, being accorded the least favoured treatment, it was nevertheless hailed as the foundation of the state. But this
glorification of hard work and low standards of living is no longer
accepted by the farming population. Farmers today no longer consider
consumption a vice and cultural aspirations a luxury. Agriculture is
just another business that is expected to produce a profit; hence the
growing awareness that it is less rewarding or profitable compared with
other sectors.

The overall difficulties facing agriculture in recent years have strengthened this awareness. If farmers find it impossible to lower their present
standard of living in spite of the impasse, they will have to reconsider
the most basic props in their life style. Life style or culture does not
change easily, and the present transformation in the life of farmers is
by no means a smooth one. Certain aspects lag while others are moving ahead. The purchase of colour television and cars, for example, has
stunted development of other undertakings in their lives. The rise in
standards of living among farmers has not, therefore, been well balanced
or even. Competition based only on vanity or concern for appearances
has also affected cultural development. Farmers are, in any case, demand-
ing much more in the realms of recreation, culture and education than
ever before.

To follow such pursuits, farm families want to do additional work to
supplement farm income. So long as their total agricultural and extra
income continues to increase, approaching income levels of wage and
salary earners, the overall attitude of farmers toward society and nation
may stay unchanged. When this particular group, however, begins to
hit a 'ceiling' and experiences difficulty in maintaining and raising its
new standards of living, both its attitude and its behaviour will probably begin to change. Change in political orientations and attitudes
toward government may even effect change in political alignment and
power. One can speculate that farmers' support for government policies might then weaken sufficiently to force political change, but no
such shift would occur quickly. Though rural society has undergone
great change, in many respects it remains stagnant.

Change and stagnation in village society

We have seen how farm families now tend to fall into either the small
category of those engaged exclusively in agriculture or the much larger
one of those working at additional occupations. Another rural group
is the great number of non-farming families who live in farm villages.

A considerable number of settlements have developed in which non-farming families are in the majority while only a few farm families remain. According to a 1960 worldwide census of agriculture and forestry, the average rural settlement consisted of 39 agricultural households and 25 non-agricultural ones, for a total of 64. But the same census, conducted in 1970, found 37 agricultural households to 44 non-agricultural ones, for a total of 81 in the same average settlement. In all settlements, the average number of non-farming families rose. Purely agricultural villages in which farm households are 80 per cent or more of the total still amount to half of all rural settlements; hence, the average number of non-farming families exceeding farm families in agricultural villages all over Japan most probably stems from the increase of non-farming residents in villages around cities. Considering both the large non-farming population in farm villages plus the fact that half or more of 'farm families' are engaged in additional occupations similar to those of the non-farming population, the rapid break-up of these settlements into heterogeneous units becomes clear.

At the same time the social character of these settlements is undergoing striking change. In the first place, they are no longer close-knit communities encompassing a small area, with more or less determined patterns of class composition. Prewar farm villages varied in composition, including owner-farmers and tenant farmers, or groups of families who worked exclusively in agriculture and those who had additional occupations, but the farm settlement of the past had a design. It centred around the landlords and a class of prominent people next to them who managed production and the life of the settlement as a whole. The break-up of the landlord system, however, has made the formation of common goals difficult in a settlement whose members are divided between those engaged solely in agriculture and the promotion of farm production and those who earn additional income in other industries, farming only for their own food supply and for security in retirement. (A young or middle-aged man will plan to carry on farming after retirement from the other occupation; in the meantime, the farm work will be done by women and old people.) Also, because many non-farming families now live in farm villages and commute to work simply because they cannot have houses in the town or city, it is difficult to unite all the inhabitants into a community within the framework of the village.

In the second place, differentiation within the rural settlements has been reinforced by external stimuli. Links with outside society have become stronger since the war, and the life of the villagers has become more varied and far-ranging. The development of agricultural production for the commercial market and the rise in consumption have forged new ties between village and city, while the growing numbers of farmers who take other jobs, some of whom commute to the cities, have created a steady urban–rural interchange. Furthermore, mergers that were effected under the 1953 Law to Promote the Consolidation of Towns and Villages superceded a town and village system dating back to 1889. The law of 1953 was enacted in a profoundly different environment from that of the middle Meiji-period, and the new municipalities were several times larger than their predecessors, while villages on the outskirts of a city were incorporated into the central city. Thus they virtually became urban areas that were part of the same administrative district and formed a single local self-governing body. As the bonds between city and village grew stronger, one could no longer speak of a purely rural society living by means of agriculture. The idea of being 'cut off' from the city has become inconceivable today.

Another agent of change is the location of industry. The drawbacks of overcrowded industrial facilities have begun to outweigh the advantages of concentration. When the dispersal of industry and the formation of new industrial regions is carried out through regional development plans, decisive changes will take place in the structure of rural villages within such a region. It is possible that rural settlements will be completely broken up or left with only vestiges of what they were. This trend is conspicuous now in only a relatively few rural villages, but small industries everywhere seeking factory sites where land and labour are cheap, are hoping to move into the rural areas. In addition to 'urban sprawl' and the urban housing shortage, industrial relocation is changing the entire aspect of rural village society.

The degree of structural change in village society differs according to region, but in all cases the prewar rural village is breaking up. The controlling power of the traditional group within the village has weakened. The neighbourhood groups, which were once active in all aspects of village life, have become merely the final transmission points of municipal administration. The functions of the co-operative organisation for assisting with funeral services have been reduced. With the decline of religious faith and the abundance of recreational opportunities, religious associations, too, are becoming shadows of what they used to be. Of the groups formed after the Meiji town and village system came into effect, the young men's associations and the women's leagues have declined the most; the latter find it difficult even to stay in existence. The organisations which are replacing them – the Agricultural

Co-operative's (*Noukyo*) young men's and women's divisions – also find it difficult to function. The diversification of the farm families has weakened the function of the Agricultural Practice Union (*Nouji fikkou Kumiai*). Instead, industry-oriented associations of fruit growers, dairy farmers, chicken and pig rearers, and co-operative shipping organisations, cutting across village lines and unrelated to any one village unit, have become the key administrative and commercial facilities for farmers. The era when the members of a village, regardless of occupation, formed a single community and co-operated in all aspects of its life, when the village itself controlled and regulated its inhabitants, is a thing of the past. Nevertheless, villagers have not been freed from the traditions of the village and its groups. Village control of water is still considered necessary for paddy cultivation, for example. The effect of these traditions has been a failure to develop rationally organised groups operating as independently functioning bodies to meet specific group needs apart from the village. The 'village' has not become just another organisation; its all-encompassing authority is still recognised, at least in theory.

Traditions of the past are deeply rooted in the structure and operation of village self-government. The idea that local affairs should be handled by the villagers themselves has left a wide margin for village self-government alongside municipal self-government. It is considered a duty for each family to share the burden of village expenses and to contribute equal amounts of volunteer labour for community work. Village official positions have lost their prestige and are considered merely troublesome and unremunerative, and no movement has developed toward a democratic or egalitarian method for selecting officers nor reformed the operation of self-government.

Economically, agriculture should be divorced from the village itself and run by specialised organisations set up for specific purposes. The village will then become an entity whose purpose is to promote the common interests and welfare of its inhabitants, regardless of whether they are farming or non-farming families, but at present the gap between the two – agriculture and village – is simply glossed over. There is no clear-cut division of functions between them, despite the growing heterogeneity of village inhabitants and the need for different modes of organisation. Yet the old-time 'village spirit' survives: the attitudes that made solidarity and tranquillity the goals of village society and that gave priority to the common interests of those living in it.

Thus the village continues to emphasise communal interests over class interest even after it has been incorporated into the broader

Table 13.4 Population of cities of 100 000 or more and percentages of total population

	1960			1970		
	Cities	Population		Cities	Population	
		(in thousands)	(per cent)		(in thousands)	(per cent)
1 000 000	6	16 688	17.9	8	20 856	20.1
500 000	3	1 804	1.9	7	4 562	4.4
300 000	12	4 262	4.6	21	7 890	7.6
200 000	21	5 134	5.5	41	9 802	9.5
100 000	71	9 914	10.6	73	10 416	10.0
Total population		93 419	100.0		103 720	100.0

municipal self-government. Its behaviour is governed by the 'village first' principle: the old principle of giving priority to the interests of one's own town or village that dates back to the pre-consolidation era. The emphasis on local interests becomes the basis of town and village politics and affects the way farmers relate to prefectural and national governments. It strengthens the role of the prefectural assembly and Diet members as intermediaries between villagers and prefectural or national government. Old political attitudes, therefore, and the tendency to push action through representatives persist. In this respect village society has still not clearly emerged from the way of life of the old village community. Startling change has occurred against the background of tenacious traditions.

The increase of cities and urban growth

As far back as the 17th century Japan's cities, such as Edo (Tokyo), Kyoto and Osaka, were among the largest in the world. The urban population at the time of the Meiji Restoration in 1868 was, nonetheless, less than 10 per cent of the national total. Even as late as 1920, when the first national census was conducted, the urban population had not reached 20 per cent. The following quarter-century reflected the growth of capitalism in a rapid increase in the number of cities; their population grew to more than 40 per cent of the total.

The Pacific War brought a stop to this trend. Immediately after the end of the war a steady flow of population back to the rural areas reduced urban population to less than 30 per cent. Even by 1950 it was considerably less than 40 per cent. From the mid-1950s, however, the economy began to shift from restoration to growth, and cities gradually returned to prewar levels of population. Thereafter they entered a period of rapid growth. From 1950 to 1960 population steadily gravitated to the large cities; as we have already seen, the areas of cities peripheral to large metropolises began to expand after 1960. Both the number and size of cities have grown remarkably. Merely having city status as administrative units does not necessarily qualify a city as an urban centre, yet if a city with a population of 100 000 or more is taken to be an urban centre, then urban centre population in 1960 amounted to 41 per cent of the total population, and then reached 52 per cent in 1970 (see Table 13.4). In other words, half the population today lives in metropolitan areas. If we add cities of 50 000 or more to this number, the proportion exceeds 80 per cent.

Modern Japanese cities have typically developed as consumer cities, evolving out of castle towns of the Tokugawa period to become prefectural capitals after the Meiji Restoration. Needless to say, there are newly developed cities which were agricultural or fishing villages in the Tokugawa period. Such industrial cities as Yawata, Kawasaki and Hitachi, which developed only after the Restoration, are good examples of this pattern. Others, such as Yokohama, Niigata and Aomori, which grew into important cities after the opening of ports to foreign trade, also developed into prefectural capitals. Most of Japan's cities, however, originally developed out of political or administrative centres, whose populations later increased with the growth of industry. The same pattern has repeated itself often in the postwar growth of cities, as well.

The formal administrative structure of Japan duly recognises local autonomy and decentralisation of authority, but in fact, functions to centralise authority both on the national and prefectural levels. Thus, along with the concentration of population in Tokyo, the population in prefectural capitals has also expanded. Even in recent years many cities, by virtue of being political centres, have continued to attract more people and develop industry on the outskirts. The main trend in rapid urban growth, however, has been expansion of industrial, rather than political, centres. The shift from coal to oil as a source of power has had a particularly great influence on the location of industry, through the formation of large petrochemical complexes in areas close to existing industrial regions. The complexes have accelerated rapid urbanisation in such areas.

Another factor in Japan's urban growth is the great number of new cities recently sprung into existence. As is generally known, consolidation of towns and villages after the war extended the scope of municipalities, doubled their number, and created innumerable cities. Yet many of these were nothing more than small towns that included adjacent or nearby farm villages spread over a fairly wide area. Another type of new city includes those which developed more recently on the outskirts of the large cities as a result of the sudden population increase in towns and smaller cities within the metropolitan area. It is the increase in number and rapid growth of this kind of city which accounts for the fact that while population growth in the six largest cities has come to a standstill, the populations of the metropolitan areas are still rapidly growing.

The overall conclusions to be drawn from the rapid growth of urban population are: first, the large cities are already overcrowded and, because of high land prices that stem from an inappropriate official land policy, they are approaching the limits of population growth.

Without a drastic programme of urban reconstruction and redevelopment, such limitations cannot be overcome. Second, all regional urban centres are growing, but growth is especially marked in those which are also industrial cities. Third, the old industrial cities expanded as the economy grew, and the new manufacturing–industrial cities, especially on the Pacific coastal belt, were among the fastest growing. From 1963 onward the development of new industrial cities pushed the spread of such cities beyond the Pacific coastal zone. Among the latter are cities built where formerly there was nothing but farming or fishing villages, thus creating urban areas very suddenly. Fourth, and this is related to the first and second trends, urbanisation is also taking place on the periphery of regional central cities, as on the outskirts of large cities. This may be considered characteristic of urban trends – the expansion of urban society.

Thus, rapid city growth is taking place not as population expansion in established urban areas and redevelopment of existing facilities and installations, but in a mushrooming kind of expansion which is rapidly taking over areas which were once only rural villages. In other words, the rapid growth of cities is swiftly turning Japan into an urban society; villages are literally being 'citified'. The dynamism of urbanisation is spreading throughout Japan as a whole and consequently throughout the life of the Japanese people, even those who are living in what are still rural community areas.

For more than 70 years after the Meiji Restoration Japan encouraged more and bigger cities, at a rate that was rapid even by world standards. Nevertheless, Japan remained essentially a rural society; its social system and the fundamental character of the dominating political trends were rural. Each family was responsible for its own livelihood, and social life was the responsibility of the community. There was little interest in the social institutions and public facilities necessary in an urban society. Political patterns and thinking were geared to assumptions that were valid when the traditional community prevailed. They have remained fundamentally unchanged since the end of the war. To augment national wealth and military strength, prewar Japan concentrated almost exclusively on the development of industry and showed almost no concern for developing the institutions and facilities for life in an urban environment or for social guarantees of the people's livelihood. After the war economic growth became the single most important national goal, pushing all other considerations aside. It spurred industrialisation on at an even more rapid pace, and resulted in unbalanced and unplanned urban growth. The imbalances in urban life have been allowed to run their course, and industrialisation and urbanisation have, therefore, progressed in an even more uncontrolled manner. The process has become a vicious circle that seems doomed to repetition. The cities of Japan have today reached a point where many aspects of urban life will be destroyed if nothing is done to control their growth.

References

Dore, R.P. (1967), *Aspects of Social Change in Japan*, Princeton.

Dore, R.P. (1987), *Taking Japan Seriously: A Confucian Perspective on Leading Economic Issues*, London.

Fujita, Y. (1984), *Employee Benefits and Industrial Relations*, Tokyo: Japan Institute of Labour (in Japanese).

Fukutake,T. (1967), *Japanese Rural Society*, Tokyo.

Fukutake,T. (1974), *Japanese Society Today*, Tokyo.

Gordon, A. (1985), *The Evolution of Labour Relations in Japan*, Cambridge Mass.

Kosai, Y. and Y. Ogino (1984) *The Contemporary Japanese Economy*, London and Basingstoke.

Minami, R. (1986), *The Economic Development of Japan*, London and Basingstoke.

Index

'3 Jingi' 128–9
'3Cs' 132

Adenauer, Konrad
increasing democratic pressure
162, 163, 164
laissez-faire liberalism 156, 157,
158, 160
public opinion 109
affluence 2, 103
Agricultural Cooperative, Japan
245–6
Agricultural Practice Union 246
agricultural sector
Japan 4; changes 240–4;
employment 86, 87, 88, 89;
modernisation 237; social
democracy 167–8; wages 95
Western Europe; modernisation
213–15, 221–4, 226; wages 74,
75, 76; workforce 214, 215,
218–20, 226;
see also rural society
Akihito, Emperor 130
Allied Occupation in Japan (GHQ)
155, 156, 159, 160
Antimonopoly Law, Japan 49, 50
Aomori 249
Arisawa, Jiromi 46, 47
Arnold, Karl 155
Atkinson, A.B. 201, 205–6
austerity 1–2
Australia 35
Austria
emigration 65
exports 61
rural society: characteristics 212;
definition 211; earnings 229,
233; population 214;
transformation 219, 222, 226
social democracy 145
welfare state 179

automobiles see cars

Bank of Japan 120
Barr, N. 192
Basic Law on Agriculture (Japan)
238–9
Belgium
affluence 2
exports 30
female employment 67
foreign direct investment 33, 34
industrialisation 147
labour surplus models 60
machinery industry 30
property income 79
rural society: characteristics 212,
213; definition 211; earnings
229; landholding patterns
216; migration to urban areas
214; transformation 217, 222
welfare state 145
Bell, Daniel 102
Berlin crisis 143
Beveridge plan 175, 181, 182, 192,
196
big government 189–90, 193
Bismarck, Otto von 180
birth rates, Japan 83, 84
black market, Japan 88
Bockler, Hans 162

cars
Japan 8–9, 43–4, 48, 130–2
Western Europe 8, 32, 105–6, 110,
111
Catholicism 143, 163
central–local government relations,
Japan 166–7
centre-left parties 139
centre-right parties 101–2, 114, 139
Cercle National des Jeunes
Agriculteurs (CNJA) 225

chemical sector 29
China 42
Chirac, Jacques 170
Christian democratic parties 145
Christian Democratic Union (CDU,
    West Germany) 109, 113, 141
    Emergency Bill for Economic
        Control 155
    founding 154
    increasing democratic pressure
        163, 164
    laissez-faire liberalism 156,
        157-8
Christian Democrats (CD, Italy) 139,
    141, 144
Christian Social Union (CSU, West
    Germany) 154, 155
cinema visits, West Germany 109
Clay, General Lucious 157
Clout, H. 224
coal industry, Japan 88
cold war 143, 176
combine harvesters 221-4
Common Agricultural Policy (CAP)
    225
communication 22
Communist Party (France) 140
Communist Party (Italy) 139
Communist Party (Japan) 154, 166
Communist Party (West Germany)
    154, 156
computer industry, Japan 50
conservative parties 142, 145, 182
Conservative Party (Japan)
    rural society 240
    social democracy 154, 166, 167,
        168, 169
Conservative Party (UK) 105, 112,
    113, 139
construction sector, Japan 89
consumption 22
    American model 103-5
    Japan 6-9, 14, 15-16, 90, 120-3,
        135-7; and education 95;
        investments and savings 4,
        133-5; living standards, rise
        123-5; role of consumer
        durables 128-33; rural society

241-2; trends 125-8; and
    wage levels 91
Western Europe 6-9, 14-15, 63-4,
    99-100, 105-12, 117; from
    collective provision to affluence
    102-3; new sensibility
    114-17; politics 112-14; rural
    society 229-30; unique
    character of 1950s 100-2
convergence theory 194
co-operative organisations, Japan 246
corporate governance, Japan 43
countryside *see* agricultural sector;
    rural society
credit 105, 113
Crosland, Anthony 144
Currency Reform, Germany 156,
    157, 159, 161

dance bands 116
death rates, Japan 83, 84
debt repayment, Japan 135
de Gaulle, Charles 113, 140, 146
democratisation
    Japan 3, 164-9
    West Germany 161-4
demographic trends
    Japan 83-5, 87, 238
    Western Europe 65-6, 216-18
Denmark
    emigration 65
    exports 30
    rural society: characteristics 212,
        213; definition 210, 211;
        earnings 228; housing
        conditions 231; landholding
        patterns 216; transformation
        217, 222, 226
    welfare state 145
depreciation system, Japan 88
destalinisation 143
direct foreign investment *see* foreign
    direct investment
discomfort index 99
Dodge, Joseph 157, 159
Dodge Plan 46
    social democracy 157, 159, 161,
        164, 166, 168

Draper, William   157

Eastern Europe   175–6
East Germany   158
economic planning, Japan   42–3
Economic Planning Agency, Japan
   165
Economic Rehabilitation Plan, Japan
   46–7
Economic Stability Board, Japan
   156, 164, 165
education
   Japan   85, 94–6, 160–1, 242
   Western Europe   149
   West Germany   160
efficiency, welfare state   190, 191–2,
   201–2
Eisenhower, Dwight D.   112
emigration from Western Europe
   65–6
employers' social security payments
   77, 78
employment
   full *see* full employment
   Japan   13–14, 82–3; composition of
      labour force   83–7; source of
      economic growth   94–7;
      transformation phases   87–94
   Western Europe   12–13, 80;
      income   71–7, 78; from
      income to expenditure   79;
      internationalisation of trade
      29–30; property income   77–9;
      self-employment   77–9;
      tensions in labour market
      64–71
   see also workforce
employment exchange ratio (EER),
   Japan   91, 92, 93–4
energy sector, Japan   54
Engel's coefficient   125, 241, 242
engineering industries   30, 31
enterprise welfare   193–4, 206
equity, Japan   190, 192–3, 201–2
Erhard, Ludwig   157, 159, 162
Ethier effect   55
Euro-dollars market   11, 36
European Coal and Steel Community
   37

European Economic Community
   (EEC)   26, 29, 32, 33–4, 35
European Free Trade Association
   (EFTA)   26, 29, 32
European Payments Union   36
exports
   and economic growth   61
   from Japan   3–4, 51
   from Western Europe   25, 28, 30

Fair Trade Commission (FTC)   49–50
family, Japan
   social welfare   193, 194, 195, 206
   workers   86
Federal Republic of Germany *see* West
   Germany
Federation of German Refugees (FGR)
   162–3
female employment *see* women's
   employment
Finance Ministry (Japan)   120, 165,
   166, 167
Finland   30, 179
First World War   184–5
food processing   29
fordism   146
Ford Motors   43, 44
foreign direct investment
   in Japan   43–4
   in Western Europe   10–11, 32–4
France
   ageing   84
   balance of payments crises   2
   consumption   6–9, 110–12, 113,
      229, 230
   exports   30
   foreign direct investment   33, 34
   GDP   5
   immigration   66
   intraindustry trade index   53
   labour surplus models   60
   machinery industry   30
   rural society: characteristics
      212–13; consumption   229,
      230; definition   210, 211;
      earnings   229, 233; housing
      conditions   231; landholding
      patterns   215; transformation
      219, 221, 222, 224–5, 226

France – *continued*
  social democracy 140–1, 145, 146,
    147, 148
  welfare state 175, 181, 182
Free Democratic Party (West
    Germany) 163
Free Farmers (Netherlands) 225
Friedman, M. 204
Fuji Steel 50
Fukutake, N. 195
Fukuyama, F. 99
full employment
  Japan 94
  Western Europe 3, 67, 70–1, 80,
    141–2; welfare state 179

General Agreement on Tariffs and
    Trade (GATT) 48
General Motors (GM) 43, 44
Germany *see* East Germany; West
    Germany
Gonin Gumi Seido 194
Goodman, Benny 116
Goto, Yonosuke 46
Great Britain *see* United Kingdom
Great East Asian Co-prosperity Area
    41–2
Greece 30, 210, 211
gross domestic product (GDP)
  Japan 5, 63
  USA 63
  Western Europe 5, 25–6, 63
gross national product (GNP)
  Japan 123, 124–5
  Western Europe 30–1, 186
growth accounting exercises 60
Grundgesetz 158

Hamilton, R.F. 111–12
Harrod-Domar model 44
Hatoyama, Ichiro 167
Hayashi, F. 129
Hayek, F.A. 204
health insurance 178–9, 196–7
Helpman, E. 55, 56
Hitachi 249
Hitoshi, Ashida 154
holidays 106
home ownership, Western Europe
  106–7, 109

horizontal equity, Japan 192–3
housing conditions, rural society 231

IBM Japan 50
Ichimanda, Hisato 165
Ikeda, Hayato 44, 47, 48, 124, 159
immigration to Western Europe 12,
    25, 65, 66
imports
  to Japan 48, 51–3
  to Western Europe 28, 29, 30–1
import substitution, Japan 45–6
income distribution, Japan 192,
    201–2
income doubling, Japan 44–5, 47,
    49, 124, 198
income support
  Japan 200–1, 203
  UK 200
industrialisation
  Japan 3–4, 165
  Western Europe 146–8, 174, 176
industrial production, Western Europe
    26
Industry Rationalisation Policy, Japan
    88
industrial relocation, Japan 246
inflation
  Japan 88
  Western Europe 99
interest groups, Japan 168–9
internal promotion, Japan 96, 97
internationalisation of trade
  in Japan 10, 11–12, 41–2, 57–8;
    development path and
    intra-industry trade 53–7;
    process 42–5; protectionism
    and export promotion 51–3;
    trade structure and trade policy
    45–50
  in Western Europe 10–11, 25–8,
    38–9; foreign direct investment
    32–4; international markets
    28–32; international money
    34–8
international markets 10, 28–32
International Monetary Fund (IMF)
    48, 49
international money 11, 34–8

intraindustry trade, Japan   53–7
investment
    and economic growth   61
    foreign direct *see* foreign direct
        investment
    Japan   91, 95, 134
    portfolio   35
Ireland, Republic of   30, 211
Ishihara, Kanji   44
Ishisaka, Taizo   48, 49
Italy
    consumption   113
    emigration   66
    export-led growth   61
    exports   28, 30, 61
    female employment   67
    international money   35
    labour surplus models   60
    machinery industry   30
    population growth   65
    rural society: characteristics
        212–13; definition   211;
        earnings   228, 229, 233;
        housing conditions   231;
        landholding patterns   215;
        transformation   217, 222, 226
    social democracy   139, 140,
        141–2, 144, 145–6, 148;
        industrialisation   147, 148;
        secularisation   149; welfare
        state   145
    unemployment   138
    welfare state   179, 182
Iwasaki, Teruhiko   45

Japan   3–4
    consumption   6–9, 14, 15–16, 90,
        120–3, 135–7; and education
        95; investments and savings
        4, 133–5; livings standards, rise
        123–5; role of consumer
        durables   128–33; rural society
        241–2; trends   125–8; and
        wage levels   91
    employment   13–14, 82–3;
        composition of labour force
        83–7; source of economic
        growth   94–7; transformation
        phases   87–94

erosion of affluence   24
GDP   5, 63
internationalisation of trade   10,
    11–12, 41–2, 57–8;
    development path and
    intraindustry trade   53–7;
    process   42–5; protectionism
    and export promotion   51–3;
    trade structure and trade policy
    45–50
political culture   23
rural society   21, 236–40; farm life
    240–4; urban growth   248–51;
    village society   244–8;
social democracy   17–18, 153–4,
    169–71; immediate postwar
    period   154–6; increasing
    democratic pressure   164–9;
    laissez-faire liberalism   156–61
welfare state   4, 18, 19–20, 188–9;
    chronological development
    194–206; objectives   189–94;
    path toward reform   206
and Western Europe: differences in
    transformation process   23;
    trade between   31
Japan Employers Federation
    (JEF-Nikkeiren)   93
Japanese Council for Economic
    Development (Keizai Doyuukai)
    154
Japanese Federation for the Welfare of
    the Bereaved   169
jazz   116
John XXIII, Pope   143
just-in-time (JIT) inventory
    management   43

Kanban system   43
Kawasaki   249
Keidanren   48, 49
Kennedy, John F.   48, 143
Keynes, John Maynard   70, 182
Keynesianism   23, 101–2
    social democracy   142, 143, 144
    welfare state   173–4, 177, 185
Kishi, Nobusuke   44, 45
Koike, K.   96
Korean War   159, 168

Krugman, P. 11, 51, 55, 56
Kuznets, S. 121–2, 123, 202

labour force/market *see* employment;
  workforce
Labour Party (UK)
  income policy 146
  modernisation 143–4
  progress towards government 139,
    141, 142, 154
  supporters 148
labour relations
  Japan 43
  see also trades unions
labour surplus models 60
laissez-faire liberalism 156–61
land fragmentation, Western Europe
  221, 223
land reform, Japan 3, 237
leftist parties 101–2, 114, 139, 154
Liberal Democratic Party (LDP, Japan)
  157, 159
liberalisation
  of capital, Japan 49–50
  of trade: Japan 47–9, 51–2;
    West Germany 162
life expectancy 124
linear expenditure system (LES)
  125–8
liquidity constraints, Japan 129–30,
  133, 134, 135
living standards
  Japan: consumption 123–5, 128;
    employment 88; rural society
    241, 246; savings levels 4,
    134; welfare state 192
  Western Europe 12, 176
Local Autonomy Agency, Japan 167
local government, Japan 166–7
Luxembourg
  exports 30
  female employment 67
  foreign direct investment 33
  immigration 66
  rural society 211, 212, 213

machinery industries 30, 53–4
Macmillan, Harold 112
manufacturing sector

Japan 87, 88, 89, 90
Western Europe: internationalisation
  of trade 28–30, 31, 32; wages
  and salaries 72–3, 75, 76
Marshall, Alfred 182
Marshall Plan 162
mass production, Japan 91
medical insurance 178–9, 196–7
Medicare 199
metal making 29
metal-using industries 29
Michiko, Empress 130
middle class, Western Europe 105–7,
  109, 110, 151
Ministry of Commerce and Industry
  (Japan) 165
Ministry of Finance (Japan) 120,
  165, 166, 167
Ministry of International Trade and
  Industry (MITI, Japan)
  car industry 48
  computer industry 50
  consumption 120
  new industrial system 49
  protectionism 51
  social democracy 165
multinational corporations 38
Murakami, Y. 51

Nakamura, T. 43
Nakasone, Yasuhiro 170, 205
Namiki, Shokichi 46
National Electric Company 92
National Governors Association 166,
  167
National Income Doubling Plan,
  Japan 44–5, 47, 49, 124, 198
National Mayors Association 166
NATO 102
Nau, H.R. 101
neighbourhood groups, Japan 246
neo-corporatism 173, 174, 185
Netherlands, the
  consumption 6–9, 64, 229–30
  economic growth 62, 63, 64
  employment 12, 85; income 72,
    73–4, 75, 76, 77, 78; from
    income to expenditure 79;
    self-employment and property

Netherlands, the – *continued*
  income   79; tensions in labour
    market   65, 66, 67, 68, 69, 70–1
  exports   30, 61
  GDP   5
  rural society: characteristics   212,
    213; consumption   229–30;
    definition   211; earnings   228,
    229; housing conditions   231;
    landholding patterns   216;
    population growth   214;
    transformation   217, 222, 225,
    226, 233
  welfare state   145, 179
'new   3Cs'   132
New Nippon Steel   50
New Zealand   35
Niigata   249
Nissan   44, 50
Noguchi, Y.   43
Nokyo   168
North America   31
  see also United States of America
North Atlantic Treaty Organization
    (NATO)   102
Norway
  emigration   65
  employment: female   67; wages
    72–3, 228, 229, 233
  exports   30
  rural society: characteristics   212;
    definition   211; earnings   228,
    229, 233; transformation   226
  welfare state   145, 179

occupational injury insurance   178,
    179
Oda, Yutaka   46
OECD   49
OEEC   32
Ohkawa, K.   45, 47
oil shocks   56–7, 203–4
Okita, Saburo   46
old-age pensions   164, 178–9
Olympic Games   130
on-the-job training (OJT), Japan   96
Organization for Economic
    Cooperation and Development
    (OECD)   49

Organization for European Economic
    Cooperation (OEEC)   32
output, Western Europe   26, 29,
    30

Pacific War   248
participation in employment
  female *see* women's employment
  Japan   85–6
  Western Europe   66–9, 85
pensions   164, 178–9
Petty-Colin Clark Law   86
Phillips, Sam   115
polipoly   51
political culture   22–3
  Japan   14
  Western Europe   4–15, 109,
    112–14
  see also social democracy
population growth
  Japan   83, 84, 87, 124
  Western Europe   65–6
portfolio investment   35
Portugal   30, 211
Postan, M.M.   28
poverty relief   192
Preferential Production Plan, Japan
    120
Presley, Elvis   115, 116
pressure groups, Japan   168–9
Prince   50
production doubling   44, 45
promotion, Japan   96, 97
property income
  Japan   202
  Western Europe   78, 79
protectionism, Japan   4, 47, 48–9,
    50–3, 168

radios   7
Reagan, Ronald   117, 160, 170,
    205
refrigerators   91
religious associations, Japan   246
rice   239, 241
Rinpo Sofu   194
Robinson, G.M.   210
rock and roll   115, 116, 117
rubber sector   29

rural society
  Japan 21, 236–40; farm life
    240–4; urban growth 248–51;
    village society 244–8
  Western Europe 20–1, 209–13,
    232–3; economic transformation
    213–16; incomes and living
    standards 226–32;
    transformation of 1950s and
    1960s 216–26, 227

Sabashi, Shigeru 50
salaries *see* wages and salaries
savings, Japan 4
  consumption 129, 130, 132–5, 136
  welfare state 198
Sawyer, M. 201–2
Schaffer, Fritz 162
Schmitter, P.C. 174
Second World War 185
  Europe 9–10
  Japan 3, 9, 10, 42, 196
secularisation, Western Europe 149
self-employment
  Japan 86, 95
  Western Europe 75, 78–9
service sector
  Japan 87, 8
  Western Europe 75, 76, 77
Shaw, Artie 116
Shimomura, Osamu 45
Shonfield, Andrew 25, 26, 38, 100
Shunt? 92
sickness insurance 178–9, 196–7
small government 190
social citizenship 182
social democracy
  Japan and West Germany compared
    17–18, 153–4, 169–71;
    immediate postwar period
    154–6; Japan 164–9;
    laissez-faire liberalism
    156–61; West Germany
    161–4
  Western Europe 16–17, 138–9,
    150–1; new voters for renewed
    parties 146–9; political
    management of mixed
    economy 142–6; progress

  towards government 139–42;
    welfare state 182–3
Social Democratic Party (Sweden)
    140
Social Democratic Party (SPD, West
    Germany)
  Emergency Bill for Economic
    Control 155
  increasing democratic pressure
    162, 164
  laissez-faire liberalism 156
  policy co-ordination 146
  progress towards government 139,
    140, 141, 155
  revision 143, 148
  supporters 109, 148
social integration, Japan 193
socialisation 156
socialist parties 139, 142, 145, 148
Socialist Party (France) 140–1
Socialist Party (Italy) 140, 141, 144,
    148
social security *see* welfare state
social security payments, employers'
    contributions 77, 78
Sôhyô 92
Soldiers' Protection Society, Japan 169
South Africa 35
Soviet Union 143, 154, 158, 161
Spain 30, 211
sporting events, West Germany 109
standards of living *see* living
    standards
steel industry, Japan 88
Storch, Anton 163
Strachey, John 101
Strange, Susan 37
Stresemann, Gustav 160
suburbanisation 217–18
Supreme Commander for Allied
    Powers (SCAP) 46
Sweden
  affluence 2
  ageing 84
  consumption 6–9, 64
  economic growth 62, 63, 64
  employment 13; income 72–3,
    74, 75, 76, 77, 78; from
    income to expenditure 79;

Sweden – *continued*
   self-employment and property
      income   78, 79; tensions in
      labour market   65, 66, 67, 68,
      69, 70–1
   exports   30
   GDP   5
   rural society: characteristics   212;
      consumption   229, 230;
      definition   211; earnings   228,
      229, 233; housing conditions
      231; landholding patterns
      216; transformation   217, 218,
      219, 220–1, 222, 225–6
   social democracy   140, 145
   welfare state   175, 178, 179, 182;
      Keynesianism   173;
      supplementary pensions   183;
      taxation   177
Switzerland
   affluence   2
   immigration   66
   property income   79
   rural society: characteristics   212,
      213; definition   209–10, 211;
      landholding patterns   216;
      migration to urban areas   214;
      transformation   219, 220, 222

Tachibanaki, T.   202
Takeo, Miki   154
taxation
   Japan   192–3, 197, 203, 206
   Sweden   177
   welfare state   183–5
   West Germany   162
technology transfers   34
television sets
   Japan   8, 91, 130, 131, 132
   Western Europe   8, 105–6
textile sector   29, 88
Thatcher, Margaret   117, 160, 170,
   205
'three Cs'   132
'three Jingi'   128–9
Tokyo Olympics   130
Toyota   43, 44
tractors   221–3
Trade and Capital Liberalisation Plan,
   Japan   47–8

trades unions
   Japan   88, 91, 92–3, 156, 161
   Western Europe   80, 148, 174
training, Japan   96–7
Tyson, L.   53

unemployment
   Japan   88, 89, 91–2; insurance
      201
   Western Europe   69–70, 99, 138;
      insurance   178, 179
United Kingdom
   ageing   84
   balance of payments crises   2
   from collective provision to
      affluence   103
   consumption   6–9, 64, 105–7;
      politics   112, 114
   economic growth   60, 61, 62–3, 64
   employment   85; income   71, 72,
      73, 74, 75–7, 78; from income
      to expenditure   79;
      self-employment and property
      income   78–9; tensions in
      labour market   65, 66, 67, 68,
      69, 70–1
   GATT   48
   GDP   5
   internationalisation of trade:
      exports   30, 61; foreign direct
      investment   32–3, 34;
      international markets   29;
      international money   35, 36, 38
   occupation of Germany   155
   rural society: characteristics   212,
      213; definition   211; earnings
      228, 229; housing conditions
      231; landholding patterns
      215; migration to urban areas
      214; transformation   217–18,
      223
   social democracy   139–40, 141–2,
      143–4, 146, 148;
      industrialisation   147; welfare
      state   145
   unique character of 1950s   101
   welfare state   145, 175, 179, 181–2,
      197; income support   200;
      unemployment   201
United Nations   35

United States of America
affluence 2, 104
ageing 84
from collective provision to
affluence 103
consumption 6, 7, 103–5, 112
GDP 5–6, 63
GNP 124
household size 124
industrial development model 100
intraindustry trade index 53, 54
and Japan: cars 43–4; direct
investment 43–4; influence
128; Joint Committee on Trade
and Economic Affairs 48;
occupation 3; Security Treaty
44, 48
life expectancy 124
New Deal idealism 154, 155
Second World War, impact of 10
and Western Europe: co-operation
between 26; direct investment
10–11, 32–4; influence 113,
156, 157; international capital
35, 36–8
youth culture 115, 116
universities, Japan 94, 95–6
urbanisation
Japan 248–51
Western Europe 148, 213

vertical equity, Japan 192
village society, Japan 243–8

wages and salaries
Japan 90, 92–3, 94, 96–7; rural
areas 239, 240–1, 243
Western Europe 13, 71–7; rural
areas 228–30, 233
washing machines 91
Watanabe, U. 96
welfare state
Japan 4, 18, 19–20, 188–9;
chronological development
194–206; objectives 189–94;
path toward reform 206
Western Europe 18–19, 173–86;
social democracy 145,
164

Western Europe 2–3
consumption 6–9, 14–15, 63–4,
99–100, 105–12, 117; from
collective provision to affluence
102–3; new sensibility
114–17; politics 112–14;
unique character of 1950s
100–2
erosion of affluence 24
internationalisation of trade
10–11, 25–8, 38–9; foreign
direct investment 32–4;
international markets 28–32;
international money 34–8
and Japan, differences in
transformation process 23
political culture 4–15, 22–3, 109,
112–14
rural society 20–1, 209–13, 232–3;
economic transformation
213–16; incomes and living
standards 226–32;
transformation of 1950s and
1960s 216–26
social democracy 16–17, 138–9,
150–1; new voters for renewed
parties 146–9; political
management of mixed
economy 142–6; progress
towards government 139–42
welfare state 18–19, 173–86
see also named countries
West Germany
balance of payments crises 2
from collective provision to
affluence 103
consumption 6–9, 13, 64, 107–10
economic growth 62, 63, 64
employment 85; income 71, 72,
73, 74, 75–7, 78; from income
to expenditure 79; self-
employment and property
income 79; tensions in labour
market 65, 66, 67, 68, 69–70,
71
GDP 5
GNP 124
internationalisation of trade:
exports 28, 30, 61; foreign
direct investment 32;

West Germany – *continued*
    international money   35;
    machinery industry   30
    intraindustry trade index   53
    labour surplus models   60
    life expectancy   124
    NATO   102
    rural society: characteristics   212,
        213; definition   210, 211;
        earnings   228; landholding
        patterns   215; transformation
        219, 222
    social democracy   17–18, 139–43,
        146, 153–4, 169–71; immediate
        postwar period   154–6;
        increasing democratic pressure
        161–4; industrialisation   147;
        laissez-faire liberalism   156–61;
        unionisation   148; welfare
        state   145
    welfare state   145, 175, 179, 181,
        182, 199; Keynesianism   173
Wilson, Harold   139, 143
women's employment
    Japan   85–6, 88, 192
    Western Europe   12, 67–9, 74, 76,
        77; agricultural sector   218–19,
        220

women's leagues, Japan   246
workforce
    Japan   83–7, 192
    Western Europe   12, 147;
        agricultural sector   214, 215,
        218–20, 226; tensions   64–71
    see also employment
working class, Western Europe
    consumption   102, 105–7, 109,
        110, 114
    welfare state   174–5

Yagi, T.   202
Yawata   249
Yawata Steel   50
Year-1940 regime   43, 45
Yokohama   249
Yoshida, Shigeru   46
    social democracy   159, 160, 165,
        166, 167, 169
young men's associations, Japan
    246
youth culture   22, 107, 110, 114–17
Yugoslavia   30

Zaibatsu, dissolution of   3
Zysman, J.   53